The American School Superintendent

The American School Superintendent

Leading in an Age of Pressure

Gene R. Carter

William G. Cunningham

 JOSSEY-BASS
A Wiley Company
www.josseybass.com

Published by

JOSSEY-BASS
A Wiley Company
989 Market Street
San Francisco, CA 94103-1741

www.josseybass.com

Jossey-Bass books and products are available through most bookstores. To contact Jossey-Bass directly, call (888) 378-2537, fax to (800) 605-2665, or visit our website at www.josseybass.com.

Substantial discounts on bulk quantities of Jossey-Bass books are available to corporations, professional associations, and other organizations. For details and discount information, contact the special sales department at Jossey-Bass.

We at Jossey-Bass strive to use the most environmentally sensitive paper stocks available to us. Our publications are printed on acid-free recycled stock whenever possible, and our paper always meets or exceeds minimum GPO and EPA requirements.

Wiley also publishes its books in a variety of electronic formats. Some content that appears in print may not be available in electronic books.

Library of Congress Cataloging-in-Publication Data

Carter, Gene R., date.
 The American school superintendent : leading in an age of pressure
/ Gene R. Carter, William G. Cunningham. — 1st ed.
  p.   cm.   — (The Jossey-Bass education series)
 Includes bibliographical references and index.
 ISBN 0-7879-0799-5 (cloth : acid-free paper)
 1. School superintendents—United States. 2. Educational
leadership—United States. 3. School management and organization—
United States.   I. Cunningham, William G.   II. Title.
III. Series.
LB2831.72.C37   1997
371.2'011—dc21
                                                    96-45874
                                                      CIP

FIRST EDITION
HB Printing   10 9 8 7 6 5 4 3

The Jossey-Bass Education Series

Contents

Foreword

In my more cynical moments, I have often thought of school superintendents as bearing the same relationship to their communities as fire hydrants bear to dogs. The superintendency is a job that attracts criticism and problems. But while the American school superintendency is one of the toughest jobs in America, it is also one of the most rewarding. No other role calls for the same intense emphasis on what Robert K. Greenleaf termed "servant leadership" and creativity in bettering the lives of children. Superintendents search for the best possible futures for our children.

Gene Carter and William Cunningham have written an important book that will help anyone trying to better understand this most difficult and complex job. They have painted a "right on" picture of the perils and possibilities of this role as we near the turn of the century. By blending a thorough overview of the superintendent's role with the words of more than 250 superintendents who live the job, the authors allow readers to walk in a superintendent's shoes. Cunningham's extensive research and higher education experience offers the critical academic perspective, and Carter speaks from the solid background of someone who served as an urban superintendent and lived to tell the story. In fact, Carter was selected as the nation's first Superintendent of the Year by the American Association of School Administrators in 1988, so he not only survived but thrived in the role. He and his coauthor know what they are talking about.

This book presents a historical context for the role of the superintendent, which started in 1837 and has been an "express ticket" ride ever since. The role has evolved considerably from the time when elected boards of education decided they simply needed someone to oversee the schools on a daily basis. It has evolved from the job of secretary to one of benevolent dictator.

Today, the role is again changing—toward one of less unilateral authority but with even higher expectations attached.

Carter and Cunningham do a masterful job of presenting the past and present in clear, and sometimes painful, detail. In fact, reading only the first few chapters leaves one wondering why any sane person would think of tackling this job. The authors' description of the job as a "lightning rod" reminded me of a school board member I once worked with who told me my job was to be a "quick-healing dartboard." The current role is indeed a troubled one. The condition of children in this country has deteriorated, while the challenges facing them have escalated. And the critics are out in full force. Superintendents find themselves defending the system they lead, demanding accountability so they can keep the doors open and morale up, while at the same time they must search for ways to transform the system to meet an uncertain future.

Much of the heat that superintendents face comes from surprise issues. Carter and Cunningham call these "time bombs." Sometimes they arrive like letter bombs delivered in anonymous fashion, such as the little undermining actions from board members or staff members who create a furor over something that could have been defused. Other times, the pressure comes in a more public forum. I have sometimes felt that in doing away with the ducking stool and the pillory America really did not give up public humiliation as a form of punishment. We just moved it to the school board meeting.

There are plenty of reasons why this is so. Public schools are democratic institutions and readily accessible by the public. They are also beset by the most fundamental and intractable problems of our society. And they are supposed to be all things to all people. As other institutions in our society deteriorate, the schools are asked to step into the breach and take on added responsibility. When I get around to writing my own book on the superintendency, the title will be *What Are You Going to Do About It?* because that was the question I most frequently faced during my seventeen years in the role.

Yet the irony of the job is that it requires one not so much to *answer* the question as to *ask* the *right one*. The appropriate role is not to be where the hurricane winds blow the hardest, but to be its eye, where dwells the calm amidst the chaos. As the authors point out, the "challenge of the superintendency is not to provide solutions, but to facilitate a process by which discordant voices, disparate interest, and conflicting points of view can work for the best interest of the community and the school system" (Chapter Nine).

While much of the wind driving the job comes from the community that surrounds the school system, at least half the job is to lead what is inside the system. I once characterized the role as trying to ride two dolphins simultaneously, with a foot on each. One dolphin represents the slippery and often unpredictable expectations of the community, and the other the sensitive and sometimes difficult feelings and performance of the system. I remember from physics that it is harder to get an inert body moving than it is to keep it moving. Imparting motion to a system that is nearly immobilized by vested interests, history, and the multiple expectations placed on it—a system that places many hands on the wheel—is most difficult. Retooling is not merely a matter of putting in new technology; it requires changing the minds and sometimes the hearts of those who are doing the work. The authors cite efforts to develop learning organizations as efforts that are central to changing school districts. The role of the superintendent is to help build capacity for the organization to move itself forward. To stick with the earlier metaphor, the role is not to try to rein in the dolphins as much as it is to help them discern where together they can find the fish needed to sustain their life.

As Carter and Cunningham point out, to be a superintendent today is to provide leadership in an age of pressure. Many conflicting messages are sent to a school district. People like high standards—until the standards adversely affect their own children. They want schools to be better—but not different. There has been a lot of scapegoating of schools by business and political leaders, and this very vocal pressure has led to loss of credibility and diminished faith in the institution. Much of the solution to this problem rests in the ability of school leaders to build coalitions of support for schools from among those most interested in seeing schools succeed. This coalition building requires excellent communication skills. As the authors state, "the secret for superintendent success beyond the year 2000 will be to have an effective and broad-based system of communication, one that builds a coalition of advocates for the improvement being made. Effective communication will be the lifeline for the schools" (Chapter Nine).

Unfortunately, the pressures on the superintendent take a personal and professional toll. This book serves in part as a warning label, because far too often the job can be quite literally hazardous to one's health. From board politics to life threats, from long hours to scant personal time, the pressures mount. But there are ways to cope. Seeking balance and perspective by creating time to reflect is critical. I have always called this self-renewal "refilling the well." So much of the job entails giving out. The role of servant leader is, after all, to serve. But to continue the possibility of service, one must make certain that as the well is emptied by others, it is allowed to refill. This replenishing can be achieved through a personal plan that involves a balance of physical, spiritual, and intellectual renewal. Often, those who fail to provide for these personal needs fail.

The role of superintendent in the future is to be the voice promoting system change. As the book points out, the superintendent must be a compass for the system. He or she must help the system find and articulate its vision and build capacity for meeting that vision. That role requires a new set of skills. Carter and Cunningham do a beautiful job of outlining the skills needed to meet this new demand. Leaders in the future will lead amidst ambiguity. They will create and nurture relationships. They will help others make order out of chaos. They will build collaborations, coalitions, alliances, and affiliations.

Perhaps it is because I so strongly agree with their views that I feel Carter and Cunningham really "get" what the role of superintendent is all about. The real challenge to school leaders of the future is captured by a quote herein from Patricia Graham, former dean of the Harvard Graduate School of Education: "for 150 years, American schools kept the pedagogy constant and let the results vary; for the future, we must vary the pedagogy and produce high levels of accomplishments for all. In other words, we must raise the standards and then vary the means—not the ends—of education in ways that respect the particular differences of children." The authors end the book by drawing a portrait of the future role for schools. They describe some of the current innovations that might be combined to create schools for the twenty-first century.

There is much I like about this book. It is well-written. It includes the case studies and voices of those who know the job best. It provides a powerful treatise on the challenge of the job. But best of all, it gives one a sense of hope. Yes, those who stop reading partway through will wonder why anyone would want this job. But those who stay with the authors to the end will see that there are solutions to the problems and answers to the questions. Savvy leaders who can master the skills and attitudes necessary to navigate the perilous conditions of American education will be rewarded by success in fulfilling the most difficult—and potentially one of the most rewarding—jobs in American public life today. Fire hydrants do not exist for the convenience of dogs; they represent the potential for saving our homes from the fires that might otherwise consume them.

Paul D. Houston
Executive Director
American Association of
School Administrators

Preface

This book grew out of recognition by the coauthors that the American superintendency is under a great deal of pressure. We participated in a Danforth Foundation School Administration Fellowship Program that ran over a five-year period. The program included superintendents from fifty different school divisions across the United States. One year after this program ended, only two of the fifty participating superintendents remained in their jobs. At the same time, one of the authors, Gene Carter, who was then superintendent of schools in Norfolk, Virginia, decided that it was time for a change in his professional life. In discussing this exit phenomenon with a number of superintendents, we saw clearly that there were many pressures on superintendents that were not well understood. At the same time, there was a need for massive educational reforms. Superintendents often found themselves in a sea of criticism and advice, at a time when the turbulence had never been greater.

The prevailing concern over the present condition of the superintendency is summarized by Dr. Donald R. Draayer, superintendent of schools in Minnetonka Public Schools in Minnesota: "one of my greatest apprehensions about the future of the superintendency is the short tenure in a key position. Important and needed organizational change occurs over many years. Leadership that is in constant flux can rarely bring about effective change which truly impacts student learning."

In examining the literature, we recognized that very little had been written on the superintendency in general and about the challenges superintendents face in improving American education in particular. *Urban School Chiefs Under Fire*, written by Dr. Larry Cuban in 1976, addressed the lack of understanding of the American superintendency—twenty years ago. In describing why he chose to write this book, Cuban stated that " . . . within this large body of advice (on how to be a good superintendent) there is precious little agreement on where the superintendency has come from, where it is moving or even what its present nature is. . . ." The same fundamental questions on the superintendency go unanswered today. Therefore, twenty years later we decided to revisit these issues from a new perspective.

The need to understand the superintendency is much more compelling today than it was in the 1970s. The turnover rate among superintendents hit an all-time high in 1991, when it reached two-and-a-half to three years for urban school systems and less than five years as a national average. The length of time to fill superintendency positions has increased, and some suggest that the quality of the application pool has decreased. This potential lack of leadership is compounded by a serious breakdown between means and ends in education and a lack of community trust and support. Neighborhood and childhood problems are becoming more serious at a time when families, communities, and governments are even less able to deal with them.

In the foreword to a 1985 book on the superintendency, Seymour Sarason (Blumberg, p. ix) wrote: "In recent decades the conventional wisdom about the job of being a superintendent of schools has been that it is a thankless role in which one survives, if one survives at all, for only five years or so in one district and is then forced to go elsewhere to learn what one already knows; it is not only that you cannot win, it is that you can do little more than nothing. . . . It is surprising how few studies of the role have been carried out, and not many of those have particularly illuminated its public and private aspects."

In the past, innovations have addressed the need for change within the existing paradigm; however, today the call is for providing leadership in a completely new paradigm of education. This greatly challenges the superintendent to provide the needed leadership during this period of transformation to twenty-first-century schools.

Political and business leaders across the country are calling for improved standards and assessment. Experts suggest that educators are handicapped by obsolete approaches and tools as they ponder what a twenty-first-century school should look like. Certainly, technology is one of the driving forces for change, but so are new constructivist, authentic approaches to learning; new assessment of quality performance; and new, dynamic career opportunities and worldviews. As the types of schools needed in America change, so do the expectations and the role of the American school superintendency.

Notwithstanding the importance of the superintendency, very little is known about its present condition, or what past and present superintendents believe about its present stage of evolution, or the most promising directions for the future. We decided to write a biography of the American superintendent with the help and approval of a large number of individuals who hold or have recently held the job. Our intent was to create overall understanding of this position and the direction it needs to take if education is to appreciably improve in America.

This book is written to provide a better understanding of the pressures related to the position and its changing role and expectations. The reader gets a firsthand sense of what it feels like to serve in this crucially important position, and of what must be done if this position is to support an improved American education system. The reader feels the pains and the pleasures, the challenges and the frustrations, the joys and the stresses, and the struggles and the rewards. The reader actually walks in the shoes of the American superintendency.

Much of the content of this book is drawn from superintendents themselves. Superintendents nationwide participate in describing the conditions in which they find themselves and their school divisions. They provide extensive discussions of successful attitudes and responses to these conditions. This description of the superintendency provides the background to consider how the position can best contribute to improved education. The book represents many frames of reference and points of view and a variety of different situations, perspectives, and possible directions. Both practitioners and researchers openly discuss the challenges that must be faced and the approaches that hold the greatest promise. The reader is taken on a journey into the personal and professional life of the American superintendent. The result, we hope, is increased awareness of the awesome responsibilities and difficulties of the role, along with increased hope for the future of our American youth.

Contained in this story is the legacy that each superintendent across America hopes to leave to future generations. It reflects frustrations, but also the spirit, dedication, and creativity that forge the redesigning of American schools. The first part of the book, "The Superintendency in Question," defines the superintendency and places it within its contemporary context. The six chapters within Part Two, "Challenges and Dilemmas," provide a clear portrayal of the internal and external challenges that face superintendents across the nation; they discuss the challenges that are faced daily and the awesome responsibilities and difficulties that are a part of the American superintendency. The third part, "Responses and Remedies," addresses what superintendents will need to do if schools are to achieve success in the future. This is the lifeblood that superintendents are expected to infuse into the education system. The final part, "New Directions and Responsibilities," provides a glimpse of what the new paradigm of education will look like and what we believe are the best pathways to travel toward creating schools for the twenty-first century. Thus Part Four helps chart the way for pioneers, champions, and catalytic agents to create the future of American education.

GENE R. CARTER
WILLIAM G. CUNNINGHAM

The Authors

Gene R. Carter is executive director of the Association for Supervision and Curriculum Development in Alexandria, Virginia. He earned his B.A. (1960) in history at Virginia State University, Petersburg; his M.Ed. degree (1967) in educational administration and supervision at Boston University; and his Ed.D. degree (1973) in instructional and curricular practice at Teachers College, Columbia University.

Instructional innovation and curriculum development have been the hallmarks of Carter's career as an educational leader. During his tenure as superintendent of schools, he was lauded for helping reduce the school dropout rate, building a strong partnership program, implementing a districtwide school improvement program, and establishing an early childhood education center for three-year-olds and their parents. He has published articles on school reform, school improvement, organizational development, leadership, and curricular innovation. He was selected the first national Superintendent of the Year (1988) by the American Association of School Administrators. In 1990 he was the recipient of the AASA's Annual Leadership for Learning Award.

Carter has provided leadership training throughout the nation and the world. He works with a number of organizations, including school districts, chief state school offices, professional associations, and state commissions.

William G. Cunningham is professor of educational leadership at Old Dominion University in Norfolk, Virginia. He earned his B.A. degree (1964) in industrial technology and management at Miami University and his Ph.D. degree (1974) in educational administration and research at Duke University. He has served in various roles in both business and education.

Cunningham is the author of several books and many articles. His main research focus has been on leadership, planning, and continuous educational improvement. He is an innovative consultant; has made over one hundred presentations at national, state, and local conferences; and is often interviewed for the print media and radio. His most recent book (1993) is *Cultural Leadership: The Culture of Excellence in Education* with Donn W. Gresso of East Tennessee State University.

Cunningham has received a number of grants, most recently on "multidisciplinary approaches to community leadership" from the Danforth Foundation. As department chairperson at Old Dominion University, he was instrumental in the successful revision of the Principal Preparation Program and is also credited with a quality revision of the doctor of philosophy in urban services program, for which he was the concentration area director. He received the 1992 Sara and Rufus Tonelson Award for Excellence in Teaching, Research, and Service.

The Superintendents

This book is what it is because of the superintendents nationwide who participated in this study, and those who read the manuscript. A list, by name and school district involvement, of those who had direct input when developing this book follows.

Superintendent	*School District*
Janet Barry	Central Kitsap School District, Silverdale, Washington
Brian L. Benzel	Edmonds School District, Lynnwood, Washington
Irwin Blumer	Newton Public Schools, Newtonville, Massachusetts
Thomas Bobo	Montgomery Public Schools, Montgomery, Alabama
E. Kathleen Booher	Berkeley Schools, Michigan
Kenneth S. Burnley	Colorado Springs Public Schools, Colorado Springs, Colorado
Ramon Cortines	New York City Public Schools, New York, New York
Beatriz Reyna-Curry	San Elizario Independent School District, San Elizario, Texas
Daniel Daste	St. Bernard Parish Public Schools, Chalmette, Louisiana
Donald Draayer	Minnetonka School District #276, Excelsior, Minnesota

Harry E. Eastridge	Cuyahoga County Schools, Valley View, Ohio
Raymond Farley	Hunterdon Central Regional High School District, Flemington, New Jersey
George Garcia	Tucson Unified School District 1, Tucson, Arizona
Shirl Gilbert II	Indianapolis Public Schools, Indianapolis, Indiana
Lois Harrison-Jones	Boston Public Schools, Boston, Massachusetts
Paul Houston	Tucson Public Schools, Tucson, Arizona
Ruben Ingram	Fountain Valley School District, California
Donald Ingwerson	Jefferson County Public Schools, Louisville, Kentucky
Leslie Johnson	Hinds County Public Schools, Raymond, Mississippi
Joan P. Kowal	Volusia County Public Schools, Deland, Florida
Diana Lam	Dubuque Community School District, Dubuque, Iowa
Raymond A. Lauk	Cerro Gordo Community Unit School District No. 100, Cerro Gordo, Illinois
David Mahan	St. Louis Public Schools, St. Louis, Missouri
Deborah McGriff	Detroit Public Schools, Detroit, Michigan
John Middleton	Columbus Public Schools, Columbus, Ohio
Larry Mixon	Columbus Public Schools, Columbus, Ohio
John Murphy	Charlotte-Mecklenburg Public Schools, Charlotte, North Carolina

Mary Nebgen	Washoe County School District, Reno, Nevada
Peter Negroni	Springfield Public Schools, Springfield, Massachusetts
Jerry Patterson	Appleton Area School District, Appleton, Wisconsin
Carol G. Peck	Alhambra School District No. 68, Phoenix, Arizona
Frank Petruzielo	Broward County Public Schools, Fort Lauderdale, Florida
Patrick J. Russo	Savannah-Chatham County Public Schools, Savannah, Georgia
Norbert Schuerman	Omaha Public Schools, Omaha, Nebraska
Franklin Smith	District of Columbia Public Schools, Washington, D.C.
Robert Spillane	Fairfax County Public Schools, Fairfax, Virginia
Michael Strembitsky	Edmonton, Alberta
Robert Wentz	Wake County Public School System, Raleigh, North Carolina
John Whritner	Greenwich Public Schools, Greenwich, Connecticut
Joe Work	Little Axe Public Schools I-70, Norman, Oklahoma
Gary Wright	Lindbergh School District, Lindbergh, Missouri
Larry Zenke	Duval County Public Schools, Jacksonville, Florida
Isa Kaftal Zimmerman	Acton-Boxborough Regional School District, Acton, Massachusetts

Part One

The Superintendency in Question

Chapter One

Changing Conditions and Rising Expectations

As we enter a new century, we see that the profession of the school superintendency is more important than it has ever been. Today's superintendents must be well grounded: from solid pedagogy to financial management, from child growth and development to political acumen, and from organizational and group behavior to staff development and student personnel. Certainly, the superintendent must be knowledgeable in matters pertaining to instructional options; application of the most promising research, assessment, and evaluation; and allocation of human, financial, and material resources. Most superintendents, however, find that this knowledge is insufficient given the existing climate in American education. Before the superintendent is able to apply any of this knowledge, he or she must first learn to survive in a very difficult, highly politicized, conflictive job. The success and prosperity of American education may well depend as much on the survival of the superintendent as it does on his or her ability to be an effective educational leader.

Today's superintendents deal with forces and incidents that are far more complex and threatening than those of their predecessors. At the same time, the need and demand for massive reform of the educational system has never been greater. One cannot be a successful superintendent today without having a broad understanding of the challenges, issues, and dilemmas, as well as of the necessary remedies and responses, for contemporary education. Key among the desired attributes are the ability to enunciate a clear, shared vision and the ability to inspire others to work toward realizing that vision. Equally important is serving as a beacon among the conflicting ideologies, political pressures, and shifting economic and social conditions. The *Washington Post* called the school superintendency "the impossible job" because it is a role in which the forces are so difficult to understand, much less control. Nowhere is there a job with higher expectations but so little trust and confidence.

It requires exceptional leadership skills to preside over the education of thousands of young people in an age of full media attention, where everyone claims to be an expert; where elections on each level bring new, often ill-advised, solutions; and where there seems to be a general deterioration in the family and community. The beleaguered superintendent is peppered with questions by critics; reporters; business, civic, and government leaders; parents; and school board members. They are expected to answer these questions without offending people whose demands are often neither well grounded nor funded. Superintendents must direct the energies of those working within the system to continually improve student learning—while shielding educators from the cross fire of community ideology.

The superintendency requires "fire in the belly," physical stamina, leadership skill, vision, and a strong desire to use one's power to improve the lives of children. It calls for good judgment, solid political acuity, and willingness to subordinate one's private goals to those of the community. The superintendent can have a profound impact on community life for generations to come. In their recent book on the school superintendency, M. Scott Norton and others (1996) said of the superintendent that

> he or she is often the target of criticism and at the center of contro-
> versy, forced to become the defender of policy and the implemen-
> tor of state and federal mandates, and the orchestrator of diverse
> interests seeking to influence the schools. Conflicts with the school
> board are common, as are the financial pressures under which su-
> perintendents operate. Superintendents in the 1980s and 1990s
> have faced the challenges brought on by the reform movement.
> Many of the proposals that have grown out of this movement (e.g.,
> site-based management, teacher empowerment, and parental
> choice) have brought additional challenges to the superintendent's
> authority and leadership [p. 21].

The Condition of the Superintendency

Before superintendents can provide the leadership needed for the twenty-first century, they must clearly understand the conditions within which they find themselves, the role they are expected to play, and the types of schools that are needed for the times.

Today, over fifteen thousand superintendents are responsible for continuously improving our nation's schools. They work in large school districts (fifty thousand or more students), in small school districts (two thousand students or fewer), and in districts somewhere between. They lead school districts with a majority of high-income families, and districts where large numbers of families fall below the poverty line. There are very stable and supportive districts, and those in which there is constant turmoil and conflict. Regardless of the type of district, all superintendents face overwhelming daily and long-term issues and challenges. They lead schools in an era when astonishing technological changes are routine and the pace of progress shows no signs of slowing. Yet all this is occurring at a time when community support for children seems to be at a low ebb.

The superintendent is often the lightning rod for everything related to the youth within a community. Although all educators feel the heat related to the responsibility for American youth, the superintendent best exemplifies the pressures that are brought to bear on educational professionals. Recently the heat has been so intense that the average tenure of superintendents has reached an all-time low. Reports examining the superintendency suggest that the average tenure ranges between two and one-half years and six years, depending on district size. A front-page article in the *New York Times* on December 26, 1990, characterized the condition of the superintendency: "school superintendents around the country have been quitting in droves or have been dismissed or have retired early, often because they have failed to deliver the quick educational fixes demanded of them. More than 15 major cities are now scrambling to find school chiefs, nearly three times the usual number in a given year, experts say. And, the searches for superintendents are getting harder. Cities are finding fewer candidates willing to apply for these jobs, despite salaries that in many cases top $100,000 a year" (Daley, 1990).

By the end of the 1990–91 academic year, a total of eighteen superintendents of larger school districts—Los Angeles, Atlanta, Boston, Cleveland, Columbus, Charlotte-Mecklenburg, Charleston, St. Louis, Kansas City, Washington, D.C., to name a few—had lost their jobs. The problems in smaller districts, although not as well documented, were very similar. This represented a significant increase in the number of positions that were open at any one time in previous decades. In the 1950s the average term in office for incumbent superintendents in large school districts was 6.5 years. By the 1980s, it had dropped to just over four years (Cuban, 1989, p. 46). Recent reports by the National School Boards Association suggest that the average term of large-district superintendents is now 2.5 years. Although the drop is not as significant in smaller districts, tenure is on the decline. A 1991 nationwide survey, completed for the *Executive Educator* (Heller and others, 1991), found that more than 53 percent of the superintendents in the United States had been in their present position for five years or less. Only about 40 percent of the superintendents felt that they had much job security in their present positions.

The conditions of the early 1990s have continued to worsen. As reported in *Urban Dynamics: Lessons Learned from Urban Boards and Superintendents,* released by the National School Boards Association (NSBA), "During 1991, approximately 30 school boards governing some of the nation's largest school systems replaced their superintendents. Some of these vacancies were due to retirement, others to new opportunities and upward mobility; but most were attributed to the pressures of an extraordinarily stressful job. As vacancies occur, urban school boards are finding fewer applicants willing to assume the considerable demands of administering these multimillion dollar education systems with their greater number of social problems and political factions, proportionately less funds per student, and intensive public scrutiny" (National School Boards Association, 1992, p. 5).

In the 1992–93 academic year, more than three dozen urban superintendency positions were unfilled. The number of well-prepared candidates to fill these positions was dwindling. It was not uncommon to hear those leaving the superintendency make statements such as "You couldn't pay me enough to take another superintendency of a large school district at this time."

Susan Moore Johnson (1996) followed the work of twelve newly appointed superintendents through the first two years of their tenure. This proved to be a much more difficult study than had been expected. Johnson found that half of the districts in her sample had experienced repeated turnover in the past decade: "Counting both acting and permanent assignments, one school district had named its seventh superintendent in six years; another had appointed five individuals in three years. I had not completed interviews in a third district when the superintendent announced that he was leaving after little more than a year on the job. The district was on the brink of fiscal collapse and no one had warned him" (Johnson, 1996, p. 60).

The financial and organizational costs of such turnover weigh heavily on the school district and the staff who are trying to hold it together. One of the few coping techniques that seem to provide any level of protection from this rapid turnover is closing the doors and ignoring the craziness occurring at the top. Commitments to programs of ex-superintendents dry up and the programs are abandoned; staff become disillusioned and resist future change. At the same time, few aspire to ever want to be in central office administrative leadership, particularly the superintendency.

Paul Houston, executive director of AASA and former superintendent of public schools in Tucson, Arizona, said that "Most of the urban superintendents I know—the good ones, anyway—are trying to figure out how to get out" (Rist, 1990, p. 14). A search consultant for Harold Webb Associates said that a superintendent he was recruiting for a position in a large system told him, "I've gotten beaten up enough." One of Boston's string of nine superintendents in an eighteen-year period stated that being superintendent in Boston "is like being made to walk the gangplank slowly."

Ken Scott, of the Kentucky School Boards Association, says his state is short on superintendent applicants: "We have a tight market for superintendents now" (Mulligan, 1996). The state averages about thirty vacancies a year and is having a progressively harder time filling them, particularly from applicants within the state. Tim Kremer, from the Ohio School Boards Association, agrees. Ohio typically has 120 superintendent vacancies each year among the more than 700 school districts in the state. He notes, "Our candidate pool seems to be drying up" (Mulligan, 1996). There were also fewer candidates participating in the 1996 American Association of School Administrators (AASA) Jobs Central placement center than in previous years. Glen Burdick, superintendent of schools in Winchester, Virginia, is completing a dissertation at the University of Virginia on the seriousness of this pipeline shortage. His initial findings affirm that the problem is real and may have a significant impact on the reform efforts in many states.

Many in the superintendency suggest that the future of the superintendency—and of American education, for that matter—depends on whether policy makers and the public gain a clear understanding of the conditions that are driving the most qualified individuals from the superintendency and other educational positions. If unchecked, this trend in American education could cause greater upheaval in the profession, and lost promise for American youth and ultimately the nation.

The Education Pressure Cooker

The superintendency has always been described as a hot seat, a pressure cooker, a highwire act. Today it is described more bluntly as a very unpleasant, even impossible, job. Floretta McKenzie, president of the McKenzie Group, says she worries about a future dearth of experienced candidates interested in competing for superintendencies. She fears that "we'll be in serious trouble if something is not done. A 1992 *Education Week* article discussing the Superintendents Prepared Consortium maintained, 'the pipeline will remain almost empty and those in it will remain ill-prepared for the job'" (Bok, 1992, p. 48). This problem is just becoming visible as it becomes more difficult to attract competent candidates and the competition among districts for those candidates begins to heat up.

Even school board members are beginning to question the sanity of an individual who would take on such a position. A board member explained his feelings during interviews for a new superintendent: "I wanted to ask these people, 'Why do you want to come here and be captain of the *Titanic?*'" People are starting to ask, "what type of person wants to be the superintendent of schools in a district with five thousand students or more?"

Even worse, all the struggle and flailing takes place in the public eye. It is a local media event. Reporters will take an already difficult situation and fuel what could be described at best as an inflammatory condition. The superintendent faces one contentious situation after another as the press stokes the heat to an unbearable point. This may make for interesting press; however, it has also made being a superintendent a painful experience. One superintendent explained the feeling: "For a number of reasons, including discomfort and embarrassment, members of the community don't speak to you or, worse, disassociate themselves from you. Other administrators within the district become confused about or concerned for their jobs and begin distancing themselves from you. People who unanimously supported your coming to the district and that you have gotten along well with throughout your tenure go silent every time you approach."

Compliments are rare as criticisms abound. The culture is such that it becomes impossible to carry out the herculean feats expected of today's superintendents. She or he starts fighting feelings of disbelief, disgust, distrust, and depression. These feelings often turn to outrage when the superintendent learns that board members and administrators are leaking items to the press, distorting the truth, and ultimately destroying his or her ability to salvage the situation. Gradually, almost everyone around the superintendent becomes skillful at embarrassing him or her in public. Associates grow reluctant to speak out about the successes the superintendent has had within the school division, as others begin taking the lion's share of the credit. Political alliances form to distance themselves from the superintendent. Those involved keep chipping away at public support, causing enough infighting to paralyze the system. Then the superintendent is blamed for not making much headway on needed educational reforms.

Robert McCarthy has described the hostility and helplessness he felt long months after he was fired from a superintendency. He had been a superintendent for nineteen years in four different states before he was fired in the middle of a three-year contract. McCarthy said that "the rage I felt still smolders—eighteen months after I last worked as a superintendent, nine months since my last paycheck. I was forced to resign—terminated at the beginning of my second year of a three-year contract. The official reason: philosophical differences and leadership style." (Nationally, this reason is the one most cited by far for removing superintendents.) He explained the difficulty in regaining employment as a superintendent: "Their school boards and search consultants are reluctant to consider me seriously, because they view me as overqualified or think their small districts won't be enough of a challenge for me. That rules out the vast majority of districts in the country. Large school systems, on the other hand, question whether I can handle the demands of the job, in view of what happened in my first large superintendency. I'm fearful of the future. I don't understand why my former colleagues shun me, why search consultants consider me damaged goods" (McCarthy and Bennett, 1991, p. 15).

One thing that almost all superintendents can agree upon is this: they are always alienating someone with their decisions, and over time there is very little gratitude for this job. Support will not last very long after the day a superintendent is hired, and some superintendents wonder if it is even there when one first arrives. The immediate warring factions are the neighborhoods, businesses, school board members, administrators, teachers, unions, elected officials, religious leaders, etc. Each faction has its own set of expectations for the new superintendent.

The qualities that typically allow these factions to work together are communication, trust, and understanding of differences among these groups. Such supportive organizational attributes all tend to break down as each faction begins to push its educational agenda at the expense of the others. The superintendent becomes the underappreciated referee—and, as time passes, the lightning rod. This problem is even more evident when the different factions become involved in micromanagement of areas that should be left to professionals. Heat is generated, as the primary motives of one faction are to promote its own agenda, or ones advocated by their constituents, at the expense of all others. These problems are compounded as they are decided politically and not on the basis of what is in the best interest of the youth of the community. Major problems begin as the factions use the media to help further their cause.

Where the Heat Comes From

Few people question the difficulty of providing leadership in the public domain. Public leaders are the targets of constant criticism and public attack. The opportunities for missteps are endless, and public scrutiny is intense. Public figures live in a fishbowl. Beyond the very demanding nature of the job itself are the constant opportunities for disorder, crisis, and pressure. Charges and countercharges are fired off in a barrage of attacks, with the superintendent caught in the middle. As a result, superintendents live in a permanent condition of turbulence and pressure. The concept of the "vulnerable superintendent" developed in the 1970s by Larry Cuban is truer today than at any time in the history of the position (Cuban, 1976).

Often, apparently benign problems turn into major crisis points in the tenure of a superintendent. One has only to read newspaper headlines to become familiar with many of the problems that besiege our schools. The turbulent environment surrounding schools has caused an erosion of the superintendent's ability to govern effectively. Superintendent Beatriz Reyna-Curry from the San Elizario Independent School District in Texas finds, "Most of the pressures come from keeping focused on the goals despite the day-to-day distractions. Pressures come from staff relationships, community involvement in gossip, board members occasionally slipping into administrative roles, keeping staff focused on self-improvement, political pressures, and ideological battles." Although the sources of pressure vary, almost all superintendents feel some form of pressure.

The Horace Mann League reported the results of a study of the "top ten destructive factors influencing public education" at the 1996 AASA national conference on education (Dlugosh and others, 1996). These forces, as seen by superintendents, are:

1. *Perpetual negative myths:* continually misleading information and an inability to convert the resulting negative myths to more positive ones (that is, to get out a positive message).
2. *Decline of the family:* breakdown of family structure with a resulting lack of parental responsibility.

3. *Funding of public education:* not providing the resources to successfully implement demanded improvements (regressiveness
of taxes).
4. *Lack of community interest and responsibility:* communities have
an isolationist, balkanization mentality that does not provide
support for schools other than the ones that close relatives
attend.
5. *Inability to see differences in schools:* all schools expect to get the
same results regardless of resources, technology, support, stim-
ulation at home, etc.
6. *Working with school board members:* problems in confronting
board members involved in power politics, micromanagement,
special interests, excessive fiscal conservatism, pandering to
electorate, lacking strategic thinking skills, etc.
7. *Lack of attention to social issues:* community members who ignore
issues of intolerance, imbalance of wealth, blight, etc., and look
out more for family and friends than others.
8. *Religious right:* this group tends not to embrace diversity and is
very conservative, looking more toward maintenance during
times calling for continuous improvement and reform.
9. *Limited funding:* not enough money to provide adequate facilities, instructional support, and salaries.
10. *Nothing is moving:* unions, community, parents, business leaders, politicians, etc., seem resistant to educational efforts; result is a never-ending system of roadblocks.

A major theme seemed to be "We want better schools, but we
don't want them to change." The pressure comes as much from
employees of the school systems as it does from the parents whose
children attend the schools. This is exacerbated by communities
overwhelmed in dealing with existing problems. Given these circumstances, superintendents must strategize in new ways to move
the school systems forward.

Picking up on the second concern in the list, communities
have begun to realize that they have lost something precious: physical and emotional safety for their children. Children are often left
to fend for themselves in a fast-paced, hostile—even dangerous—
materialistic world that provides little or no direction and support.
Instead of acknowledging that schools must deal with this legacy,

members of the public often accuse schools of being part of the cause. The real problems are rooted in economics, crime, violence, discrimination, neglect, stress, instability, unemployment, conflict, divorce, inadequate parenting, abuse, mobility, vulnerability, disabilities, destructive relationships, social and psychological dysfunction, general alienation, and greed. These are examples of the types of problems with which schools now contend.

In recent years, the family structure has changed drastically, as have extended support systems. The problems of society have greatly increased, while the resources available to solve those problems have dwindled. The violence that has been afflicting society in general is slowly creeping into the schools. These changing social conditions have placed pressure on our schools to find ways to meet students' needs. These and other growing demands have made the work of the superintendency much more complex, as they move education beyond its traditional boundaries. Issues creeping into the schools include intolerance, violence, homelessness, alcohol and drug abuse, physical and sexual abuse, sexually transmitted diseases such as AIDS, suicide, abortion, birth control, condom distribution, and many other hot topics. In the face of these issues, significantly large numbers of American youth are at risk of not realizing their potential, and superintendents are being challenged to ensure that this does not happen.

The Condition of American Youth

Children of both rich and poor alike are experiencing a life that few would consider healthy. Michael Kirst (1991) states:

"Johnny can't read because he needs glasses and breakfast and encouragement from his absent father; Maria doesn't pay attention in class because she doesn't understand English very well and she's worried about her mother's drinking and she's tired of trying to sleep in her car. Dick is flunking because he's frequently absent. His mother doesn't get him to school because she's depressed about having lost her job."

We might add that Mary doesn't turn in her homework because she is a latchkey child who receives very little supervision at home or in her neighborhood from adults who are too involved in high-pressure careers. These children are reported to watch three and one-half hours or more of television each day. Neighborhood activities are more likely to have eight-year-old girls in high heels, perfume, and lipstick competing as Madonna look-alikes than doing their homework. High divorce rates, conflict-filled families, prenatal and birth-related problems, psychological disorder, extramarital relationships, violence, government mistrust, anger, abuse, and poverty are all areas that the schools are expected to overcome (Children's Defense Fund, 1991).

These conditions have presented an almost overwhelming challenge to already heavily burdened school systems. According to the Children's Defense Fund, 10.2 million American children experienced one or more developmental, learning, or emotional disorders in 1991. The suicide rate has tripled in this age category over the past thirty years. Twenty percent of children live below the poverty line, and that percentage is increasing. An astounding 11 percent of all newborn babies have been drug-exposed, and 40 percent of teenagers have tried drugs by the time they reach eighteen. Approximately 60 percent of all children will spend part of their growing up in single-parent homes, with 40 percent of the noncustodial parents seldom seeing their children. Almost 20 percent of school-age children report that they have less than a ten-minute conversation with a parent per month. Every thirty seconds a teenager becomes pregnant, according to the U.S. Centers for Disease Control, and every thirteen seconds one contracts a sexually transmitted disease. AIDS is now the sixth leading cause of death for people aged fifteen to twenty-four.

Parents who feel guilty for not spending enough time with their children overspend on them (if they can afford to). This practice has not resulted in happier children. Students rent expensive limousines, hotel rooms, and "entertainment" at proms. Marian Wright Edelman has expressed her deep concern for the nation's "backseat" children in the 1991 Children's Defense Fund report on the state of American children: "Our children are growing up today . . . where instant sex without responsibility, instant gratification without effort, instant solutions without sacrifice, getting rather than giving, and hoarding rather than sharing are the too-frequent signals of our mass media, popular culture, business, and political life. . . . Nowhere is the paralysis of public and private conscience more evident than in the neglect and abandonment of millions of our shrinking pool of children, whose future will determine our nation's ability to compete and lead in a new era" (1991, p. 7).

Anyone giving serious consideration to the condition of children in the United States finds overwhelming evidence that it is threatened. "If you could convict a nation for child neglect, you could convict the United States far more easily than any European or Asian nation," asserts Harold Hodgkinson, director of the Center for Demographic Policy at the Institute for Educational Leadership in Washington, D.C. (Natale, 1992, p. 23). What happens to many children in the United States, Hodgkinson says, "borders on the criminal."

We as a society have moved from asking "What's best for the child?" to "What can the child tolerate?" A *Newsweek* article (Adler, 1994, p. 42) raises the question, "Who killed childhood?" The article concludes: "We all did" (p. 49). The decline in children's quality of life is explained by changes inside and outside the home. Major changes inside the home are the prevalence of single parents, working mothers, neglect (36 percent of children make their own meals), crime, and abuse. Outside influences include child abuse, sexual abuse, and lack of financial and civic support. Children must be very resilient for these conditions not to lower their potential for success in school. They must be able to navigate the troubled condition of childhood if they are to achieve the high expectations being placed upon them.

In addressing the National Forum for Youth at Risk, then-Gov. Bill Clinton (1987) stated: "Whether you are in direct contact with at-risk children or not, whether you have any or not, it is perfectly clear that your interest, your future, your children's future is bound up in what happens to them, because people are the most important factor in the economy and in the society of any advanced country in the world today. And, frankly, we're doing the worst job of any of the countries with whom we compete in developing the capacity of our children." According to statistics prepared by the Office of Educational Research and Improvement, U.S. Department of Education, 35–40 percent of American students in grades K–12 are classified as at-risk (Withrow, 1990).

The Resulting Evolution in Roles and Responsibilities

The times are calling for a shifting form of leadership in order to address reform agendas. This means that the roles, responsibilities, and procedures of the superintendency will continue to evolve in order to serve the needs of children, families, and communities. Superintendents must be in a position to distribute power and influence in such a way that it supports the capacity to continuously improve schools. Superintendents must develop shared visions that address the needs of students and communities while holding firm to high standards established by government, business, and their profession. In a study of twelve newly appointed superintendents, Susan Moore Johnson confirmed "that political and managerial expertise are essential for today's superintendents. However, being a proficient manager or effective politician is not enough to carry a school district through sustained and meaningful change. For while managers and politicians may successfully address the immediate problems of unbalanced budgets, ineffective control systems, or lagging public confidence, they are not likely to engage teachers and principals in the responsibilities of collaborative leadership. They must also impress their constituents as educational leaders who demonstrate an understanding of what happens in the classrooms, who share a commitment to the cause of public education, who relish the teaching mission of the superintendency, and who are teachers of the first order—advising school boards, persuading mayors, coaching administrators, informing the public, and convincing those in the schools to join them in leading to change" (1996, pp. 289–290).

The conventional role of the superintendent, in many cases stipulated by local law, is to assist the board in policy making and to carry out policy. This role has proven to be an oversimplification that tends to cloud understanding almost as much as it clarifies it. Many school districts have tried to develop lists of superintendents' responsibilities along with performance evaluations that are based on these published lists.

Over the years, opinions have varied greatly among school districts as to the role of the superintendent. As a result, superintendents have been pulled in different directions by politicians, interest groups, communities, school boards, other superintendents, central office staff, principals, teachers, students, and parents. Realizing the importance of helping local school districts create consistent and effective lists of responsibilities, the American Association of School Administrators (AASA) and the National School Boards Association (NSBA) met in 1980 to develop a set of guidelines (Joint AASA-NSBA Committee, 1980, p. 5) for roles and responsibilities. These two groups met again in 1992, and in 1994 they jointly approved an updated position statement. The new statement reflected the "constantly changing environment and evolving roles and relationships." The introduction of this publication states that "When roles are clear and relationships are sound, communities feel a sense of confidence in their school leadership, and ultimately, students in each community and in our nation receive an even better education " (Joint AASA-NSBA Committee, 1994, p. 2). The responsibilities from the revised AASA-NSBA joint publication (1994, pp. 11–12) appear in Appendix A.

Such guidelines have often been used to develop requirements to gauge the quality of performance of superintendents. These efforts have helped to clarify responsibilities; however, the expectations among districts will never be fully defined or regulated because of the divergent interests and expectations that exist in each district. To further define the superintendency as a profession, the AASA Commission on Standards for the Superintendency, chaired by John R. Hoyle, developed a set of professional standards (American Association of School Administrators, 1993b). It was hoped that these standards, when coupled with defined professional responsibility and a means of gauging quality of performance, would enhance the public's belief that "superintendents are responsible executives worthy of the public trust." This standard setting was an effort to further enhance the professionalism of the superintendency in hope of stabilizing the profession.

The commission believed that "all superintendents should be held accountable for the eight professional standards." Exhibit 1.1 summarizes the commission's Professional Standards for the Superintendency.

These standards are to be used as guidelines for ongoing professional development. The standards help describe what superintendents need to know and be able to do.

Exhibit 1.1. Professional Standards for the Superintendency.

Standard 1: Leadership and District Culture.
This standard stresses executive leadership, vision, shaping school culture and climate empowering others, and multicultural and ethnic understanding.

Standard 2: Policy and Governance.
This standard centers on developing procedures for working with the board; formulating district policy, standards, and regulations; and describing public school governance in our democratic society.

Standard 3: Communications and Community Relations.
This standard emphasizes skill in articulating district vision and purpose to the community and media. Also, it stresses responding to community feedback and building consensus to strengthen community support.

Standard 4: Organizational Management.
This standard calls for skills in gathering, analyzing, and using data for decision making; framing and solving problems; and formulating solutions to problems. It also stresses quality management to meet internal and external customer expectations and to allocate resources.

Standard 5: Curriculum Planning and Development.
This standard tests the superintendent's skill in designing curriculum and a strategic plan to enhance teaching and learning, using theories of cognitive development, employing valid and reliable performance indicators and testing procedures, and describing the use of computers and other learning technologies.

Standard 6: Instructional Management.
This standard measures knowledge and use of research findings on learning and instructional strategies and resources to maximize student achievement. It also centers on applying research and best practice to integrate curriculum for multicultural sensitivity and assessment.

Standard 7: Human Resources Management.
This standard assesses skill in developing a staff evaluation and assessment and supervisory system to improve performance. It also requires skills in describing and applying legal requirements for personnel selection, development, retention, and dismissal.

Standard 8: Values and Ethics of Leadership.
This standard stresses understanding and modeling of appropriate value systems, ethics, and moral leadership. It also requires the superintendent to exhibit multicultural and ethnic understanding, and to coordinate social agencies and human services to help each student grow and develop as a caring, informed citizen.

Source: AASA Commission on Standards for the Superintendency (American Association of School Administrators, 1993b).

The standards have their critics. Some suggest they are too broad and cover too many expectations. Others suggest they might cause superintendents to lower their job expectations to the minimum standards. Some argue that the standards are beyond the reach of most, while others suggest they do not capture the true complexity of the superintendency. Some critics are worried about the absence of outcome indicators with which to hold superintendents accountable, while others are concerned that such indicators might needlessly limit the dynamics and direction of the superintendency. Still others suggest that the standards tend to focus on technical skills and ignore the important intangibles that are often the heart and soul of a school district's spirit. To date, the standards have tended to have minimal impact on the profession.

What Is Expected of the Superintendent

Superintendents are often held to very high standards in a very public arena. A number of contemporary studies examine the responsibilities of the superintendency. Perhaps the most comprehensive study of the superintendency was completed by Thomas Glass (1992) and entitled *The 1992 Study of the American School Superintendency*. It is the most recent of a "Study of the Superintendency" series conducted every ten years under the sponsorship of the American Association of School Administrators. According to Glass's study (p. 43), the criteria used by school boards to evaluate superintendents are, in rank order:

1. General effectiveness
2. Board/superintendent relations
3. Management functions
4. Budget development and implementation
5. Educational leadership/knowledge
6. Community/superintendent relationships
7. Staff/superintendent relationships
8. Personal characteristics
9. Recruitment and supervision of personnel
10. Student/superintendent relationships

These factors for evaluation are quite vague and subject to varying interpretation within districts. Glass found that superintendents
are not really evaluated against criteria in their job descriptions,
but more according to a sense of whether the superintendent is
doing a good job and has a good relationship with the school
board and/or community leaders. Yet, the demands on the superintendency are to meet the needs of the changing population of
students, who are affected as never before by the realities of shifting demographics, advancing technology, and the demands of an
uncertain future.

Chapter Two

The Superintendent's Changing Role

The superintendent is the chief educational leader and spokesperson for the school district. To ensure quality education, the school district must be managed and led by an effective school superintendent. This is not to ignore the key role of the school board in supporting effective leadership; however, the superintendent has the expertise, responsibility, and position to manage the school district's future. To quote the American Association of School Administrators' (AASA) Commission on Standards for the Superintendency:

> To a great extent, the quality of America's schools depends on the effectiveness of school superintendents. These executives of our nation's schools have complex leadership responsibilities, and those who hold the position must be among the brightest and best our society has to offer. Their vision and performance must focus on creating schools that will inspire our children to become successful, caring Americans, capable of becoming contributing citizens of the world.
>
> The superintendency requires bold, creative, energetic, and visionary school leaders who can respond quickly to a myriad of issues ranging from dealing with social changes, diverse student populations, and demands for equity to improving school quality for every child and making effective use of new technologies [Commission on Standards for the Superintendency, 1993, p. 3].

Evolution of the Superintendency

The superintendency is nearly 160 years old. It was created in recognition that the education enterprise had become too demanding for a board of education composed of volunteers who donated part of their time to public service. A full-time leader was needed to carry out the policies initiated by the board, which met only occasionally. Buffalo, New York, is commonly credited with establishing the first superintendency, when the Buffalo common council appointed a superintendent on June 9, 1837. Soon after, the mayors and aldermen of Louisville, Kentucky, and Providence, Rhode Island, also appointed superintendents of public schools (Bateman, 1996).

By the end of the nineteenth century, the superintendency had become generally recognized as the only promising solution to the administrative problems facing public education. In a few states, school boards were given the statutory authority to appoint superintendents; however, in most cases, boards made such appointments without specific legislative authority. By 1880, thirty-four of the thirty-eight states had made provisions for the position of superintendent. As of 1890, all large cities had superintendents; but it was not until well into the twentieth century that superintendents were found in small cities and towns.

The average age of superintendents increased from forty-three in 1923 to around fifty in 1992, while the average salary during the same period increased from $3,390 to more than $60,000. Concurrently, it became more unusual for a superintendent to remain in one school district for an entire career. The first baby boomers hit the schools in 1952, and superintendents focused on building new schools and locating badly needed teachers. By the end of the 1950s, approximately 50 percent of the adult population had earned a high school diploma. The 1960s brought universal recognition that the superintendency was a distinct profession in its own right.

The school superintendency evolved with little guidance from legislative directives. School codes in only about half the states contain language defining the relationship between the board of education and the school superintendency. This lack of legislative guidance has resulted in confusion regarding the status, authority, and responsibility of the superintendent of public education. In general, the board has been given the freedom to determine the level of trust placed in the superintendent's judgment to guide the direction of schools. This discretionary power has made it essential for the effective superintendent to maintain a good relationship with the board.

The AASA has periodically expressed concern over the ambiguous role of the superintendent, as in its 1994 resolutions: "AASA believes there is a vital relationship between effective school district leadership and successful schools and learners. This relationship is enhanced when roles and responsibilities between superintendents and boards of education are clearly defined and implemented. Therefore, AASA shall lead efforts to define the roles, responsibilities, and qualification of superintendents and boards of education" (American Association of School Administrators, 1994, p. 19).

Shifting Roles

The American public school superintendency has gone through four major stages since its inception.

Its earliest role was *clerical,* assisting the school board with the day-to-day details of school activities. As pedagogical matters became more complex, the board began to expect the superintendent to serve as the instructional leader of the schools. In this second stage, the superintendent was seen as a *master educator* providing direction on curricular and instructional matters. The growth of education and the focus on efficiency in the first half of the twentieth century created the expectation that the superintendent would be both the instructional leader and the business manager. Some larger school districts actually appointed dual superintendents—one for business and one for education. The superintendent came to be seen as an efficiency expert concerned more with "administrivia" than with the education of children. In this third period, a strong push for hierarchical bureaucracy and scientific management caused the superintendent to be viewed as the *expert manager.* This was the era of the four Bs: bonds, buses, budgets, and buildings.

Reforming, Restructuring, and Another Role

During the second half of the twentieth century, American education underwent a shift caused by a number of reform and restructuring issues. Perhaps the decisive moment in thinking about the role of the superintendent occurred in 1957, with the Soviet Union's highly technical success of the Sputnik launch. We had been teaching in our public schools that the people of the Soviet Union did not have electricity or running water in their homes, yet that country had mastered a technology far more sophisticated than anything we had then developed. Worst of all, Sputnik potentially jeopardized our national defense. Our government studied this significant blow to the American ego and decided that there was only one institution to blame: American schools. The resulting political activity led to congressional passage of the National Defense Education Act (NDEA) in 1958, which placed much greater emphasis on mathematics, science, and foreign languages. In school systems, emphasis quickly shifted from the four Bs to the three Rs: reading, writing, and arithmetic.

The call in American education was for leadership, political savvy, reform, community responsiveness, and improved education. It ushered in the fourth and current view of the superintendency, that of *chief executive officer for the board*. As a result, the superintendent serves as the professional advisor to the board, leader of reforms, manager of resources, and communicator to the public.

The 1960s ushered in a period of social tensions that placed great responsibilities on school superintendents and the schools they managed. This period was marked by violent resistance, civil disobedience, legal subterfuge, delay, and conflict related to a number of civil rights issues. Education was seen by minority and poor families as the only hope for improving conditions, if not for themselves then for their children. But the NDEA, with its focus on improving the math and science curriculum—especially for gifted students—was often viewed as closing off educational opportunity for underprivileged groups. This perception was aggravated by segregation and the racial antagonism that black Americans and other minorities experienced in their communities.

The frustration of these groups became manifest to Americans watching the riots in inner cities across America during the sixties.

The Kerner Commission, studying the riots and destruction within the inner cities, learned that the rioters were typically black males who had dropped out of high schools that were not serving their needs. The counter-rioters, those trying to stop the riots, were better educated, most having graduated from high school and attended some college. Education and income therefore seemed to be the only factors that distinguished the counter-rioters from the rioters and the noninvolved. The commission concluded that, apparently, higher levels of education and income not only prevented rioting but were more likely to lead to active, responsible opposition to rioting (U.S. Riot Commission, 1968, p. 132).

Congress quickly passed the Civil Rights Act and the Economic Opportunity Act, both in 1964, and the Elementary and Secondary Education Act of 1965 to address inequities. The latter has since served as the cornerstone for efforts to improve educational programs for families with poverty-level incomes. Another important goal of this bill was to strengthen state departments of education. The act greatly increased both federal and state influence on local education. Government involvement was enhanced by the multiplier effect of public interest. As a result, superintendents often found themselves responding to mandates as much as providing educational leadership.

A number of other factors continued to whittle away at local superintendent/board control of schools. An important one was the large and ever-growing number of groups and individuals who were attempting to influence school decision making. The diversity of these groups and the intensity with which they advocated their views continued to increase as they learned to use more sophisticated tactics. Certainly the most visible, and probably the most powerful, were the teacher unions. The National Education Association and the American Federation of Teachers emerged as strong advocates for teacher interests during the 1960s. Teacher unions became a formidable force in the operation of American schools.

Yet another challenge to the authority of the superintendency was the encroachment by a more involved citizenry and school board. The superintendent's traditional role as "expert" was being challenged on a number of different fronts. He or she often became the target of criticism when schools would not respond "appropriately" to pressure. Superintendents were once again being forced to reexamine their role in American education.

The 1970s heralded widespread concern that American schools were insensitive to the desires of communities, parents, and students. According to a number of education polls, including the *Annual Gallup Poll of Public Attitudes Toward Education,* the level of public confidence in education declined, particularly among young adults and the college educated. The theme of the 1970s for school superintendents was "accountability." Parent advisory councils and national assessment were two major initiatives that gained headway during this decade. A major concern of the period was to provide equal opportunity for all individuals in American society. This concern prompted efforts to improve school attendance, to provide needed services, and to ensure that all American youth achieved a minimum standard of learning. The mission of most schools became: "All children will learn." Money was lavished on special programs for students having trouble learning (they were later to be called "at-risk" students). A new U.S. cabinet-level position, secretary of education, was created on September 2, 1979. There was a string of teacher strikes over issues related to salary increases, cost of living adjustments, lesson planning time, class size, and extra-duty pay. The new cabinet position was a response to fulfilling a hopeful promise, coming out of the 1976 presidential campaign, to the National Education Association to improve relations with America's teachers.

The 1980s

The eighties began with teachers openly expressing dissatisfaction with their jobs; 41 percent responding to an NEA teacher poll said they would not become teachers if they had to do it over again. For the superintendent, the stress of balancing diverse interests and initiatives reached the breaking point in the 1980s. Superintendents were torn by conflicting desires to carry out the laws of the land, the policies of the board, the advice of school administrators and teachers, the demands of a diverse community, and the agendas from an ever-growing number of focused interest groups (business leaders, religious leaders, ecologists, chambers of commerce, the National Rifle Association, civil rights groups, social services, the National Bar Association, builders' associations, universities, and textbook suppliers). The superintendents were called on to make school decisions affecting not only these groups but, more importantly, the youth of America. Superintendents' decisions became more complex as interested parties learned to challenge them through the political and court systems.

In 1983, a prestigious ad hoc policy panel, under the direction of the newly created U.S. Department of Education, issued a widely publicized report, entitled *A Nation at Risk*. The National Commission on Excellence in Education report (1983) was packed with apocalyptic rhetoric and military analogies. It was purposely alarmist in tone: "Our nation is at risk. Our once unchallenged preeminence in commerce, industry, science, and technological innovation is being overtaken by competitors throughout the world. . . . [T]he educational foundations of our society are presently being eroded by a rising tide of mediocrity that threatens our very future as a nation and a people. . . . [I]f an unfriendly foreign power had attempted to impose on America the mediocre educational performance that exists today, we might well have viewed it as an act of war" (p. 5).

The report's major points were that American students compared unfavorably to students in other countries and were weaker in inferential skills, science achievement had declined, and there existed a national problem of illiteracy. The recommendations were to launch a core curriculum, raise academic standards, lengthen the school day and year, improve teacher quality, and attract more capable teachers.

Release of the report was followed by hundreds of national, state, and local commissions; task forces; study groups; committees; hearings; and legislature reports that were critical of education, offering all sorts of suggestions on how to improve the American educational system. Many of the recommendations were in the form of mandates to which boards, superintendents, and local school divisions were expected to respond. From almost every facet of America, reforms, proposals, and policies were being suggested. Superintendents had never seen such a large volume of differing suggestions from so many vocal groups regarding how American

education could be improved. Superintendents and, later, researchers were to use the term "waves" of reform to describe the
tumult of the 1980s. The waves seemed to increase in size; each
new one washed over a public school system still trying to respond
to the last one.

Thomas Glass said the 1980s "will be remembered as the time
in American public education when the private sector and citizens
of all races and socioeconomic levels became sufficiently displeased
to trigger a nationwide reform movement. With the publication of
A Nation at Risk, a diverse group of civil rights and corporate interests led a national movement inspired by concern over equity
issues and the inability of industry to compete successfully in world
markets because of low education and skill levels of graduates"
(Glass, 1992, pp. 3–4). The decade is best described as a period of
reports outlining what various groups viewed as deficiencies in the
education system, along with mandates on what needed to be done
to improve the system. Education had entered the political arena
full swing, and politicians felt compelled to make their mark on
education. There is no sign that they will retreat from this position
anytime soon.

The Role of the U.S. Office of Education

In hindsight, it is somewhat ironic that the second secretary of education, Terrell H. Bell, serving in a position that the National Education Association had been instrumental in creating, produced
this most scathing attack on education to date. In fact the 1980s
might be described as a decade of ironies in education. The Education Consolidation and Improvement Act passed in 1982 was intended to deregulate education by reducing federal controls of
education and decentralizing them to state and local authorities.

The idea was to reduce the level of federal involvement in education. But the response to *A Nation at Risk* would soon derail the
transfer of authority and place education close to the top of the
federal agenda. Bell resigned his position approximately a year and
a half after the release of the report. Later, when assessing his own
first term in office, President Ronald Reagan reflected, "If I were
asked to single out the proudest achievement of my administration's first three and one-half years in office, what we've done to

define the issues and promote the great national debate in education would rank up near the top of the list" (Reagan, 1984, p. 2).

One thing was quite clear by the end of the 1980s: the pendulum of public concern had swung from equality of educational opportunity to excellence. The focus of attention was now on setting higher standards; strengthening the curriculum in core subjects; increasing homework, time for learning, and time in school; more rigorous grading, testing, homework, and discipline; increasing productivity and excellence; and providing more choices regarding education. In addition, a big T had been added to the classic three Rs: a focus on technology and computers. Nationwide, Americans began to talk about excellence and world-class education. Superintendents were made painfully aware of the links between education and economic competitiveness in a global economy, at a time when American business was not faring well.

In 1989, school reform was developing within the most ideologically conservative political climate of recent times. In this setting, President George Bush and the nation's governors came together at a historical education summit in Charlottesville, Virginia. All agreed that "the time has come for the first time in the United States' history to establish clear national performance goals, goals that will make us internationally competitive" (U.S. Department of Education, 1991, p. 2). There was a clear call for a "renaissance in education." The meeting of the president and governors was clearly a response to the perception of a rising economic challenge from highly productive industrialized nations.

The prevailing mood was best summed up in a February 9, 1990, *Wall Street Journal* article that appeared in the first education supplement the *Journal* had ever published. The supplement began:

> Jobs are becoming more demanding, more complex. But our schools don't seem up to the task. They are producing students who lack the skills that businesses so desperately need to compete in today's global economy and by doing so, they are condemning students to a life devoid of meaningful employment.
>
> Better corporate retraining may serve as a stopgap. But ultimately the burden of change rests with our schools. While debate rages about how change should come, almost everyone agrees

that something has to be done. And quickly [*Wall Street Journal*, 1990, p. 1].

During the 1980s, morale among classroom teachers declined as they became more cynical about the nation they were serving. They believed that criticism reflected a naïveté about the challenges they faced and a misunderstanding about the outcomes being achieved. They expected the U.S. Office of Education to provide support, when in fact it was providing fuel to criticisms they felt were unjustified. The Carnegie Forum on Education and the Economy (1986, p. 26) found that many teachers "are immensely frustrated to the point of cynicism" regarding reform activities which they saw as bringing about very little change and showing a lack of respect for classroom teachers. They observed bureaucratic structures becoming more rigid, opportunities for exercising professional judgment decreasing, little to no real gains for students, and lack of professional respect for teachers.

The 1990s

With the 1990s has come recognition that growing up in America can be very risky. An increasing number of children are not being well cared for by their parents. Two-parent income earners, single-parent homes, and divorce have changed how children experience "the family." Children are directly confronted by social issues such as crime, neglect, poverty, abuse, disease, addiction, violence, and unemployment. In *Beyond Rhetoric,* the National Commission on Children (1992, p. 5) characterizes the state of American children this way: ". . . among all races and income groups, and in communities nationwide, many children are in jeopardy. They grow up in families whose lives are in turmoil. Their parents are too stressed and too drained to provide the nurturing, structure, and security that protect children and prepare them for adulthood. Some others are unsafe at home and in their neighborhoods. Many are poor, and some are homeless and hungry."

One might conclude that "if a nation can be judged by the way it treats its children, America is not faring too well." The reality has caused David Tyack, a prominent educational historian, to conclude, "Once again, educational reform and social pathologies have become prime-time, first-page news. If Americans do not help and heal the children at risk, the nation's social fabric will be in quite as much danger as its standing in the world economy" (Tyack, 1992, p. 30).

With the alienation of teachers, communities, and children came formal recognition of the importance of collaborative relationships among diverse groups in order to improve schools and ultimately student learning. The push was to achieve greater understanding through exchange of information and ideas among both internal and external groups; the goal was to ensure that all the groups that were needed to support public education were full partners in the process. The Goals 2000: Educate America Act, which was passed in 1993, encourages "communities to develop their own reform plans and provided seed money to support these efforts" (Riley, 1994). The law requires innovation in teaching and learning, increased parental and community involvement, professional development of teachers, and reduction in educational bureaucracy. The first four titles codify the six national education goals and establish the National Education Goals Panel and National Education Standards and Improvement Council. The legislation provides for a framework and resources to support state and local systematic educational improvement and establishes a National Skills Standards Board. Where the legislation of the 1980s was on shifting responsibility for education to state and local bureaucracies, the shifts in the 1990s seem to be to the local schools and communities. As Ted Sizer suggests (O'Neil, 1995a), "Lasting reform requires creating a climate for local educators and community members to craft their own improvement strategies. . . . [O]ur research suggests that you're not going to get significant long-term reform unless you have subtle but powerful support and collaboration among teachers, students, and the families of those students in a particular community . . . we strongly believe you have to look at reform school-by-school-by-school" (p. 4).

In March 1996, forty-nine corporate leaders, forty-one governors, and thirty educators, staff advisors, and policy experts (observers) attended the second National Education Summit, seven years after the historical summit in Charlottesville. The second summit was cochaired by Louis V. Gerstner, Jr., chairman and chief executive officer of IBM, and Gov. Tommy G. Thompson of Wisconsin; it was held at the IBM Conference Center in Palisades, New York. As Gerstner said, "Until we set standards and learn how to measure against them we can't assess the effectiveness of all the ideas that bounce off the walls of the educational establishment." The attendees endorsed the idea of each state developing "internationally competitive academic standards" and rigorous new tests to measure whether students meet the standards. They also agreed to establish an independent, nongovernmental body to review the new standards and monitor each state's progress toward them. Companies pledged to support governors by changing hiring practices to require academic transcripts, portfolios, or certificates of mastery from new high school graduates seeking jobs. However, concerns were expressed about the summit's setting standards for the workplace, the chaos of a separate set of standards in each state, and different levels of expectation.

State officials and proponents of reform responded by calling on school boards and superintendents to raise their standards and to build in accountability based on student performance. The state role would be to exert considerable influence on education through mandates and personal influence. This theme was initiated in 1986, when all fifty governors issued a joint report stating their willingness to act as "strong and eager partners in educational reform" (National Governors' Association, 1986, p. 60).

The 1990s have seen a significant increase in the number and variety of groups that have focused attention on educational issues, even though their primary interest is elsewhere. The schools have become the focal point for the resolution of broad economic, ideological, and societal issues. These groups tend to form around education issues such as standards; taxes; textbooks; curriculums; religion; and educational concepts including outcome-based education, family-life education, cooperative learning, school prayer, portfolio assessment, technology, and authentic learning. Superintendents across the country have experienced vigorous challenges against specific efforts to implement changes in the schools. Such challenges are often based upon economic, political, social, family, or religious values, with challengers showing less interest in academic impacts. These challenges often convert educational policy development and implementation into a war zone, and as attacks intensify the superintendent is often caught in the middle.

The distinguishing characteristic of the 1990s is that these groups are better organized and financed than at any period in the past.

Balancing Countervailing Forces

Superintendents and local school divisions are feeling pressure and counterpressure from all these very powerful agents, who are often opposed to one another's ideas. Decisions are being made less and less on values and the benefits of alternatives, and more on the basis of powerful political rhetoric. Finding and maintaining a reasonable balance within the existing context of education has become increasingly difficult for American superintendents. Superintendents are immersed in a vague and uneasy harmony of opposing forces. The fragility of the relationships often becomes apparent as superintendents attempt to balance the countervailing pressures, at the national, state, and local levels, in the development of school plans.

At the same time they are balancing these conflicting expectations and responding to mandates, superintendents are also asked to empower teachers so they can both design and carry out the curriculum. The staff members themselves must be considered in any decisions because they are the ones who must implement them. Everyone who works within the system must support decisions, through appropriate involvement and development, if the decisions are ever to have an impact on American children. It is at this teacher-to-student level that services are delivered and the success of the school system is determined.

In this context, the superintendent is being called on to decentralize and democratize public education, to involve school administrators, teachers, and parents in determining what will work best for their schools. After all is said and done, this local group best knows the demographics, histories, values, resources, and needs within their schools. Thus, the superintendent is being asked to support and facilitate school-based decisions, shared leadership, and other site-based approaches to school leadership. In describing the important role of superintendents in building effective schools, Joseph Murphy (1991, p. 224) says, "the chief executive officers of reformed schools act, not as they traditionally have, as directors and controllers, but as coordinators and 'enablers'—their job is to facilitate, not dictate. One of their major functions is serving and assisting schools. In this role, central offices act as service providers or support centers that offer technical assistance to schools." He later concludes, "Without their [the superintendents'] endorsement and support, their willingness to commit valuable tangible and intangible organizational resources, the seeds of restructuring are likely to fall on barren ground."

The problems that need to be addressed in education are not acute; they are chronic. Teachers must constantly change curriculum and instruction to meet the needs of the children and communities they serve. As we move up and down the local, state, and federal hierarchies, essential differences among local schools and communities are often lost and schooling is incorrectly viewed as having a sort of uniformity. Programs mandated by those who spend their professional lives outside the classroom often generate hostility, frustration, or helplessness among teachers.

The challenge for the superintendent in the 1990s is to find ways to manage all of the various national, state, and local pressures for improving school performance while working with the local school board and staff members to develop the most effective schools possible. This is the balancing act that most superintendents and boards find themselves called on to perform as they struggle to improve student learning and outcomes. Each entity has a legitimate role in the process of education; however, the superintendent and board are responsible for deciding how those roles play out within their school districts. This process has proven to be very difficult. Each decision further shapes the school agenda in a direction that favors one group, generally to the disadvantage of another.

These decisions are made more difficult by a sense of the urgency of school reform. Education reform has captured public interest and seems to remain a major national issue of debate and discussion regardless of what decisions are made. No other area has dominated the interest of Americans for so long a period as American education. National, state, and local groups of all kinds form commissions and make countless recommendations and reports. Candidates for public office usually have a number of educational planks in their election platforms. Political appointees, bureaucrats, business leaders, educators, and ministers all tout ideas for major school reform. Few issues on the American scene engender more experts and more controversy than does education. Consequently, the nature of the superintendency is to confront a perpetually changing set of conflicting expectations.

Responsiveness to the Needs of the Twenty-First Century

The key to successful superintendency in the next millennium will be responsiveness to the diverse demands placed on education. Superintendents must establish trust, focus interest and attention on student learning, and create a positive community paradigm if they are to have any hope of maintaining control of American education. If people lack confidence in the chief executive officer of the school division, they will neither trust nor support his or her difficult decisions. Therefore, the superintendent must be responsive to all the groups that are drawn into the educational arena, as well as to those who are there permanently. The superintendent talks—but listens more—to all those who have a legitimate interest in education. He or she works with members of the staff, the public, and the school board, as well as the countless interest and pressure groups who have an impact on education.

A major responsibility of superintendents is to deal with conflicting expectations, multiple political agendas, and varying ideas without unduly creating enemies or distrust. The superintendency can crumble from the outside or from the inside. Either way, the most-often-heard symptom of a superintendent who is in trouble is that he or she lacks rapport with—and respect from—important constituents in the education process. In these cases, communication and ultimately cohesion breakdown, and the superintendent is no longer able to manage the multiple pressures on the school district. This failure generates public dissatisfaction, which typically ends with the superintendent's being fired.

Movers and shakers exist among all groups that are involved or interested in education. A superintendent should meet regularly with these powerful individuals and seek their advice on issues that are sure to become controversial. This bridge building helps gain support within those groups that have the greatest potential for influencing the entire community. In this way, the superintendent can be sensitive to the feelings and beliefs of interested parties without becoming overwhelmed in the process. The superintendent should be sensitive to the diverse needs of interested parties but able to judge the relative merits of the wide range of input received when making educational decisions.

Superintendents are responsible to ensure that schools do not move in a narrow range inconsistent with the major purpose, spirit, and intent of public education. Effective superintendents are not paralyzed by divergent interests, and they do not merely tack until they determine where the winds of influence are blowing. They are capable of tackling gale forces to reach decisions on controversial matters and to articulate and defend the basis of those decisions so they are well understood and supported. Decisions should be based on a clear understanding of the positions taken by all interested parties and an accurate assessment of the conditions and desired outcomes. The superintendent's decisions should be based on well-grounded core values and policies, not reaction under pressure.

In a study of successful and unsuccessful superintendents, Edward W. Chance found that

> Superintendents who have a tenure of twelve years or more in a
> district identify open communication with the school board and
> community as one of the most important leadership attributes.
> The board members interviewed where superintendent turnover
> has been the norm identified lack of open communication as the
> primary reason for superintendent change. Finance was also listed
> as an area of importance by both groups as were such issues as per-
> sonnel and public relations. Clearly, those who enjoy a long tenure
> and are viewed as successful strive to communicate fully with the
> community as well as the board. . . . It is evident that the superin-
> tendent who does not succeed fails to practice open communica-
> tion. . . . They do not strive for an understanding with the board
> and often are more autocratic than democratic. The result is that
> the local school board, school district, and community and school
> staff are constantly in a crisis mode in any substantial interactions
> with the superintendent [Chance, 1992, pp. 22–23].

The keys to being a successful and responsive superintendent, then, are open communication, integrity, hard work, positive direction, core values, sound judgment, and effective decision making. Superintendents should strive to ensure that they clearly understand the diverse interests involved in each decision and are well informed. The successful superintendent is open, accessible, and responsive in all activities.

Part Two

Challenges and Dilemmas

Chapter Three

Negotiating Community Politics and Controversy

Clearly, many of the pressures that the superintendent confronts do not originate with the school board. In fact, they are felt by board members as well. They come from outside the day-to-day operation of the schools. External forces include demands for specific policies from interest and pressure groups; increasing intervention from federal, state, and local governments; heightened public expectations for schools; and social and economic problems existing within communities. Thomas Glass says that "working with many groups of citizens, parents, and staff who display adversarial stances is one of the most difficult public challenges facing superintendents" (1993a, p. 66). Amid the plethora of pressures, what's a school executive to do?

More people are demanding that schools do more things than ever before in the history of American education. If the typical problem with the school board is micromanagement, the problem with those outside the school division is hyperinterest and hypercriticism—paired with a reluctance to pay for needed improvements. These pressures are heightened by a growing number of social problems finding their way into the schools. An undercurrent of all these pressures is a new outpouring of political activism. This increased political turbulence has given rise to the often narrow, single-issue mentality exhibited by many of these groups. Daniel Yankelovich, president of the Public Agenda Foundation, suggests that "It's a peculiar moment in our history, where people feel mobilized and empowered, and somehow leadership is paralyzed."

What is peculiar about this increased pressure is that it is really paradoxical. Superintendents have realized that schools cannot be successful unless everyone is involved. A Senate forum on December 12, 1994, sponsored by the Center on Families, Communities, Schools, and Children (1994) and the Institute for Responsive Education, reinforced this open invitation to participate. Entitled "Connecting Policy Makers, Practitioners, and the Public," the forum stated its theme:

> In order for significant and enduring change to occur, all groups must be willing to convey their own expectations, and to acknowledge the validity of others' perspectives, in an ongoing dialogue. Written commitments to a collaborative process, local compacts, will help to ensure the dialogue. State and federal policies could enhance the success of local partnerships. Education reform must involve not only policy makers, but also parents, educators, business leaders, community organizers, health and social service professionals, and students for it to be successful. The collaboration must not be a one-time effort, but rather an established and continual process of working together to develop a shared vision of improved education in the classroom and the home, to redefine the work of the school building and the central office, and to articulate constructive, supportive policies on the state and federal levels [p. 1].

A major theme in school reform is that change in education cannot be expert driven but must be shaped by all those who have an interest in the education process. Richard Riley, as secretary of education, has picked up on this theme and developed national initiatives for community involvement in education. The Goals 2000 legislation requires schools to build broad-based panels and to develop programs to enable community members to participate. The legislation targets resources to those school divisions that link schools, parents, and communities.

A paradox in all of this is the problems that superintendents face in trying to identify a real sense of community in America. A small example of this void occurred in Raleigh, North Carolina, in 1992. Superintendent Robert E. Wentz succeeded at achieving greater integration and reducing involuntary busing by developing magnet schools in downtown Raleigh that drew white students.

As a result, his administration proposed a "reverse magnet campus" outside downtown Raleigh to draw African-American students out from the inner city and further reduce involuntary busing. Wentz was surprised at the polarization of community factions in response to this proposal. "Cost was a factor," he said, "but I don't believe it was the major reason that our board rejected our proposal. There was pressure from the angry parents in the area of the K–12 campus who did not want African-American students taking seats away from their children. Also, the magnet high school was in downtown Raleigh, and certain community and board members wanted more for this magnet school."

Trying to build collegiality and consensus, superintendents begin to recognize—and perhaps provide visibility and a forum for—many disparate groups with narrow agendas. Superintendents try to bring the community together in support of education but actually end up further dividing the community and school district. In addition, issues emerge whose proponents use the schools as a social and ideological battleground. Social, religious, economic, and cultural agendas often take precedence over the academic one. Superintendents end up scratching their heads and wondering, "Where do we go from here, and how do we reach a consensus?"

Communities have also been wary of placing too much trust in any form of government. Today, the public attitude toward public administrators and public service employees is one of almost total mistrust. It is easy to understand these feelings as the legacy of Watergate, Vietnam, savings-and-loan scandals, "middle-class" tax breaks that benefit only the wealthy, a crushing national debt, failing Medicare and Medicaid, troubled social security, loss of buying power, increased violence, and a general decline of political values and government viability. Derek Bok said in his 1988 annual report as president of Harvard University: "At present, the American people and their political leaders seem willing to tolerate a state of affairs that is impossible to defend on rational grounds. On the one hand, they demand a government that will take responsibility for the most difficult, most important tasks to be performed in our society. On the other hand, they exhibit a distrust of government and a disdain toward those who devote their lives to public service. Such feelings have many unfortunate consequences . . . [including] a constant preoccupation with malfeasance and scandal rather than creativity and success" (1988, p. 33).

This attitude has not been lost on the American superintendency. Citizens often vent their concerns on superintendents, wrapping them in that general mistrust of government and the belief that it is letting its citizens down.

Types of "Political" Issues

In 1992, a program was launched to help superintendents deal with community disputes by enabling them to better handle various interest groups, the media, and the general political process. The program, which was sponsored by five foundations, was called Superintendents Prepared. It attempted to help aspiring urban superintendents to solve conflicts between different segments of the community or among special-interest groups; to communicate effectively with the news media and the general public; to work collaboratively with staff members and motivate people to meet common goals; to manage the business and financial sides of complex organizations, and to coordinate efforts with municipal leaders and human-service providers. Such a program reflects the very difficult expectations placed on school superintendents. As they become enmeshed in the web of issues debated by various constituencies, they find themselves at the center of controversy. An Ohio superintendent said in his resignation address in 1990 that "I was spending so much time going after funding, trying to talk to people, to the legislature, that sometimes that seemed like that's all there is time for."

Political differences among various groups both inside and outside education are placing increasing pressure on the way superintendents operate. The differences are caused more by events or disparate views than by any specific actions or decisions made by the superintendent. For example, a Prince George's (Maryland) county executive called for the resignation of the superintendent despite a long tenure in the school system. One possible explanation was that a number of educational shortcomings had occurred in the county during the executives' terms in office; and the school system and education problems became an important political issue in the gubernatorial race. The superintendent was accused of a "lack of vision" and a "lack of ability to inspire others to follow," even though he was supported by the elected board and respected by colleagues within the region.

As is clear, superintendents find themselves facing two types of issues with political and pressure groups. The first is a situation where they are aware that an issue or action is going to draw fire. In these cases, the superintendent is fairly well prepared for the flak and the struggle. But the other type of issue comes out of the woodwork, with an incident suddenly seeming critical as an issue is blown out of proportion. Robert Spillane (whom we take as an extended case study later in this chapter) said that "as superintendent in Boston it seemed that a train was always about to come through my office wall. This is because everything was politicized there." These situations can take over one's time and attention to such an extent that progress is stalled.

The Inevitability of Political Decision Making

The decision arena of the superintendent becomes smaller and smaller as public officials become embroiled in political debate related to schools. Policy makers broaden their involvement in decisions and policy statements regarding education, which narrows those left to educators. As a result of this trend, many education decisions are being subsumed under larger political agendas. World events, political decisions, and economics are closely tied to education as these larger forces often influence the balance of political power and community life in American school districts. No longer can superintendents focus their attention only on issues within the education community—or even in the immediate community of the schools. What occurs inside is quite likely to be part of a larger political process outside the school system.

Superintendents seldom survive or succeed if they ignore the reality of the various power structures in the operation of the school system. The most important is the politics within the local school district; but every year local, state, national, and international politics seem to become more intertwined. The most obvious concern is recognizing the potential dangers inherent in confronting a politically influential individual, group, or position. This experience has often been a difficult lesson for educators, who tend to scorn anything that even smacks of being political. Jack Kaufhold (1993) sums up the sentiments of many superintendents: "If I'd wanted to be a politician, I would have majored in political science and taken a law degree instead of a doctorate in education. . . . I don't want to be a politician. . . . I wanted to help kids and provide the best education possible for them" (p. 42). Politics occurs, however, in any setting where different interest groups compete for power and decide upon the distribution of scarce items, such as resources, participation, information, influence, and prestige.

The complexity of the political process can immobilize some superintendents. They must have a stomach for politics. Superintendents can't expect a clear consensus or a cohesive set of political forces in making decisions on what is best for the education of children. Ultimately, they need extraordinarily good political acuity—including knowing how to apply power and effectively communicate to diverse groups.

Conflict is everywhere, thanks to differences in the needs, perspectives, interests, and power of different participants. Bargaining, negotiation, collegiality, coercion, and compromise become part of everyday political life of the superintendent. The dynamic activities of politics produce temporary coalitions that provide enough stability to allow the exercise of leadership. However, making decisions requires great courage, because the stability of this political process is fragile at best and the superintendent is held accountable if the coalitions break down and the decisions are no longer supported. The coalitions that form around specific interests change as issues come and go. Effective superintendents are able to gain needed political support. They recognize that issues are constantly changing but that relationships stay (for a while, anyway).

Political Acumen

Many of the decisions faced within schools are converted into political campaigns. Interest groups use flyers, public meetings, proselytizing speeches, letters to the editor, talk show appearances, marches, filibustering meetings, and personal influence to ensure that school decisions turn out as they desire. Patricia Howlett (1993) documented a situation in which politically active minority groups in Oakland, California, applied intense political pressure to get the local school and elected representatives to reject state-approved textbooks as being racist. Howlett concluded:

> The facts were clear: the new series was a marked improvement over anything in print; the publisher had promised to work with teachers and volunteers to provide supplemental materials about underrepresented ethnic and cultural groups; and a review team of district teachers and citizens had praised the books as "the best to be printed to date." Rejecting the entire sequence meant a frantic scurrying to develop a course outline and to accumulate instructional materials for the next school year. In spite of all of those facts, the majority of the members of the local school board did the politically correct thing: they rejected the textbook series, making whatever political statement the loudest pressure group in their district demanded [p. 14].

This resulted in anger at the state level, community fragmentation, loss of confidence in the superintendent and board, and expanded involvement of political groups in educational matters.

The literature is replete with examples of political activities that became the basis for decisions related to effective student learning. Everyone wants to call the shots on the basis of his or her personal interpretation of what is right or wrong for America. This begins with members of the staff, runs into the community, and goes all the way to state and national politicians. It is not uncommon for assistant administrators and principals to build support structures that bypass the superintendent; the staff members try to control the school board through involvement in board elections or maneuvering to take power away from the superintendent. These employees seek to become the power behind the scenes, and they sometimes succeed.

Governors often use political clout to obtain the superintendent's support on issues related more to party platforms and political negotiations than to sound educational practice. The challenge for today's school administrators is to find ways to deal with the politics and obtain needed support while ensuring important student outcomes. Schools are no longer pure and clean, governed by precise rules, unsullied by interest groups, and clearly defined by appropriate practice.

Confidence in the superintendent and the schools comes as much from influential individuals and political support as it does from student outcomes. Therefore, developing coalitions and hammering out agreements that gain wide support becomes a key task for an effective superintendent. This, of course, is much more difficult as the views of power groups grow more divergent. The superintendent must find ways to align the various views both inside and outside the schools so that as many of the powerful groups as possible can support the initiatives. Once these individuals and groups are aligned with the direction the school is to take, public opinion soon follows, and the superintendent is seen in a positive light.

The task of bringing powerful constituents online is complicated by the complexity and volatility of the contemporary issues working their way into schools. These issues often have very little to do with student learning but everything to do with the superintendent's survival. The political goal is to help the community power structure work through disputes with the least amount of permanent damage. This goal sometimes can get in the way of idealistic views about improved education, which stand in the way of harsh political pragmatism. The superintendent cannot afford to lose his or her power base if long-term employment is important. This means that the superintendent must constantly test the waters on any project that is potentially controversial or needs widespread support. This also means lots of meetings with those in the power structure and efforts to participate in social and civic activities with the important power brokers. Superintendents need to attend important civic affairs and be part of the inner circle of power within the community.

Special-Interest and Pressure Groups

Beyond responding to federal, state, and local politics, the school division is expected to define and respond to community interests. The problem becomes one of defining common interests despite the pressures exerted by special-interest groups. How do the superintendent and school board identify common interests that encompass the aggregate interests of all those different groups within the boundaries of the school district and state? This feat is particularly hard when groups are created to counter each other's efforts. It is even more difficult when small but very vocal and energetic groups do not represent the larger, quieter community at large, which shows no inclination to take an active role. The superintendent and board's evaluation and decision regarding the common good will be influenced by opposing representations from the activists within the various interest groups. Thus, education policy and practice is at least partially formed as a result of the interplay of the competing demands of group interests.

Many types of interest groups exist at the national, state, and local levels. In fact, the 1989 *Encyclopedia of Associations* lists 1,221 national and international education associations. This list includes only permanent organizations on the order of the American Association of School Administrators (AASA), the Association for Supervision and Curriculum Development (ASCD), the National School Boards Association (NSBA), the National Association of Secondary School Principals (NASSP), the National Education Association (NEA), and others. There are also countless temporary groups that form around various interests and are quite active over shorter periods of time. Interest groups may be very narrowly focused on school policy, or they may see the schools as a means to a larger end: reducing the tax burden, teaching Christian values, or supporting free-market principles.

There is no simple way to categorize interest groups. For example, foundations, textbook manufacturers, and the media maintain that they are not interest groups, yet they exercise a major influence on various school issues, particularly curriculum issues. They often create new knowledge and demands around which others rally their support. A policy network newsletter of the National School Boards Association states:

> Schools are the places where young minds are molded, thought processes are developed, social values are reinforced, and acceptable social behavior is fashioned. Increasingly, individual citizens, as well as religious and civic groups and organizations across this nation, are developing a keen interest in what is taught, read, viewed, and discussed in our public schools. Parents, students, school board members, and administrators all have an obvious interest regarding what goes on in our schools, but so do people with no local affiliation or direct connection to the district.

People representing the political spectrum of ideas and beliefs, people worried about social mores and the future of a sometimes less than admirable society look to the public schools as a mechanism either to foster change or to stifle it [cited in Morris, 1992, p. 1].

Interest groups clarify and articulate demands, placing them within the context of decision making and applying pressure to decision makers to conform to their interests. They often attempt to achieve their goals at the expense of competing values or desires by providing organized representation for those who think as they do. The danger inherent in these groups is that they might go beyond acceptable limits in trying to influence the public and ultimate decisions. The superintendent and board must ensure that this does not happen. Obvious misuse of the political process by such groups is when they attempt to wield scarce resources such as money and power to purchase decisions—or employ violence to try to force decisions. Hult and Walcott (1990, p. 58) suggest that less obvious but equally destructive methods often can subvert the system, as when interest groups exaggerate or fabricate claims about the benefits of their positions. The researchers also found cases where interest groups had purposely confused the issue or spread inaccurate information to strengthen their positions, prolong debate, and heighten internal conflict.

The problem these tactics create for the superintendent is to run the schools effectively when everyone out there wants to call the shots according to his or her personal agenda, and when those people are even willing to employ deception to impose an interpretation of social need. Groups have used techniques such as dominating discussions, misrepresenting opponents' views, digging up dirt, spouting generalities, wearing opponents down, dividing and conquering, overwhelming, and obscuring the issues. This situation is sometimes further complicated when what seems like a local concern is part of a well-organized, nationally funded campaign that transcends local district interests and is thus not really open to negotiation at the district level. The constitutional principle that all pressure groups have the right to be heard governs these situations.

Educational Reform and the Religious Community

One area of disagreement among interest groups that emerged in the 1980s and has gained momentum in the 1990s is the New Christian Right's focus on "religious rights," which is sometimes closely associated with the "parents' rights" movement. The Christian Right has sometimes opposed activities that are tolerant of counseling, self-esteem, global education, drug education, independent and critical thinking, homosexuality, values education, sex and health education, abortion, outcome-based education (particularly related to ethics, environmentalism, and multicultural education), population growth, meditation, New Age thinking, visualization, journal keeping, and other issues that they see as contrary to Christian teaching. They tend to support parents' choice of their children's schools, traditional roles for women, prayer within schools, ideological purity, basics education, normative grading systems, educational accountability, and what they describe as "pro family" curriculum.

Educators' initial response was to dismiss such interest groups as an anti-school-restructuring movement with a small-city or suburban flavor. But as support has grown, the group has become a powerful political force in education. There are, however, those in the American Civil Liberties Union, People for the American Way, the Freedom to Learn Network, the Sandi National Laboratories, the American Library Association, Americans United for Separation of Church and State, and others who are fearful of the Christian Right's efforts to ban books, curriculum, extracurricular activities, and educators and board members who do not support their causes.

There is concern within some religious communities that textbooks and tests promote "leftist political agendas" and "liberal values." In extreme cases, they believe that the school superintendent might be involved in a conspiracy emanating from Washington, D.C., to destroy their children. The strength of this belief may be demonstrated by a brief excerpt from a book written by Pat Robertson, president of the Christian Broadcasting Network (CBN): "We have these things because we have allowed Christian and biblical standards to be removed from our national life. It has taken the left some seventy years to reduce us to this level" (Robertson, 1994, p. 149). He later goes on to say, "Instead of the First Amendment concept, which says that government shall not establish a religion or prohibit the free exercise of religion, the new law would recognize the universal character of religion. . . ." (p. 465) He has sometimes called this concern about the eradication of Christian beliefs religious cleansing in the American republic.

Any dilution of the Christian perspective may have resulted from the desire to honor diversity, which has tended to put a squeeze on the space left to represent Christian beliefs. The Christian community feels very strongly that this has gone too far; the resulting tension has never been greater.

One of the many challenges to current reform efforts has focused on textbooks used in the schools. These challenges have caused real problems for publishers such as Harcourt, Brace, Jovanovich and Holt, Rinehart, and Winston, that have long worked with educators to improve the curriculum. Harcourt, Brace, Jovanovich revised its *Impressions* reading series to embrace current educational thought, such as whole-language approaches. The series focuses on reading for meaning, with selections that are believed to be of interest to children. The publisher's efforts have included soliciting massive input from both parents and teachers. The conservative criticism and challenge to this series focuses on the subject matter more than the pedagogical approach. Conservatives argue that the books are depressing, morbid, and violent; invade students' privacy; attack traditional values; and promote satanism, mysticism, and the occult. Statistics indicate that one out of five school districts where challenges have been lodged no longer uses the series. Superintendents have often had trouble surviving these challenges.

Holt, Rinehart, and Winston had similar problems with a high school health series for use in Texas. Anti-abortionists, fundamentalist Christians, the Christian Right, and other interest groups lobbied the Texas Board of Education not to allow the textbooks to be used in school districts in Texas. The Texas Family Planning Association, on the other hand, believed that using the texts might help to reduce the forty thousand teenage pregnancies each year in the state—the second highest number in the nation. Texas is an important market to educational textbook publishers and is sometimes used as a test market to determine how adoptions will go across the nation (Texas and California together represent almost 20 percent of the total textbook market). In the end, the Texas board asked the publisher to make four hundred revisions to the five texts. Executives at Holt, Rinehart, and Winston decided not to accept the changes "because making scores of requested revisions was economically infeasible and because ethical issues were at stake." Corporate Vice President Peter Farwell said, "When you look at the potential sales, it wasn't feasible, especially because the changes made it a Texas-only book. We created the book by talking to a lot of administrators and teachers involved in health education, who told us what they felt kids needed to know in order to deal with health. The changes would have left out issues we feel are important" (Dillon, 1994, p. 6). In fact, a number of the requested changes were in opposition to the stated fundamental philosophy of the series. In the end, the series was not sold in the state of Texas.

Texas is one of twenty-two states where government committees must approve all texts sold in the state. Regardless of the level at which such battles are fought, they are important to school superintendents as instructional leaders for the schools. Gilbert Sewall, director of the American Textbook Council, expressed to us his concern that "this underlines how hard it is getting to produce a textbook that appeals to a general audience and to satisfy all the pressure groups. Especially in books dealing with health and sex education, highly opinionated, sometimes obsessive people come to the table and publishers are increasingly inclined to retreat from subjects that bring so many marketing headaches." The result of concessions is generic, dull books that do not address the critical issues of the twenty-first century. These same groups are now expressing concerns regarding the Internet and curricula in general.

Individuals see these groups as creating a form of paranoia that is whittling away at the support for improving American education at a time when it needs to be transformed. George Kaplan reported that "In district after district, supporters of the schools are finding themselves on the defensive, often unable to rally lasting support for venturesome but sound educational practices. Unless and until this backing materializes and becomes a permanent feature of the educational landscape, the promoters of reactionary political causes and outdated educational doctrine will continue their advance in the nation's schools" (1994, p. 12). Supporters say that this conservative movement is needed to support the rights of parents to bring up and educate their children.

The result has been that both educators and politicians are reluctant to enter the debate. Martha McCarthy is concerned that

> Instead of arguing that the challenged instructional programs are value-neutral or trying to sanitize the curriculum so that no groups are offended, policy makers and educators need to take a stand that some context (e.g., science), attitudes (e.g., respect for racial diversity), and skills (e.g., critical thinking) should not be compromised. Such instruction is necessary to ensure an educated citizenry in our democratic society, and educators should not have to defend the merits of teaching children how to think or how to get along with others from diverse backgrounds. If policy makers do not take a stand against the mounting threats to the public school curriculum, many school restructuring efforts may be doomed before they get off the ground. And, more significantly, we may produce a generation of citizens who lack the skills necessary to address the vexing dilemmas that will confront our nation in the twenty-first century [1993, p. 60].

This neutrality is becoming more problematic as conservative groups, the religious right, militia, etc., are influencing school boards and scuttling curriculum reforms across the country. Debate is being couched in terms such as conservative versus liberal, economic versus civic, environmentalism versus commercialism, and the suggestion of incompetence among tenured educational experts.

Organizations such as the Institute for Development of Educational Activities (I/D/E/A) that have attempted to clarify the debate and help educators understand the religious right have been seriously attacked. Because the religious right is a national movement and well backed by religious radio and television, it has no trouble getting its message across. Organizations such as I/D/E/A do not have the same communication systems to make their side of the story heard. The NSBA, AASA, and ASCD have provided information on the religious right while avoiding official positions on the key issues. The NEA has reacted strongly to what it believes to be consequential issues of difference. The American Federation of Teachers has been less involved. The superintendent and some-times the school board are in a difficult position when trying to rally support for innovative new programs. They are not always sure how various interest groups will respond, or where they will be able to identify support groups.

Policy, Practice, and Pressure Groups

An effective approach to dealing with interest and pressure groups includes strong curriculum review and selection policies that allow an appropriate response to legitimate concerns, along with broad community involvement in curriculum development. Strong poli-cies for the selection of curriculum materials and instructional strategies should be well defined and accessible to the community. These policies should also spell out strict procedures for challenges launched against present or proposed programs within the school district. Policies should allow the board and superintendent to keep control of potentially volatile situations.

The superintendent has a responsibility to protect the interests of the larger community that was involved in the planning process, over the challenges of special-interest groups. This is much more difficult if there are no policies and ground rules to be enforced in these areas. In an article investigating the activities of interest groups, it was noted that "nearly a third of these challenges suc-ceed in some measure. . . . Schools with review policies defeated nearly three-fourths of the challenges to their curricula, while schools without policies succeeded in turning back only half" (Ed-ucation Daily, 1991).

Sound procedures and policies, as well as core values, provide a better framework from which participants can enter into dis-cussions about whether changes are needed and why. Making ex-ceptions to established policies often backfires, placing the superintendent in stormy legal waters and diminishing the support of those who have chosen to participate. Policies and procedures provide support for the superintendent and for everyone else in-volved in the process. A good policy also supports teachers, who in implementing the results will feel a lot of heat themselves.

Interest and pressure groups are often able to succeed by in-timidating principals and teachers who fear repercussions. This factor can often create a less-than-enthusiastic response among educators to planned improvements and a self-censorship regarding ideas, values, and direction that participants in the process really believe in. Many teachers have simply stopped using effective materials or strategies to avoid the unrestrained lobbying efforts of a small but vocal group of parents or community members. These teachers do not feel supported by either the administration or the school policy and therefore feel it is easier to give up on ideas they have found to be effective with children, rather than be subjected to intense pressure with very unclear support. Henry Reichman tells us that "Where sound formal policies and procedures are lacking, censorship efforts may quietly succeed. In these types of situations, teachers, librarians, or administrators may accede to pressure without any 'incident' being registered. Perhaps more ominously, school personnel may initiate removals on their own, either to deter perceived threats or to implement their own values and orthodoxies on the educational process. In some cases, potentially controversial materials simply are not acquired in the first place" (1988, p. 13).

It is too late to establish policies and ground rules to protect those involved in the improvement process once they have been burned. Injured participants convey a message—that it is better to avoid controversy—that will not be soon forgotten. Of greater concern, such an attitude will be passed down to future participants as they are socialized into the ways of the education system. Effective policy and practice protects participants and builds a culture that supports continuous improvement efforts. Effective procedures allow for broad-based parent and community involvement in important educational decisions, before any form of board action is taken. Policy and procedures should be established to allow for communication, decision making, and challenges, and to protect those who are charged with implementing the perceived improvements. Efforts should focus on ideas and issues that people share and not those that divide.

Time is a very important ally in efforts to survive pressure group tactics. One must provide enough time for all interested parties to discuss and understand the decision. Time is needed to understand all of the ramifications, related concerns, and possibilities in any opportunity for improvement. Time is needed to allow teachers to build confidence and trust that the improvements will be supported.

As educators gain greater understanding of other participants' values, beliefs, interest, visions, and commitments, they find it easier to design and implement an overall plan. The energy and effort required to sustain a school improvement effort grow out of those who support it. The inspiration, motivation, and related support for successful renewal of American education must come from its local communities, including all of the special-interest groups. Superintendents are charged with helping communities to trust, support, and empower one another as they face the challenges required to foster continuous improvement in American schools. In *Future Shock,* Alvin Toffler accurately foretold that we need "a multiplicity of visions, dreams, and prophecies—images of potential tomorrows" (1984, p. 140). That time is upon us as we prepare our schools to handle this complex reality.

An Extended Case Study: Robert Spillane, 1995 AASA Superintendent of the Year

The true complexity of the politics of the superintendency cannot be clearly conveyed within the pages of a book. The reader can neither feel the intense pressure and emotions involved nor truly grasp the complex and intricate web of relationships that must be understood if the superintendent is to survive.

Perhaps an extended look (even if necessarily simplified) at the experiences of the 1995 AASA Superintendent of the Year, Robert Spillane of Fairfax County, Virginia, can illustrate the richly political nature of the school.

The best way to characterize Spillane is to use a motto that appears on a plaque on his desk: "The main thing is to keep the main thing the main thing." Although his schools are inundated with the social, personal, and economic problems of their students, parents, and community, the "main thing" for Superintendent Spillane is academics, quality instruction, and student learning. This solid grounding in academics provides the needed stability to weather some fairly harsh political conditions. His experiences in establishing important political ties show the difficult and often complex situations superintendents face.

Spillane has been superintendent in Fairfax County, Virginia, one of the nation's fifteen largest school districts, since 1985. He has built a national reputation as an innovator and developer of quality education. Under his leadership, the Fairfax schools have often been described as a "premier school system." While the population in Fairfax has changed to include greater diversity, the verbal scores on the Scholastic Aptitude Test, which were already fairly strong, have held steady; there has been a significant increase in math scores. Dropout rates declined significantly, and 73 percent of Fairfax graduates enter four-year colleges. He has championed the nationally recognized Thomas Jefferson High School for Science and Technology, which consistently produces large numbers of National Merit Scholarship finalists and science prize winners. Fairfax students have continued to score far above the national average on standardized tests.

On the other side of the ledger, Spillane was also caught up in a maelstrom of political pressure caused in part by shifts in ethnic and economic diversity, economic solvency, and political power structures related to both. The clashes were compounded by philosophical struggles between a Republican-controlled board of supervisors that held the purse strings and a Democratic-dominated school board that approved the school budget. Money was in short supply; he was faced with cutting $30–50 million from budgets. Spillane believed the quality of education should be maintained, even if a tax increase needed to be considered. However, the mood of the politicians and, to some extent, the citizens was that no tax increase should be incurred regardless of any resulting impact on Fairfax children. There had been a taxpayer revolt in nearby Maryland, and Fairfax politicians did not want a repeat performance in Virginia.

Spillane was charged to make massive cuts in the education budget. This task was particularly unpleasant because he was told to make cuts in his own initiatives, which had previously been supported and had been given credit for improving the schools. The most serious disagreements occurred in relation to a merit-pay plan for teachers that was one of the cornerstones of his success. In getting hefty raises for teachers during his early tenure in Fairfax County, Spillane had won the support of the political power structure, the community, rank-and-file teachers, and ordinary parents during his first three years. Support both inside and outside the school system made the critical difference during the three years of difficult work to get an evaluation system in place along with the merit-pay system and to finally preserve them both. On the basis of this system, approximately one hundred teachers a year did not measure up and ended up leaving Fairfax schools.

Now, however, Spillane launched what was seen by some board members as an inappropriate battle against the board's wishes to suspend the merit-pay plan, which provided bonuses to exemplary teachers. Teachers who had received bonuses (averaging $4,000) formed a strong pressure group to ensure that their pay would not be cut. Dr. Spillane and his group of teachers had been very supportive of one another in past years. The teachers who had not received bonuses became politically active and encouraged their teacher union and others to support the elimination of the bonus program. Both supporters and critics of merit pay waged an intense and acrimonious campaign to make the decision go their way. Ultimately, merit pay was suspended. But the Teacher Performance Evaluation program continues as a very strong, tough, and effective program.

A second disagreement occurred when Spillane asked board members to scale back a cost-cutting plan that used administrators as substitute teachers in the classroom. This problem was compounded by the layoffs of 150 support-staff employees. He was trying to head off a growing morale problem among employees within the school system, who had fought hard against these changes. "The most troublesome issue for me," he said, "is the divisiveness among employee groups that is generating anger and resentment on one level and, on another, eroding the extraordinary esprit de corps that has always characterized the school system." The board ultimately required administrators to go back into the classroom as substitutes.

Fairfax administrators were also actively fighting a plan to give them a one-time bonus rather than pay raises for the next year. At the same time, the Fairfax Education Association announced plans to sue the Fairfax board if it tried to freeze their seniority raises. Employees of the county government began to express irritation with the teachers' and administrators' insistence on raises, stating that the rest of county government was being cut more deeply than schools. The sentiment was "Why should education get any raises when we're not getting them on the county side?" The county employees began to lobby. They maintained that if raises were given to any employee of the county, they should be given to all employees. The board ultimately decided to give administrators bonuses.

Spillane's recommended budget cuts included programs as well, in programs from special education to gifted and talented classes, from boys' gymnastics to swim and diving teams. These proposed cuts inspired thousands of parents to join strong lobbying groups determined to campaign and apply pressure to save their programs. Some, such as the Fairfax County Association for the Gifted, had been around for a long time. Each group launched well-organized mailing and phone-call campaigns, packed meetings, recruited speakers, and raised questions without end. They picketed key school events, were interviewed by the press, and ultimately created so much pressure on Spillane that he often backed down. In putting one program back into the budget, he said in total frustration, "So let's go on. Let's stop this. We can do this all night long. . . . I didn't want to cut a penny of that $42 million. Let's remember that. Let's not put everyone on the defensive here about why this cut and why not some other." His approach and statements rankled some school board members, most of the County Board of Supervisors, and some of his supporters in the extended power structure. His problems were compounded when a panel of the county council of PTAs emerged from a series of meetings with a recommendation to raise taxes in order to save programs. They set up an e-mail link for all PTA members to monitor the latest moves by the board, county supervisors, and PTAs.

Spillane had had the support of the Fairfax County Council for the Arts and the Federation of Citizens Associations since first coming to Fairfax. These two groups, along with a number of others within the county, urged Spillane to extend the school day on Mondays for elementary students. This request was very much in line with Spillane's desire to increase the number of hours students had for instruction. He proposed to add a seventh period to secondary schools and to eliminate the twenty-year-old practice of closing elementary schools early on Mondays. The elementary schools had a longstanding tradition of closing two and one-half hours early on Monday for personal and community activities. The board chairperson at the time had championed the idea of extending the school day; however, the composition of the board had changed and its general consensus was to add the seventh period but not to make any changes to the Monday early closing. The teachers' unions argued very strongly against Spillane's proposal as well. One attack against Spillane came from the president of the 6,900-member Fairfax Education Association, who said, "We are not nearly as distressed by current economic difficulties as we are with Dr. Spillane's cavalier and callous actions. We know the economy will improve, but it is now clear to us that Bud Spillane will not." Elementary school teachers put up amazing resistance, eventually convincing large numbers of parents that changing this practice would detrimentally affect their children. In such matters, Spillane continues to practice the Yogi Berra rule that "issues cannot be laid to rest" and is still looking into pay-for-performance and extending the school day. "As long as the issues remain critical, one must continue the political struggle," he believes.

Even when Spillane and the board were able to cut programs, there were often strong backlashes. One such program was the Minority Student Achievement Office. The Northern Virginia Baptist Ministers Council criticized what it saw as discriminatory treatment of blacks by the public school system. The council was also concerned that layoff notices sent to teachers would disproportionately hurt minorities. According to those in the superintendent's office, the Minority Student Achievement Office was abolished because it "was not effective" and because less expensive approaches such as reducing the size of some classes were going to be tried instead. The ministers saw this as an attitude within Fairfax that blacks in the county were second-class citizens who were not provided the same level of attention as whites. The ministers were quite interested in the fate of Deputy Superintendent Loretta Webb, the highest-ranking black school official, whose job was up for elimination due to budget cuts. The National Association for the Advancement of Colored People also had a number of concerns regarding discrimination issues in all branches of Fairfax County government.

More recently, incidents occurred as a result of the national fallout over "outcome-based education" (OBE). The Mobil Foundation had funded efforts to establish high and clear academic-achievement outcomes for Fairfax students. (Chester Finn, Jr., usually associated with conservative views and administrators, was the major consultant on the project.) However, resistance developed on the basis of what had been heard about the OBE concept in the national press, and on religious radio and television talk shows. Spillane declared that "although our project focused exclusively on academic outcomes, we found that our use of the word 'outcomes' invited attacks from everyone who had heard about OBE efforts in other states. Even after we changed the name of the project from 'outcomes project' to 'Fairfax Framework,' the attacks continued. They have now substantially dissipated but will, I expect, never end." Political allies helped limit the damage from these heated attacks; in fact, they saved the essential project.

Spillane was both surprised and discouraged by how quickly and extensively his support base had declined. Interest and pressure groups had come from all corners of the community, and there were very few areas of agreement. The disagreements were harsh and ended with many hard feelings. Spillane had worked hard within the school district to gain widespread political support for a number of new initiatives; the resultant political base had allowed Fairfax County to become one of the premier school districts in the nation. Now, in a little over two years, he was watching this political support dissipate. He was determined not to let it happen.

Between 1991 and 1994, Spillane eliminated 870 administrator positions through budget cuts. He suggested that the community and school board should "twist the arms of the supervisors to come up with more revenue." He proposed charging an activity fee for the county's students. A plan to save bus operating costs included starting some schools earlier, even though it could "surely inconvenience some parents . . . but, in this kind of budget climate, parents must be willing to trade convenience for twelve million dollars." Spillane created a contingency list of items that would have to be cut if the supervisors could not come up with the needed money. This included elimination of an additional 408 teaching positions. Such proposals and many other changes caused usually by tight budgets had worn heavily on a number of important political relations. His critics suggested that it was "time to move." Spillane did not want to leave: "It's an issue of facing the realities of being here in my ninth year, with then one year left to find something meaningful." After a search for a new position and national media attention on his being a finalist for a number of positions, board and community members began questioning his commitment to the county and suggested this job search was proof that it was time for a change.

Spillane called for the healing of wounds and an end to divisiveness after a period of bruising budget battles. In a statement he said: "Somewhere in the midst of this budget season the attacks on our credibility and integrity became especially nasty and persistent, and then we circled the wagons and shot at each other. The result, I think, is that we are all wounded." Five of the eleven board members responded with suggestions that they would not vote for renewing his contract. Spillane asked for another two years to benefit the terms of his retirement.

With his nine years as school superintendent, Spillane was a veteran in the Washington, D.C., metropolitan area. The two things that seemed to make a difference for the superintendent were the strong national reputation of the Fairfax schools and resulting endorsements by local business and corporate leaders whom Spillane had worked hard to keep on his side and who saw schools as an important element of economic development. Spillane had developed a solid ally in the chairman of the Fairfax County Chamber of Commerce, who had continued to speak in his support. The official position of the chamber was that the Fairfax schools had "a stellar record of achievement by one of our nation's foremost school administrators." The board ended up extending his contract for two years, rather than the four that his supporters had sought.

Robert Spillane has ridden considerable turbulence and still remained an effective superintendent. This is because he was able to maintain both effective political support and effective schools. In fact, the American Association of School Administrators recognized him as the 1995 Superintendent of the Year, notwithstanding these tumultuous experiences. He says the key elements to achieving longevity while "changing the status quo are: (1) clearly and simply articulate the needed change and its compelling benefits; (2) build constituencies for the change both inside and outside the school system; and (3) ensure that the people and other resources necessary to bring about the change are in place, prepared, and that it really can be made to work. Articulation of the change is critical."

Spillane is still working to continuously improve the schools. His most recent proposal is for providing high and clear standards for student achievement and the means to assess that achievement. He is also interested in exploring better governance structures and going beyond elected or appointed boards to meet the needs of current circumstances. It is important, he feels, for people to look back and see what they have accomplished, even if it is very difficult. Finally, he suggests (perhaps with tongue in cheek) that no leader can be effective without "constructive criticism." He has remained able to keep his focus on the main thing, even through the excessive politicization of the job.

Reflections on the Politicized Superintendency

This story of one individual's struggle to conscientiously perform an intensely politicized job characterizes what is happening on various scales in school districts across this country. Spillane offers his impression of the process:

> I define [politicization] as becoming an issue in which some people feel they have a stake and over which they are willing to organize and fight. Politicization often leads to distortion of the issue, as people organize around one or both (or more) sides of an issue and try to score points with potential supporters. Since people who are not initially involved with an issue will not understand its complexity, much less nuance, people who believe they are stakeholders will simplify and distort in order to build support. This is as true in the issues faced by superintendents as it is in "real" politics. Dealing with critical incidents requires the same kind of political skills as "real" politics. This means keeping your goal and your message clear, explaining sufficiently and clearly, making critical judgments about when and how to respond to opposition, communicating core values, getting the message out, being patient, and many other things that those who engage in "politics" need to be able to do. An educational leader who cannot do these things will not be able to change the status quo in his or her school system.

Superintendents should not form protective peer alliances, but rather embrace the political power that can mobilize resources to achieve results. These are the key groups who can "make things happen and get things done."

The source of a superintendent's credibility, therefore, comes from his or her ability to gain support from the political structure within the community. Power is something that influential people attribute to one another—and the superintendent must be a part of the process if he or she hopes to have any impact, success, or just survival. If the superintendent does not become one of the political players, he or she will be dominated by others, powerless and at the mercy of the political system.

Political power is self-reinforcing. Subordinates who see the superintendent as a politically recognized and influential figure will naturally look to that individual for leadership. Superintendent power, when used properly, motivates subordinates, instills loyalty, and results in accomplishment of goals. This leads to more political power and support. It has been said that the measure of a person is what he or she does with power. The superintendent who moves forward without political support—or misuses it—loses the respect of subordinates. This results in the need to apply coercive force, to supervise too closely, and to become a watchdog. People understand and respect the usefulness of power when it is properly used. They realize that little is successfully achieved without it and that it has to be revalidated throughout one's tenure. Power cannot be taken lightly, and it must be continuously earned. Without power, it is better to do nothing and hope that no one notices.

Superintendents need powerful constituents to stick with them and provide support. Spillane knew that he had the support of the business community and a few essential Fairfax leaders; this provided the power that allowed him to respond proactively during some difficult times. Superintendents must be able to hold their own in discussions within the power structure of their communities. The best way to achieve a positive relationship is to listen and keep everyone well-informed, so that there are no surprises (particularly of a negative nature). The superintendent needs to move slowly, include politicians and powerful individuals early on, promote deliberation and dialogue, and allow understanding and support to build for his or her initiatives.

The process begins by personally inviting and involving the participation of community leadership, including the media. The second step is slowly developing an awareness of what needs to be done and contemplating appropriate directions. This is where the superintendent needs to be very knowledgeable about his or her audience. It is therefore extremely important to remember that attitudes and loyalties change rapidly, as does the need for research on the audience before beginning any dialogue with groups.

Third, provide lots of information to help the interested groups gain understanding of the shared vision for the schools. Communicate to selected individuals only what they need to know so they are not overwhelmed, can understand the information, accept it, and embrace it. This means providing information your audience will hear, comprehend, and accept.

The next step involves helping those in power to see why it is important to the community and to them personally. Once the overall concepts are supported, the superintendent can move forward and work collaboratively with staff and the community to refine the ideas and craft a plan for implementation.

The final phase is asking members of the power structure to build the needed critical mass of support within the community. Spillane stresses the importance of knowing how to martial power for the common good. This cannot be done unless you have established what Spillane calls "the respect and trust factor" first. "The key players in the power structure are always changing," he says, "so the political process continues throughout all phases of the effort." Innovation typically is difficult to get started and needs a lot of support so as not to be abandoned before it becomes established practice. He suggests that participants need a sense of hopefulness, support, direction, optimism, and most of all purpose and vision. They need to work toward attainable achievements and ultimately the celebration of victories and successes.

A superintendent cannot wait to form these supportive relationships. He or she must begin with the earliest interactions, upon arrival in the school district. The interactions should include lots of face-to-face communication if they are to be successful. One superintendent says, "When a superintendent feels he or she must put it in writing for people to understand it, you know the effort is destined for failure." The superintendent's success is usually inversely related to the amount of paper produced and directly related to face-to-face communication and positive community and staff relations.

The superintendent needs to know all the players and what is happening both inside and outside education. This means expecting oneself and others to be involved in civic groups and constantly exchanging information about the community and power structure: knowledge of legislation at all levels of government, actions taken by organized groups within the community, and identity of newcomers to the power scene who can be brought aboard and made aware of district issues. The top leadership's role is to position the school district in the community; doing so naturally entails being in touch, getting involved, building respect and trust, and generating broad and vital support.

Chapter Four

Responding to Reform Goals and Mandates

Superintendents have often found their hands tied by the controls, regulations, and mandates placed upon the schools. As Thomas Glass puts it: "The 1980s era of school reform, dominated by state and federal initiatives, created a backseat role for superintendents and school boards, thus putting a damper on successful results. The emergence of 'choice' movements across the country as well as advocacy for more control at the local level by principals, teachers, and students themselves have brought additional challenges to superintendents' authority and policy making leadership" (1992, p. 4).

Bureaucratic Constraints

Superintendents end up feeling just as powerless in dealing with multistructural government regulations and policies and bureaucratic rigidity as does everyone else. They often find that legal mandates create resistance, and participative decision making frequently lacks coordinated support. Superintendents have learned that there are severe limitations to what can be accomplished either by regulation or by an individual teacher's effort unless the entire school culture is supportive. Governmental and bureaucratic regulations usually require surveillance and increased paperwork; however, seldom is there any evidence of improved educational performance. In fact, the pressure on the superintendent is more for compliance than for producing educational improvement. Superintendents might agree on very little, but they all express a concern about the constraints they face in dealing with governmental and bureaucratic policies and regulations. These regulations have required them to become more heavily involved in the political process through which education-related decisions are made.

The history of mandates is one of misdirection, lack of fiscal support, and shifting players, all of which end up clogging local reform efforts. Two examples are the New American School Development Corporation (NASDC) at the national level and the World Class Education Initiative (WCEI) in the state of Virginia. These efforts enjoyed commitment of considerable energy and resources at implementation but abruptly ended. The political winds of government changed, causing NASDC to evaporate and WCEI to be canceled. There are many examples of canceled plans in almost every state of the union, as the political winds of government constantly shift.

As superintendents become dissatisfied with the barrage of shifting state and federal mandates that have drained their resources, they find themselves actively involved in trying to influence and shape those mandates to give greater freedom to local districts. This issue has become more pressing as school district revenues are increasingly drawn from state, federal, and sometimes business sources. Education becomes more tightly tied to national, state, and local economic interests and related directives. Superintendents are obligated to be informed regarding important economic matters and to offer their best efforts in areas where education and economic development are joined. They are fearful, however, that political pressures force them to overlook the most pressing needs of children to focus attention on economic development and governmental legislation.

Fiscal Constraints

Certainly a key concern of superintendents is very tight fiscal resources. Superintendents have been asked to do "more for less"— an elusive concept at best. There must be a better approach to raising the expectations we have for our schools than trimming budgets. Today, with such strong pressures to innovate; to break down traditional boundaries; and to invest in technology, research and development, school budgets are very tight. This means that as schools add one thing, something else must be cut back or eliminated; emphasizing one area means deemphasizing another. This trade-off requiem results in very difficult and painful decisions as new alliances have to be drawn, assumptions reexamined, and agreements renegotiated.

Case Study: Financial Concerns in Los Angeles

At the same time that the Los Angeles superintendent was facing pressures to reform schools to meet the needs of the city's children, the Los Angeles Unified School District was teetering on the brink of bankruptcy. In 1991, to continue educating the youth of Los Angeles, the system increased class size by three students per class and cut back on substitute teachers, counselors, custodians, field trips, classroom supplies, and teacher support staff. A massive effort was launched to streamline district headquarters and to operate a no-frills administrative complex. The system also enacted an across-the-board pay cut and unpaid furloughs for all employees, while asking them for a longer work day and school year. Travel budgets and salaries of board members were also reduced.

For one twenty-year employee of the system who became superintendent of the Los Angeles Unified Schools, the heat became too much and he resigned under intense pressure. He was caught between the teachers, who second-guessed and undercut his decisions, and the powerless position in which the school board held him, regarding the intense pain of imposing cutbacks of $400 million from a $3.9 billion budget. The district budget was already very tight prior to the cut, and the superintendent couldn't manage the schools the way he wanted—and he didn't want to be part of the system's demise. Repairs, maintenance, supplies, equipment, and teaching materials were already cut to the bone, and more than half of the additional cuts would have to come from employee salaries and benefits—in some cases pay cuts of as much as 16.5 percent. The school system had already reached the point where it could no longer carry out its charge, with more than four thousand jobs eliminated in four years.

The superintendent was bitter both that the teachers had turned against him for a problem he had little to do with and that the board was micromanaging. At the same time, he could not stand by and watch young people in Los Angeles being underserved.

Later that year, intense riots caused billions of dollars of property damage in the south Los Angeles area.

Federal, State, and Local Involvement

The ways of government and politicians have slowly infiltrated the schools. The theme of government involvement is well captured in the phrase "Time for Results," as the National Governors' Association titled its 1986 report on education. Terrell Bell, former U.S. Secretary of Education, summed up the mood of the day: "We launched the Marshall Plan to rebuild the devastated European economy because we knew it was in the best interest of peace and prosperity not only for America, but for the free world. The same self-interest and world interest should govern the need to reform and renew education in America" (Cunningham and Gresso, 1993, p. 16).

Questions arose as to who was in charge of this much-needed reform and restructuring movement of the 1980s. Federal and state governments had mandated a number of changes in the past that seemed to have only limited success. Local boards and superintendents complained that they were responding to "expanded unfunded mandates" rather than leading continuous improvement of the schools. Teachers complained that the schools were encumbered by various aspects of mandates that were constantly changing. This lack of focus resulted in a general confusion as to who was responsible for educational improvements and who was accountable.

Many of the mandates reflect the government view that the schools are responsible for remedying our social ills. In a major review of educational reform, Samuel Bacharach (1990) pointed to the need to spell out appropriate roles for the various levels of government that are involved in education. He concluded that "The current reform movement, more than any other period in history, has raised fundamental questions about the role of government in education" (pp. 14–15).

A recent theme in the reform literature is the call for liberation of local school districts from federal and state mandates and for supporting local efforts at improvement. This shift is resulting in a slow devolution of responsibility for education to local districts, with the expectation that they will be responsive to the educational consumer. Keeping decision making close to the level directly affected by the decisions has worked well in other kinds of organizations and has much to offer public education.

The recurring theme is the need to keep board members as well as state and federal policy makers from micromanaging local schools. The appropriate role at the national level (*national* instead of *federal* denotes limited involvement of the federal government and greater involvement of state policy makers) is to establish the standards to be used to assess district performance. The local level is expected to develop and implement the means of meeting the standards, based on the demographic needs of, and resources available to, the school district.

One state that has implemented a model of greater decentralization is Florida. Larry Zenke, superintendent of schools in Duval County, Florida, used a leviathan metaphor to describe the bureaucratic/mandated structure that has existed in education:

> It has been described that in piloting the *Queen Mary* it takes two miles just to get the ship stopped. . . . In this state, the legislature, up until 1991, had been perceived as a "super school board," mandating programs and categorically funding programs in school districts in an effort to bring about statewide change and improvement. In 1991, after two decades [of] attempting to bring about such statewide change through top-down, mandated legislation, the legislature, through the Accountability and Reform Act, "tipped the pyramid over" and put in place a school reform effort which calls upon individual schools to develop annual school improvement plans in each of the seven goal areas established by the state. . . . Plans are reviewed and approved by the school board prior to the notification of the state that such plans are in place for all schools within a school district.

As part of this school-improvement process, schools are expected to show incremental progress each year in the several goal areas established by the Florida legislature. The hope is that smoother coordination, faster reaction, more effective planning, and incremental progress will all begin to appear. Failure to show such improvement, over time, could result in intervention by the school district or the state. This system recognizes the importance of the local context and the need to involve those who receive services and those who must carry out plans in deliberations about educational programs. This is also a way to keep everyone well informed and thus reduce the political nature of the decision. This system gives those within school districts greater freedom to develop effective approaches to improved education.

In Florida, the role of each level of government is clearly spelled out. The national level establishes the standards to be met; the state level further refines those standards and holds schools accountable for meeting them; and the local level concentrates on finding and implementing the means to do so. Those means may be varied across schools and school districts. Table 4.1 shows the relationship of checks and balances between the state and school districts; Table 4.2 shows the relationship between school districts and individual schools.

Zenke discussed this approach:

> I am comfortable with the national goals which have been established, and I am also supportive of the seven statewide goals under which we are operating. I firmly believe, however, that once such goals are established it must be the responsibility of local school districts and, very importantly, individual schools to develop their own approaches to meeting these goals. This process provides the accountability for results for those most closely located to where the action is taking place, that being the individual schools. I am quite comfortable with the change which has occurred within this

Table 4.1. Checks and Balances Between State and School District.

	State goals (product expectations)	Program implementation (process decisions)	Evaluation
State	Decision making	Advisory	Decision making
School district	Advisory	Decision making	Advisory

state over the past three years, with the direction for instructional improvement moving from the legislature and department of education to individual school districts and schools. There seems to be a genuine effort to support change and improvement at the individual school level, but to then also hold people accountable for results.

The system of checks and balances can create problems for the school system. This is particularly true when local city or county government becomes very heavily involved in the operation of the schools. When mayors, city managers, country commissioners, and/or city council members get into brawls with the superintendent over how the schools should be financed or run, the superintendent almost always comes out on the short end. The most well-known and recognized case was in New York City, where disagreements between former Mayor David Dinkins and former Chancellor Joseph Fernandez were legendary. Ramon Cortines, the next chancellor, made a political error when he first came to New York: he solidly embraced Mayor Dinkins prior to the election. With the election of Mayor Rudolph Giuliani, battles with city hall continued and intensified. The mayor asked the chancellor to cut 2,500 employees and reduce the budget by $332 million; he even suggested some specific senior staff members who might be fired. Giuliani also wanted to place police in the schools, appoint a fiscal monitor, and get involved in school reform. The mayor created a commission to investigate the school system's handling of

Table 4.2. Checks and Balances Between School Districts and Individual Schools.

	District goals (product expectations)	Program implementation (process decisions)	Evaluation
School district	Decision making	Advisory	Decision making
Individual school	Advisory	Decision making	Advisory

safety and violence. Eventually Chancellor Cortines resigned, say-ing, "I don't work for the mayor. This isn't the first time he's said I don't exercise leadership, which is doing what he doesn't want me to do." The school board felt that the chancellor had been pushed from his job by City Hall. This was surprising since he seemed to have the support and confidence of a majority of the school board, the city council, and the city's parents. He just seemed to lack the skills needed to deal with intense political pressure from the mayor's office. In the interest of peace, the school board would work with the mayor in selecting Cortines's successor.

Although these are two of the most highly visible scenarios, such things go on in school districts across the United States. Su-perintendents are under constant pressure from various local politicians requesting changes within the schools. Without the skills to deal with this political pressure, superintendents are either over-run or replaced. Obviously, when the desires of the politicians match those of the school leaders, they make powerful allies; but when they do not they make almost insurmountable enemies. Few superintendents can survive major disagreements with the politi-cal power structure regardless of the support they receive from the school board.

Heat in the Age of Reform

Innovation cannot be successfully achieved with the same type or degree of effort that suffices to maintain the status quo. People both within and outside the school system often have difficulty putting in the energy and effort to successfully implement new pro-grams. Failures are not seen as a normal step toward continued improvement. The changes initially reduce trust and increase in-security and resistance. When successes occur, people often sug-gest that standards were lowered or the project was "doctored" to make it look good. Superintendents are not surprised at the diffi-culty of getting staff to swallow the bitter pill of failure; however, most superintendents are shocked at how difficult it is to get staff members to feel good about the system's achievements.

To build faith in legitimate improvements is very hard. It is a delicate balance because if successes are overamplified, the insti-tutionalization of change may be forced to proceed too quickly. Yet if successes are not supported, they may wither and die. Carl Glickman (1990) has studied some of the ironies that plague successful superintendents. For example, the more a school or district improves, the more apparent it becomes that there remains much to be improved. Thus improvements can increase dissatisfaction with what is currently being done and raise awareness of the awesome challenge of what must be done. As a district improves, those from other school districts increase their criticism of it, and the improving district ends up under siege.

The more that groups are brought together within a district to try to improve the schools, the more different views, tensions, and conflicts within the school district become apparent. This awareness is compounded by the fact that collegial and shared approaches tend to eliminate "the enemy out there" that is holding back progress. Thus, as superintendents empower interest groups to influence the school, the participants feel a greater sense of responsibility for the school's failing since they lose their enemy out there to blame. Over time, they may choose to divert that enemy status onto the superintendent. Those involved in school improvement tend to be more concerned with short-term gains rather than achieving the long-term goal of improved learning. Short-term gains may fade or be impossible to achieve. Innovations take time to stabilize themselves, and participants are often unwilling to wait. Most superintendents know the long term is not a luxury they will be given.

The story line is fairly similar in school districts across the nation. The school board purposefully hires a change-oriented superintendent to improve the schools and prepare them for the twenty-first century. School employees tend to resist the change. Community debate rages over the types of changes that should *not* occur. When the school board realizes the superintendent is unable to make changes without conflict, confusion, and hard feelings, the honeymoon is over. Board members who supported the superintendent are defeated. Discord intensifies as everyone spars with the superintendent. The superintendent is either chased off or fired. The schools return to the status quo and the act is then repeated, with an even more skeptical cast for the new star to work with.

Deborah McGriff, a bright, energetic, expert school reformer, was hired in 1991 as superintendent of the Detroit public schools to lead a commitment to reform the schools. She quickly won the admiration of parents, community and business leaders, and teachers. When she began to actually reform the system, including some schools of choice and self-governing schools, her popularity with the teachers union quickly evaporated. A bitter, month-long teachers' strike led to the defeat of three members of the Hope Team, supporters of the superintendent and leaders of reform on the eleven-member school board. The next year, she quit to join the Edison Project, where she felt more freedom to reform education.

Although the situations and reforms differ, the story line is very similar in school districts across America.

Academics or Well-Being

The classic debate that superintendents confront in defining outcomes to be achieved occurs over the broadness of student achievement goals. Broader reform efforts often go beyond academics to include a focus on the overall child's well-being. The rationale for this approach is that one's productivity and prosperity as an adult require an education that goes well beyond what has been traditionally defined as education for economic and civic responsibility. In addition, the argument runs, education should address the child's health, social well-being, protection, welfare, and morality. The assertion supporting this broader view of schooling is based on the belief that these "foundational services" are needed within the schools so that students will be better able to focus their attention on academics. For example, California Gov. Pete Wilson created a cabinet-level position, secretary of child development and education, to provide recommendations regarding the integration of social, health, mental health, and support services in the school. Other states—including Florida, New York, New Jersey, Kentucky, and Connecticut—are also expanding beyond the traditional academic role of education.

On the other side, while acknowledging children's needs, economic and political leaders are uncertain how far schools can delve into family and other developmental support issues without losing the focus on academic, economic, and civic well-being. The America 2000 report asserts that "Schools are not and cannot be parents, police, hospitals, welfare agencies, or drug treatment centers. . . .

They cannot replace the missing elements in communities and families" (U.S. Department of Education, 1991, p. 5). Schools have to have a focus because they can't do it all. These advocates argue that we must concentrate on the essential function of schooling while finding ways to neutralize students who interfere with the learning process.

The National Governors' Association report *Time for Results* (1986, p. 3) states early on that "better schools mean better jobs." Schools are meant to prepare students for employment and civic responsibilities that they are capable of fulfilling. Schools must focus on radically improving the academic performance of the next generation so that they are able to compete in a global economy. According to this group, asking schools to expand boundaries beyond academic services makes them even less effective in the task of improving academics.

Superintendents must often face such opposing forces in school reform. In this example, one side focuses on academic interests, international economic competitiveness, and corporate health. The other suggests that schools must also play a more prominent role in alleviating social and family problems that have a direct bearing on the child's ability to learn. Those envisioning a broader role for schools support an expanded number of nonacademic services. The superintendent feels the pressure of having to create a mutually shared vision between strongly disparate points of view.

The argument goes that if Americans do not help to heal children at risk, the nation's social fabric may be damaged and its economy may not be able to function. Those who support the more narrow focus on academics argue that the schools cannot do it all and will end up failing in both areas if they take on these expanded responsibilities. The superintendent is called upon to lead the reform movement under such conflicting ideologies.

Accountability and Test Scores

Superintendents often find their schools, school districts, and even themselves personally being compared on the basis of how well students perform on standardized tests. Rather than helping planning teams to improve curriculum and instruction and help children

develop needed skills, test scores are used as a quality-control ranking device. They are often made public and used by the community to judge the quality of principals and teachers within schools,
to compare school district performance with surrounding districts,
or to compare the present superintendent's performance with that
of past superintendents. Thus testing programs become quite
threatening as they become evaluative rather than developmental
tools.

The emphasis on test scores as the means of accountability is a
national phenomenon. Glass found that "in the educational climate of today, superintendents and districts are being literally bom-
barded by lobbyists representing parents and other interest groups
pressuring them to raise the achievement level of their children. . . . In short, public interest groups want school children to
produce improved scores on some test or indicator of achievement
in order to be satisfied that the system is working and they are getting value for each tax dollar spent on public education" (1993b,
p. 48).

School districts are not allowed the luxury of taking a long-
term perspective. They are forced to make quick fixes for those
concerned with short-term gains in test scores. Educators are expected to turn things around quickly, and turning things around
means higher test scores. Turning things around also includes
showy, highly visible improvements that gain local, state, or national prominence. However, true excellence often requires time
to stabilize and produce results and may result temporarily in lower
test scores or the need to change the assessment and testing program to be more in line with the new curriculum and instruction.
As a result, superintendents can be forced into a pattern of being
more interested in stability and assessment (test) reports than in
achieving improved learning for American youth.

Decentralization and Leadership

Society's expectations for schools call for fundamental transformation of the core business of schooling. Although studies have
examined the effects of restructuring on the roles of teachers, principals, students, and a variety of actors at the state level, much less
is known about the effects of restructuring on the roles of central

office administrators. Much of the scholarly literature on the central office focuses more on functional responsibilities within education than on what their role should be.

A growing number of schools and school districts across the nation are changing their structures to improve teaching and learning. The major focus of these shifts has been toward site-based leadership. As the shift in control from central bureaucracies to individual schools spreads, more school districts have reorganized to give power to those most directly responsible for educating children. "This transformation in the role of many school leaders has begun to change schools from places where grown-ups know and young people learn to communities of learners where all who come under their roof—students, teachers, administrators, parents—are discovering together the joys, difficulties, and the excitement of improved learning" (Barth, 1995, p. 23).

Problems can occur when members of the school staff lack experience in shared decision making. When participants do not have immediate success, or when they are not prepared for the complex process of deliberation and decision making, they can become frustrated and resort to counterproductive practices. Ramon Cortines suggests that participatory forms of leadership can be impeded when "the constituencies that compose a school community have not learned to develop common goals and strategies to achieve goals. Frustration easily sets in and leads to a tendency to resort to the old unsuccessful methods."

The bureaucracy itself is often seen as an impediment to the superintendent's efforts to support broad participation in the improvement of children's lives. Participants' lack of experience in working with the bureaucracy promotes an adversarial relationship in which "bureaucrats" are attacked, misunderstood, or just generally mistrusted. Cortines finds that "bureaucracies are generally not participant-friendly. Information is often disseminated in formats that are extremely difficult to understand. Bureaucracies also develop many mandates that draw the focus away from students and teaching and learning. Budgets are written in 'bureaucratese' and mandates are disseminated in lengthy documents that require numerous steps for implementation and monitoring." This lack of participant-friendliness means those outside the bureaucracy cannot see a legitimate role for themselves. They also view the bureaucracy as resisting their efforts to improve education. The bureaucracy seems out of their control, and there is no room for them to participate.

Richard Miller, executive director emeritus of the American Association of School Administrators, is adamant in his belief that "strategic plans for improving the school district should have the participation and input from those working within the system and the community before being adopted. Then regardless of what happens related to changes of board members or changes in the bureaucracy, you have a plan that's driving the district." The superintendent controls the bureaucracy by allowing for broader, more thoughtful communication among those within and outside the school system.

Linda Darling-Hammond has not always found this openness within the central office to be the case. She observes that "Schools largely function now by submerging talk about those things that are potentially most controversial and potentially most important. Debates about the most fundamental concerns of teaching and learning are typically squashed—or tacitly agreed to be inappropriate" (Darling-Hammond, 1992, p. 23). This is the traditional central office approach of "make no waves, keep the waters of education calm and smooth." That means complaints should not be heard "downtown."

Solutions to our problems in education can neither be discovered nor supported by professionalization; centralization; or bureaucratic, controlling approaches. Solutions must grow out of confronting concerns, responding to needs, and supporting meaningful dialogue. Superintendents must develop approaches that create support mechanisms encouraging input, conversation, collaboration, direction finding, goal setting, risk taking, significant action, and broad support for educational improvement. Darling-Hammond says the new paradigm for school reform must develop communities of learning grounded in communities of democratic discourse: "We therefore need policies that allow and encourage schools to engage in a democratic dialogue that develops trust and understanding of current conditions, a community with shared purpose. As Dewey suggested in *Democracy and Education*: '. . . What they must have in common in order to form a community or society are aims, beliefs, aspirations, knowledge—a common understanding—like-mindedness, as the sociologists say.' Such things cannot be passed physically from one to another, like bricks; they cannot be shared as persons would share a pie by dividing it into physical pieces. . . . Consensus requires communication" (Darling-Hammond, 1992, p. 27).

School-Based Leadership

While the demands of leadership require different styles for different situations, it is safe to say that bureaucracies are rapidly moving from leadership based on command and control to leadership characterized by vision, adaptability, and empowerment of others. Today, the dominant principle of organization has shifted from management that controls an enterprise to leadership that brings out the best in people and that responds quickly to change (Naisbitt and Aburdene, 1990).

Decentralization, which includes innovations such as site-based management and school-based decision making, is based on the assumption that reducing bureaucratic controls prompts teachers and principals to exert greater initiative and to tailor instruction to the needs of students. Yet shared decision making and school-based management efforts have shown that changes in decision-making structures alone rarely spur substantive changes in the quality of teaching and learning. In many places, increased teacher participation in decision making has not overcome norms of individual autonomy, nor has it increased collaboration among teachers on matters other than governance. Principals, teachers, and central office staff involved in school-based management often fail to make the needed connections between new governance structures and the improvement of curriculum and instruction.

"Though enthusiasm for decentralization shows no signs of abating," according to Bruce Bimber, "there is little evidence of better student achievement, and few schools calling themselves 'decentralized' have made major changes in established educational practices" (1995, p. 1). Bimber adds that "the main reason for the limited effects of decentralization is the inseparability of decisions. Linkages among budget, personnel, instructional, and operational decisions mean that 'decentralized' authority ostensibly given school staff over one class of decisions has effectively been limited by centralized constraints on other classes of decisions" (p. 2). But rather than abandoning school-based leadership, superintendents and other education leaders "need to learn under what conditions it works to promote substantive school reform" (Midgley and Wood, 1993, p. 252).

Although there is no single model for implementing shared decision making, there are guidelines to help central office and school-based leaders implement the approach that will work best for schools. It is unrealistic to expect school-based leadership to succeed when schools are simply given more authority over such things as budgets, personnel, and curriculum. In addition to authority, schools need four other essentials for making good and productive decisions:

1. Knowledge of the organization
2. Information about student performance and comparisons with other schools
3. Information about whether parents and community leaders are satisfied with the schools and the resources available
4. Rewards to acknowledge the extra effort school-based leadership requires as well as to recognize school improvements

One criticism of school-based leadership is that it often causes teachers to make disjointed and thus poor decisions that are not connected by a common vision for school improvement. So what is a good decision? Phillip Schlechty (1993, p. 22) says "it is technically sound, ethically defensible, and produces the results intended while employing means that are consistent with the values of the system of which it is a part." A set of shared values or principles to guide change can help school people avoid knee-jerk or quick-fix approaches and increase the likelihood that reforms will be compatible with and responsive to the context and culture of the school.

Over the years, talk about leadership has shifted from the chief executive officer—the superintendent—to a process of leadership that is shared by people within the district. This has raised many questions concerning the role of the central office bureaucracy.

Leadership Versus Maintaining the Status Quo

Employees must feel trust and support from central office leadership before they are willing to try out new ideas that might improve the schools. In the absence of a supportive central administration, principals and teachers will place all of their efforts in maintaining existing practice. After Lois Harrison-Jones resigned the superintendency of the Richmond (Virginia) City Schools, concern was expressed over the condition of the school system. Some believed that leadership from the top to the bottom was at a standstill, at a time when there was a real need for change. This stagnation could not be blamed on any one individual; it stemmed from political factors and in-house power struggles that seemed to occur within the central office. False starts, political infighting, and wasted energy had drained the organization and kept the system from dealing with changes in the community and schools. Blame was freely passed out to everyone; however, it tended to focus on the superintendent and central office staff, who were as much victims of the situation as were the children.

Many Richmond teachers believed the schools needed to move toward cooperative teaching and learning so students could improve their social skills and learn to support one another in their learning outcomes. Barbara Shade, dean of the school of education at the University of Wisconsin and a consultant to the Richmond City Schools, pointed out that learning styles were the product of different cultures. As an example, she noted that "in Afro-American culture, emphasis is placed on cooperation, the affective domain, and an orientation toward a social world, while the school district culture emphasizes individuality, competitiveness, separateness, and orientation toward the physical world and the cognitive domain." She supported the teachers' desire to implement cooperative learning. She urged them to invite children to learn; use positive communication; and develop an integrated, holistic approach to the curriculum.

Instead, the school board developed policy that opposed this intervention. Teachers were evaluated on the basis of classroom control and the behavior of students. Those whose students were held in line, whose classes were orderly, and who held noise and disturbance to a minimum were the more respected and promoted staff members. The safe response to the political turmoil surrounding the schools was to maintain the status quo within the schools. The central office responded as much to the mood of the school board as it did to the superintendent, relaying the message of tight student control and a very orderly, learning environment. This was interpreted to mean rigid control and teaching children as had always been done, despite strong indications that children needed to be taught quite differently. With the superintendent resigning, those within the schools felt that there was little likelihood that needed changes would be made within the bureaucracy, and that any momentum for change would probably not carry over to the next administration.

The teachers in the district believed that they had much to offer toward improving the schools; however, there were very few outlets for them to share or use their knowledge and experience. There seemed to be a general lack of central office respect and appreciation for what school personnel knew and what they said. Teachers were very frustrated by their awareness of the work that needed to be done to better educate Richmond youth. A few of the top teachers left the school district, some taking jobs in fields other than education. Central office administrators began focusing their attention on handling the external and internal conflicts surrounding schools. They focused their staff development on conflict-resolution skills, control mechanisms, problem solving, and political awareness. A central office administrator confided: "Personally, I have long had a problem of trying to be a nice guy too often. During this year, I have developed the ability to eliminate positions, eliminate programs, and close schools without undue trauma to myself."

The central office administrators became tougher and the teachers grew self-protective, closed, and fearful—not a great culture in which to attempt school improvement. More recently, Richmond City Schools has begun to turn this situation around.

Chapter Five

Doing More with Less: The Fiscal Crunch

Education operates on an appropriations budget in which most of the money comes from various forms of taxes. When taxes are decreased, so is the money available to support public education. Beginning with the Tax Reform Act of 1986, a shift in the federal tax base has placed more financial burden on the middle-class taxpayer and less burden on the wealthy taxpayer. Donald L. Bartlett and James B. Steel (1992, 1994) found that the reform act resulted in a 47 percent cut in taxes for the wealthy and an 18 percent increase in taxes for the middle and upper-middle classes. Where the income of the wealthiest 20 percent of Americans has increased rapidly since 1986, the Bureau of Labor Statistics shows that wages and benefits for 90 million middle-class wage earners have actually lost ground, being approximately 5.5 percent lower than they were in 1987. Most federal and state budget debates since 1986 have included figuring additional ways to lower taxes for those who have received the most from the American economic system: the high-income earner.

Income and Tax Inequities

Starting in 1995, federal debate has included the concept of a flat or proportionate tax. This runs against one of the basic assumptions existent since the inception of American taxation: progressivity. The argument against proportionate taxes is that they are not equitable to all Americans. If the proportionate (flat) tax rate is 20 percent, it affects primarily the food, housing, medical care, education, and safety of middle- to low-income wage earners, but primarily luxury items for high-income wage earners. The argument centers around whether it is fair or equitable to take basic living needs from lower- to middle-class families while taking only a few luxuries from upper-income families. The U.S. Treasury has estimated that proposals along the lines of the flat tax would amount to increases of 7–17 percent in federal taxes for families with incomes under $200,000, and a 26 percent decrease for families with incomes above $200,000 (Christian, 1996, p. 381).

At the local level, the response to reduced income taxes is to shift the burden of education onto property taxes. But such a system is actually regressive, with middle- and low-income wage earners paying a higher percent of their wages in taxes. Someone earning $10 million a year may live in a $2 million house, while someone earning $80,000 a year lives in a $240,000 house. Property taxes are on the value of one's house, not one's income. The person paid $10 million is paying taxes on something worth one-fifth of his or her income, while the person earning $80,000 is paying taxes on something worth three times his or her income. Property taxes are thus quite regressive.

All of this has resulted in a very tight dollar for American public education. The way taxes are structured, educators are forced to put the tax bite on the middle-class wage earner whose wages have decreased while taxes have increased, and not on the wealthy income earners, who have much more money available from significantly increased incomes and reduced taxes.

This means that the majority of middle-income voters tend to see taxes as too high and are unsupportive of tax increases since the impact on their worth is more serious than it is on the wealthy. The wealthy become role models sending out the message that reduced taxes are good. The superintendent, the board, and ultimately politicians are thus very concerned about suggesting tax increases on the wealthy, who are generally the major employers, service providers, and members of the power structure within the community from whom the superintendent will ultimately need support.

Labor Secretary Robert Reich says of the growing inequality of income, "I find this trend deeply disturbing. We have the most unequal distribution of income of any industrialized nation" (Ponnuru, 1995, p. 32). He is fearful that the combined wage and taxation policies are creating class warfare, and that shrinking wages and growing inequality are America's central problems. This is partially responsible for the increased number of children living in poverty; the difficulty of obtaining adequate money to fund education; and the general distrust, disillusionment, and bashing of public institutions that can lead to violence, civil disobedience, and social breakdown. Today's superintendents find themselves caught between employees who want increased wages and resources, middle-class taxpayers who are stretched to the limit, and wealthy taxpayers whose tax burden is being progressively reduced.

Fiscal Belt Tightening

When talking about where the heat comes from in a school district, fingers point to the budget process. As school budgets shrink, all issues have the tendency to be put in financial terms, with the budget process becoming the battlefield. Kirtman and Minkoff (1996, p. 17) suggest that "The school system decided to break the budget paradigm of separate camps battling for the district piece of the pie. Almost universally the tension between school systems and their surrounding municipalities creates many short- and long-term problems." One of the most prevalent causes of short tenure for superintendents is reaction to massive budget cuts. The budget is probably one of the best predictors of the level of peace or conflict in a superintendent's professional life. A slowing economy, state cutbacks, tax decreases, proportionate and regressive taxes, and local demands to do more for less reduce already tight budgets and require superintendents to achieve the impossible regarding budget management. When communities realize that it cannot be done, it is often the superintendent who is (incorrectly) blamed for failure. Eliminating layers of bureaucracy, providing minimal raises, cutting supplies, and increasing class sizes to "improve education" are traumatic experiences. Mayors, city councils, city managers, and others have no qualms about making recommendations and decisions when they know that few superintendents are able to weather them in the long run. This is particularly true when the needs are great and the schools are already operating on a shoestring. Unfortunately, schools do not operate in the high style that so often exists in corporate budgets.

The difficulty of surviving severe budget cuts is exemplified by two past superintendents of the Los Angeles Unified School District in the late 1980s and early 1990s. They were driven out of the superintendency during periods of severe budget cuts. In both cases, budget problems were aggravated by troubled relationships with the teachers' union. One was an outsider hired "to bring new vitality to a troubled school system." The other was an insider promoted because of his knowledge of the community and the players. Finances and budget planning proved to be perennial problems, fueling tensions that ultimately resulted in their abrupt resignations. Spending cuts became the critical incident with the school board, the community, and the teacher union. Superintendents don't garner much gratitude during periods of budget cuts.

A discouraging aspect of budget cutting is the pressure not to look at the impacts of cuts on students. The politically expedient approach is to swallow the cuts and make the system do more for less. Ramon Cortines, the second chancellor of the New York City schools to lose the job in a four-year period, says, "There is tremendous pressure to accept more monumental and unending budget cuts without addressing their impact on teaching and learning. There is also a great deal of pressure to cut the budget and reconceptualize the administration based on external views of the size, the cost, and the value of central and district administration."

Here again, mayors, city councils, city managers, business CEOs, and others have no qualms about making recommendations and decisions in areas about which they have minimal knowledge or data. Superintendents who question and resist pressures to cut budgets are characterized as tax-and-spend proponents of huge, inefficient bureaucracies and the wrong people for their communities. Such concerns have some legitimacy. However, for city officials to discourage superintendents from presenting data showing that budget cuts are ultimately not in the best interest of children is shortsighted and potentially harmful. This situation prevails in a growing number of school districts. The city government mood seems to be: "Don't confuse me with the facts, if you know what's good for you."

Kenneth Burnley, superintendent of the Colorado Springs public schools, puts it this way:

The major pitfalls that we face as school superintendents, in the area of instituting changes in curriculum and staff development, are contributed to by the lack of funding and available resources to fully implement the needed changes in our ever-changing school curriculum.

Funding is needed in order for school districts to properly train their staffs in curriculum development, and the lack of these resources can hamper the process. School districts are constantly reallocating and redistributing monies within their budgets to meet the heavy demands of changing the curriculum in our schools.

Lack of money for achieving needed reform results in mere window dressing—which even becomes a hidden agenda for some city officials.

These expectations, that superintendents find ways to operate and reform schools on dwindling budgets, have begun to change the job itself. Superintendents lose sight of children's learning as the reason they are there in the first place. Gene Hall, a professor at the University of Northern Colorado, is studying the budget-cutting phenomenon with Judy Berg. They have found that the absence of a financially supported ". . . strategic perspective is leading to many school district central offices' being gutted and each school left as an island. Short-term effects include (1) euphoria over all that can be kept afloat by working fifteen-hour days, (2) total loss of any concrete long-term plan, and (3) steadily increasing risk of major balls being dropped. There are also shifts in the role of the superintendent and the superintendent's staff. Probably the most pronounced of these is that little change is being initiated by superintendents, who may not be permitted to address student needs."

Superintendent Compensation: Coca-Cola and Kids

Another element that has consistently caused problems in public education is the compensation package provided to central office administrators, especially the superintendent. There is a significant gap between their remuneration and that in upper-level executive management positions in business and industry. Executive salary and benefits are so important in America because they help define one's relevance and power in American politics. One superintendent said, "It's sort of embarrassing when your salary is not even comparable to many midlevel managers who have less responsibility and pressure. We are not even compensated for the risks we take in dedicating our lives to education." Central office administrators typically have low salaries in relation to business and do not receive "performance awards" or "incentive bonuses," which are regularly paid in the business sector. The typical educator feels that he or she is falling further behind those in other professional fields.

A large school system is similar to a big business in a number of ways. It can have anywhere from one thousand to almost eighty thousand employees within the district. As such, it is often among the largest employers in its area, and the superintendent and central office administrators face the same complexities, long hours, and responsibilities that chief executive officers face in big business. In many communities, superintendents manage one of the largest budgets, especially when accounting for the number of employees, transportation services, food services, etc. Perhaps the biggest difference is in budgeting. Although overall their jobs are similar to those in the for-profit sector, superintendents operate on an appropriations budget. The significant similarities are a real bone of contention for superintendents, who see comparable CEOs in business receiving much more compensation for similar work but with less conflict and pressure. A superintendent in Delaware suggests that "In the corporate sector, someone handling this kind of responsibility would be earning from several hundred thousand to a million dollars. There has to be some way to compensate [superintendents] for the level of performance, visibility, and stress the job entails."

Superintendents and central office administrators should receive contracts comparable to what CEOs in business receive. Robert Spillane says, "There has to be some financial remuneration for spending the outrageous hours a superintendent puts in—besides the intrinsic satisfaction of doing a good job."

The frustration that superintendents experience regarding compensation is conveyed in an extreme case. Roberto C. Goizueta, chief executive officer of Coca-Cola, received $86 million in 1991 for managing the corporation. This amount included salary, bonus, and stock options. Based on Goizueta's working day, he was paid approximately $35,000 per hour. Superintendents cannot help but shake their heads when they realize that the CEO of Coca-Cola earned more in six hours of one day than one of the highest paid superintendents in the country earns in a year, in the critically important hot seat as chancellor of the New York City schools. This disparity is particularly troubling to superintendents struggling to care for and educate America's youth, when they realize that these wages reflect where Americans place value. Apparently, Coca-Cola is significantly more important than our children.

Similar examples abound, of course. Based on this logic, Mickey Mouse is even more important than Coca-Cola. In 1993, *Business Week* reported executive pay (with stock options, benefits, etc.) at $203 million for number-one-ranked Michael Eisner of Walt Disney, a company providing entertainment to youth. (His executive vice president received over $80 million; Bates and Shiver, 1992.) The combined net worth of the Forbes 400 for 1993 equals approximately $328 billion—almost one fourth the federal budget. Thomas H. Frist, president of Hospital Corporation of America, was paid $125 million in one year in part to try to figure out ways to cut doctor and hospital costs, while doctors, who work long hours under greater pressure and seldom earn even $1 million, are finding their salaries decreased.

The president of United Airlines was paid over $10 million in a year when United released more than one thousand employees because of new "belt-tightening" policy. The fortune of technology genius William Gates, founder of Microsoft, grew by $1.5 billion in 1992. In total, Gates is reported to have accumulated $14.2 billion in a little over 20 years. There are enough of these cases to make superintendents wonder if education has any importance in American society—while educators in general wonder if, based on American values, they entered the right profession.

Estimates in 1992 based on proxy statements indicate that the top five thousand chief executive officers in America each had annual compensation of more than $1 million. The estimate for all executive officers for publicly held companies is an average compensation in excess of $500,000 a year. This average does not include private corporations, where annual earnings are believed to be higher. Regardless of the exact figures, superintendents and assistant superintendents find the disparity between their salaries and those of the CEOs in business to be somewhat disheartening.

The average superintendent's salary in school districts with twenty-five thousand or more students is $104,000, according to Educational Research Service (1995). A 1993 nationwide survey of superintendents found that very few were eligible for any form of performance bonus, and only 2.6 percent of those eligible earned a bonus greater than $5,000. One of the top school salaries in the country in 1994 was that of Ramon Cortines, who was paid slightly over $200,000 for managing nearly one million students, seventy thousand employees, and the $7.2 billion budget of the New York City public schools. The next largest school system, the Los Angeles Unified Public Schools, paid their superintendent a salary of approximately $165,000 in 1992. Because of a financial crisis within the school district in 1992, the superintendent took a cut in this salary. Superintendents across the nation interviewed on this subject feel strongly that their compensation could stand some "substantial improvement" when compared to that of similar chief executive officers in business.

Another, much less critical, annoyance is the fact that some smaller but wealthier suburban districts pay central office administrators as well as, and quite often better than, those in larger districts in more urban settings. For example, the superintendent of a suburban New York public school district earned about $142,000, and the superintendent of a small school district in Texas earned approximately $157,000—salaries which at that time were about the same as that of the superintendent of the Los Angeles Unified Public Schools.

Compounding the financial problems is the volatility of the positions; superintendents and some central office staff are often finding themselves out of work and relocating. This lack of stability has an adverse effect on the money for retirement that they might have built up with an organization, because their pensions typically lack portability. Usually, they cannot carry their pension benefits with them when they leave one district and move to another state. The high cost of housing and the difficulty in selling homes in today's real estate market have caused many superintendents serious financial problems as they take bad beatings on the selling price of their homes when moving to a superintendency in another state. Housing allowances and bonuses, which are very common in business, are relatively rare in education.

The superintendent must rely on central office staff to help carry out the responsibilities of the position, while most central office administrators and school-based staff are carryovers from as many as fifteen preceding superintendent's administrations. Consequently, people may view the superintendent as just passing through, while thinking of themselves as providing the continuity in reform efforts. Others are trying to do whatever it takes to survive the revolving door at the top. All feel the pressure for reform, but few have the job security or compensation required to motivate blazing new trails. The result can be lethargic, fearful central office administrators who resist the pressure being exerted at both ends of the system: the school board/superintendent and the community/schools. However, within constraints, most superintendents and other educational leaders are seriously trying to figure out how they can most effectively help schools to improve American education during a period of rapid administrative turnover, expansive reforms, budget cuts, and minimal compensation.

Chapter Six

Resolving Conflicts with Boards

Most superintendents know how important school board relations are to their ability to be successful. A majority have experienced how impossible the job is when relations begin to deteriorate. "Deteriorating relations with the school board" is often given as the reason why superintendents are asked to step down. Robert Wentz, superintendent of the Wake County Public Schools in Raleigh, North Carolina, explained, "I am retiring at the end of December 1994 even though my contract runs through June 1996. Why? Because my board wants a change, and somewhere along the line I've lost most of them. In other words, I don't feel like I am effective any longer with board members. However, I don't feel stressed out by the recent turn of events. The focus has to be on student outcomes and continuous progress in the system, and I'm pleased that these continue to improve!"

How does one determine that the relationship between the board and the superintendent has gone sour? Things often start with one of two general indicators. First, it takes three or four tries to get an important issue passed by the board. The second is when board members interfere or attempt to interfere with the hiring of individuals who have already passed muster at the school level.

The superintendency is perhaps most clearly defined by its relations with school boards. Jack Kaufhold states, "You have no idea what it's like to be superintendent until you get into the executive session of a school board meeting" (1993, p. 41). This is the forum where the superintendent must convince laypeople—who most often have never taught a day in their lives and have little experi-

ence working with children—what is best for the education of chil
dren within the district. Public consensus conceals the behind-the-
scenes haggling and lost arguments that occur in private. This
unseen arena is where a high degree of conflict, mistrust, and un-
easiness develops.

To paraphrase Machiavelli, "there is nothing more difficult,
more perilous, or more uncertain of successes than to take the lead
in introducing a new order of things."

One of the early problems that can get in the way of relationships with the board is taking too strong a stance on the "trust me
as an educational expert" approach. The track record of this approach is especially poor since most boards operate in the political mode. The administrator must earn support and recognition
by establishing a strong record of success. This approach is most
beneficial in eliminating doubts about the superintendent as he
or she becomes successful in connecting and linking power structures in support of needed educational improvements. The effective superintendent works hard to maintain positive relationships
with the school board and all other groups that have an interest in
education. Everything depends on good relationships.

The first order of business for a school board and its superintendent is to build a relationship of trust. Unfortunately, the complex demands of a busy school district allow little time for this to
mature. Nonetheless, it is essential, for the board's trust creates the
foundation that allows the superintendent to genuinely take
charge of operations.

Case Study: Bonding with the Board

E. Kathleen Booher, superintendent of the Berkeley schools in
Michigan, discusses some issues that complicated her hiring for her
first superintendency.

To begin with, the previous superintendent had left the district
for another position three months earlier. Rather than hire an
interim superintendent, the board had asked the new assistant
superintendent—five months on the job—to assume the superintendent's responsibilities as well. Second, the board president, a
high-ranking professional in a large corporation, left his company
due to downsizing. Third, the district had completed a facilities

study and was poised to run a campaign for a bond issue shortly after the school year would begin.

The first two circumstances coincided to create a situation that allowed the board president to believe *he* was needed to help run the district. Although competent, the assistant superintendent was new to both the district and the central office role. As a result, the board president inserted himself into issues that arose in the interim, going so far as to occupy the superintendent's vacant office and call in administrative cabinet members to give instructions.

Booher reflects:

Almost from the date of my hiring, I struggled with the president's directives, yielding to some, resisting others. It was, however, the bond elections that presented the greatest challenge and opportunity—the one which would allow the board and me to build our foundation of trust. We lost the election by a slim margin and, in the aftermath, the board turned to me for leadership.

Typically, when election results are in, superintendents and board presidents speak to the press and campaign volunteers. I thanked the supporters and shared hopeful references to our future. In contrast, the president made an oblique reference to the [outside] organized opposition, who had distributed "eleventh-hour" misinformation, as "snakes." In context, his comments were not particularly offensive, but when quoted as they were in the next day's newspaper, a firestorm erupted. Thus began a barrage of indignant letters and phone calls to the editor, to our office, and to board members. The comment was soon interpreted to mean that all opponents of the bond issue were snakes. Irate residents could not be stilled. Soon after, these negative comments began to be generalized to the entire board and superintendent; suggestions about recall were made, the ability of the superintendent questioned, and an apology demanded. As with any firestorm, it was swift and demanded prompt damage control.

I talked with each board member personally and firmly asked each to recognize me as the sole district spokesperson on this issue. I asked each of them to refer all citizen or media requests for comment or discussion to me. I assured each that it was indeed my job to take the heat for them. Through my conversation with two other officers, we agreed to meet with the president and urge him to write one straightforward letter to the editor clarifying the intent of his remarks and incorporating a simple apology. In the meantime, I met with the editor and secured his agreement to print the letter immediately. Within two weeks, we had the incident behind us and it was no longer of interest to the local media.

Through this experience the superintendent and school board "bonded." The board expressed confidence in the new relationship that had developed. It was a distinct turning point in this superintendent's need to build a trusting relationship. While the district continued to face difficult issues together, without necessarily agreeing, the board as a whole readily sought the superintendent's opinion and supported her decisions. This difficult clarification process resulted in a healthy exchange of ideas and information, and a sound sense of role differentiation for the superintendent and the school board.

Relationships Between School Board and Superintendent

Most studies of superintendent-board relationships conclude that communication, trust, and understanding role differences are the main factors influencing their effectiveness. The importance of collaboration among individuals and groups was consistently stressed in a 1992 survey conducted by the AASA. Board members and superintendents who described their relationships as excellent consistently named collaboration as the most important factor. Survey respondents (McCurdy, 1992) attributed their successes to joint efforts to seek good relationships and mutual understanding. Numerous comments in the surveys stressed how they had worked together constantly—using good communication skills, sharing information, and seeking agreement on mutual expectations—to form healthy and trusting relationships. Notably absent as a secret of success was any mention of individual accomplishment, such as the board's doing something special or the superintendent's performance being exemplary. Their explanations confirm the crucial importance of the basic elements of a strong relationship.

Tensions Between Superintendent and Board

Certainly, some superintendents are unable to provide leadership or even respond to the massive number of demands. However, this is not the major reason that so many superintendents across the country continue to have such short tenure. The number one reason that most superintendents leave a school district concerns their relations with, and support from, the school board. Moreover, there are many more superintendents who remain but are basically impotent because of poor relations with the board. Superintendents can do very little, if anything, unless the school board empowers them to make effective changes. Larry Zenke, superintendent of the Duval County public schools in Florida, found that

> One of the most important responsibilities that a superintendent has, if one is to survive beyond the average tenure of two and one-half years, is to know your board members "individually" as board members and "collectively" as a school board. Superintendents who fail to give the necessary time required for such knowing usually will find themselves experiencing relatively short tenures. The superintendent must allocate sufficient time to develop open channels of communication with board members both individually and collectively, and also work to raise levels of trust between the superintendent and the board members and among board members themselves.

One of the ways that Omaha Superintendent Norbert Schuerman is able to walk the difficult line of cultivating trusting relations with individual board members without damaging his relationship with other board members is through maintaining confidentiality and openness. He is open with all board members, and he never gossips or discusses confidential information. If he ever needs to break a confidence, he always discusses it with the original party to gain his or her approval and understanding before sharing the information. "I honor confidential information," he says. "If, in fact, I am going to break that confidence, I will go back and get permission to share the information."

However, like most superintendents, he is always concerned about how the school board is evaluating him. It is not easy to read a diverse group of people who represent many factions. Being able to read the board is essential to a superintendent's ultimate success. Schuerman describes how he prepares for board evaluations: "I perspire a lot. I try to assess their behavior throughout the year. Where are their 'hot buttons'? I try to talk about where we have made progress and where we are not doing as well as we should."

Superintendents should always inform board members about the reality of what is occurring in schools by presenting it in the most positive light possible, without whitewash. The motto "Be willing to lose a few battles to win the war" goes a long way in superintendent-board relations.

A person can have all the skills needed to be an effective superintendent, but if he or she is not *seen* as successful by the school board, then he or she *isn't*. Perception is everyone's reality. That means one needs to be seen in a very positive light. One cannot maintain board support if various factions within the school and community turn against the superintendent. This poses a real problem as different groups perceive the superintendent from their point of view, which can be quite different from the way the superintendent sees himself or herself. This "perception gap" is why it is important to have good communication within and outside the school board office, so that the superintendent can have a reading on what the public thinks. Relations with the press are especially important, and at the same time potentially dangerous. Controversy sells newspapers (and broadcast media time), and reporters can't help but look for a little controversy.

Daniel Daste, superintendent in the St. Bernard Parish public schools in Chalmette, Louisiana, has recommendations:

> Keep the press informed and establish good relations with them before you need them. Expect to be misquoted from time to time and be prepared for the possibility they will plant ideas, make controversies out of nothing, and help stage the story. This can jeopardize relations with board members if you are not careful. In fact, one of the stories that the media likes to stage is disagreements between school board members and superintendents. Turn to board leadership and legal advisors when incorrect and false stories are circulating in the press. When there is a fair amount of truth to the stories, it pays to have others face the music with you—spread praise *and* blame.

Don't stand out to defend a position which others have not supported with you. Boards don't like media questions or stories that they are not prepared for and [that] were not considered as part of the superintendent-board deliberations. There is very little chance of recovering if money is spent improperly, audits are not clean, or there are questions regarding purchasing procedures. The key to surviving difficult times is to build strong relations with as many factions as possible in advance. Making regular contact with the key people in your district is essential to a long, successful tenure.

If trust, communication, respect, and collegiality form the basis of superintendent effectiveness, major factors that often destabilize the superintendent's relationship with the board are confusion about roles, poor communication, and personal agendas. Problems with effective communication have increased over the past two decades, resulting in growing hostility and strain between boards and superintendents. Pressures on boards and superintendents have increased the potential for tension and the need for improved communication and understanding, at a time when both seem to be at a low.

Factors Affecting Superintendent-Board Tensions

Evidence as to the causes of increased tensions and poorer communication tends to vary from school district to school district; however, a pattern of factors is emerging. Conflicts and tensions often result more from misunderstanding than from an inability to come to consensus on issues. The problems arise from the way people work together or the expectations they have of one another. The reasons for deteriorating relationships are often encapsulated as "Well, the superintendent and the board just didn't get along."

A number of studies have identified factors that explain these increased tensions, and the resultant high turnover among superintendents. By far the most often-mentioned problems are related to (1) effective communication and (2) financial matters. A majority of the problems identified led to a change of superintendent. Herd and Estes (1993) found that superintendents expressed a healthy respect for the latent power of the board. Nearly every superintendent surveyed reported troubling incidents with particular board members that for the most part had resulted in their premature departure. Boards that tend to regard themselves as representatives of the "school organization to the community," rather than as representatives of the "community to the school organization," make it possible to plan strategically what needs to be done to identify and address district priorities. Board members should, as one very seasoned respondent reported, "be strategic leaders focusing on tomorrow, next month, next year. However, many don't have a clue about what being a strategic leader means, and that ignorance makes it risky business for the superintendent to act strategically. The superintendent will get his head handed to him, figuratively speaking, if he or she is quite evidently out of step with the board."

According to Ross and Kowal (1994), there are a number of potential causes for deteriorating relationships between superintendents and school board members. They include weighing the agenda too heavily in favor of business matters, lack of knowledge or commitment, attempts at domination, lack of community trust or confidence, relinquishing responsibility, avoiding conflict, and practices that stifle vigorous discussion. Many of these problems are the result of good intentions and trying too hard to get things done efficiently. Yet the end result is alienation between board members and the superintendent.

It is safer to do too much than it is to do too little. Although most boards can forgive a superintendent for trying too hard, very few accept halfhearted effort. The superintendency is one job that demands full attention, and superintendents must be highly motivated to make an impact. Effort is probably the single most important factor in a board's assessment of a superintendent's performance. This factor is most often determined by how well the superintendent is prepared to handle various situations. It is not harmful to say, "I don't know; however, I will get you the answer tomorrow" a few times. But if it becomes a matter of normal operations, the superintendent's relations will deteriorate quickly.

Consistently weak—or worse, incorrect—responses are sure death for a superintendent. The advice that all seasoned superintendents give to those entering the position is, "Come prepared for your board meetings, don't introduce surprises, and keep your board well informed." Patrick Russo, superintendent of the Savannah-Chatham County public schools in Georgia, finds that "proper preparation for any situation is the key to success. Not being properly prepared may impact a superintendent's recommendation for approval, hurt his or her credibility, and lend a general perception of incompetence when dealing with a situation. The best approach is preparation, preparation, and preparation. Being prepared to anticipate various questions, and having answers to those anticipated questions, will allow for perceived competence in any situation." There is very little tolerance for a superintendent who is not fully informed about his or her field and school district.

In large school districts, it becomes impossible for the superintendent to know details about everything that is happening across a broad range of topics. In fact, the superintendent may be unable to answer very specific school board questions on all agenda items. In these cases, the superintendent should invite well-informed central office administrators to attend the board meetings and be prepared to respond to specific questions. The administrators should be well informed on issues or matters that they deal with more closely than the superintendent. However, the superintendent needs to be sure that these administrators know the details of items in their areas of expertise and responsibility. The superintendent must delegate and trust colleagues with contributing to effective communication with the school board. This provides an opportunity for administrators to develop their communication skills while ensuring that someone from the administration has clear responsibility in areas important to the board and community. It is also wise to review with administrators the items and or issues that will more than likely be addressed during the board meeting to ensure that all are prepared to provide a united front.

A much-quoted study of internal factors that undermine effective relationships was completed by Marilyn Grady and Miles Bryant at the University of Nebraska, Lincoln. These researchers "found the principle cause [of turnover] to be problems in the relationship between district leaders and their school boards or individual board members" (1991, p. 21). They grouped the causes for poor relationships, as reported by superintendents, into eleven categories:

1. *Family and friends.* Problems originate from disciplinary action and favorable or unfavorable treatment of the children, relatives, and/or friends of board members or other influential people.
2. *Employing relatives and friends.* This category includes not hiring, terminating, giving undesirable assignments, and being involved in generally unfavorable experiences for family members and friends, of influential people, employed within the school.
3. *Board members' roles.* Incorrect interpretation of roles include arranging facility use, assessing staff performance, job appointments, communicating with and confronting staff about personnel matters, purchasing items for schools, awarding contracts, approving all superintendent's decisions, making decisions based on outside advisement, and extreme micromanagement.
4. *Election with an ax to grind.* Election campaigns that focus on one issue, such as firing the superintendent, teacher rights, school prayer, reducing spending, extended school year, etc., which creates divergence, conflict, and disagreements at every meeting.
5. *Lack of support.* These are cases where the board does not back the superintendent's recommendations in matters such as personnel issues, maintenance recommendations, disciplinary actions, salary schedules, promotions, etc.
6. *Board malfunctions.* Incidents precipitated by the board, such as stagnation, ineffective standing committees, encouraging attacks, lack of focus, vacillation, emotional instability, and general inability to function effectively.
7. *Athletic coaches.* This category is similar to 1., 2., and 3. above, except that problems related to termination, release, reassignment, and remuneration package for coaches seem to be especially prevalent.
8. *The community.* Community groups apply pressure on single issues, such as cutting taxes, reducing administrators, keeping schools open, supporting religious speakers, or terminating/hiring staff.
9. *Individual members.* Personal problems or personalities of individual members, whose actions—such as holding private meetings outside regular board meetings, conducting unsolicited

polls, spending excessive time with the superintendent and staff, and serving on multiple boards—interfere with the superintendent's functioning effectively.

10. *Contracts.* This category deserves special consideration because it so often signals trouble, especially regarding the superintendent's contract.

11. *Superintendents.* The superintendent can create a critical problem when his or her behavior does not fit the community, for example, smokes and drinks, is flamboyant, is paranoid, spends too much money, or engages in unseemly conduct (Grady and Bryant, 1991, pp. 23–24).

Poor Relationships

Another problem is the need to work around the egos of some school board members. Board members can believe that they are far superior to any of the "mere educators" who work in the school district. They are sometimes offended when their ideas or issues are challenged, regardless of the diplomacy or effectiveness of logic applied to the situation. Some board members may even carry this to the point where they push to have an employee fired or punished for not treating them with proper respect. These board members expect the school administrators to stay out of board deliberations, not to speak until requested, and to always remember that they are working at the board's pleasure and can be easily replaced.

The degree to which any of these relationship problems affects the superintendent's tenure depends on how skilled the superintendent is at defusing difficult school board behavior. The general belief of superintendents is that it is bad personal disagreements and poor relationships, not the reasoned evaluation of competency and performance, that so often results in involuntary turnover.

The American Association of School Administrators' (AASA) critical issues report on *Building Better Board-Administration Relations* (McCurdy, 1992) found that the evidence pointed to increasing pressures on and between school boards and district superintendents. The report concluded: "A broad array of survey findings, expert analysis, and opinions of superintendents, board members, and others all indicate that while the relationships remain solid by and large, board-superintendent tensions have risen in recent years" (p. 30). The findings suggested a trend toward more active board involvement in school leadership. Some of the internal factors that were found to add to tension and friction are

- Misunderstandings about roles
- Favoritism with individual board members
- Insufficient time communicating to board members
- Losing contact between meetings
- Not feeling involved in the thought process
- Overwhelming the board with information
- Domination by the superintendent, board, or individual members
- Interference by the board in management functions (micromanagement)
- Growing independence of the board
- Single-issue, single-region, or single-interest members
- Leaking discussions from executive sessions
- Involvement in personnel matters
- Attempts to get favorable treatment for friends and relatives
- Lack of skill, knowledge, and experience
- Pursuing political pressure, careers, and activism
- Board turnover (McCurdy, 1992)

Many superintendents suggest that board turnover is the major reason they lose their jobs. With turnover of board members, initiatives are abandoned and relationships deteriorate. New members on a board tend to mistrust the superintendent and view the person as an adversary. This situation is especially difficult when the new member has a mandate from constituents that he or she pursues with significant energy. This is especially true in cases where board members' specific intention is to get rid of the superintendent. School board members who are ex-district employees can also be a source of potential trouble.

Board members are increasingly concerned with political constituents and with getting reelected. Superintendents suggest that some decisions are viewed more with an eye to what will gain the support of voters than what is best for the children. Tough decisions that alienate voters can result in loss of support from the board, even if the decisions are best for the school system over the long haul. Superintendents have learned that they must have board support if they are to weather the heat from an unpopular decision that is best for student learning.

A good example of this phenomenon occurred in a very hotly debated vote to approve condom distribution in schools in Philadelphia and New York. The Philadelphia superintendent, Constance Clayton, was able to get the school board to propose and support the idea, which is a testimony to her political acumen and long-term tenure. The New York chancellor, Joseph Fernandez, was eventually unseated by his political battles with the board and community over just such issues as condom distribution. He was called "King Condom" by a number of board and community members.

Superintendents face controversial issues, and they are in trouble if their boards do not stick with them and provide support. Superintendents now believe that the balance has shifted to the point where political astuteness matters more than job performance. "Absolutely, politics plays a big role," said Frank Petruzielo, superintendent of the Broward County (Florida) Public Schools. "Competency in many instances is not the issue, and that's what makes these jobs more difficult to perform than any other in public or private sectors."

Reforming School Boards

The problems over the past ten years in New York City, Boston, Chicago, Los Angeles, and many other school districts have not been completely blamed on the superintendents. In fact, a number of communities have called for a complete restructuring of how schools are governed. Across America, school boards are being criticized by state governments, education experts, and the public in general. Reports from the Institute for Educational Leadership, Committee for Economic Development, and the Twentieth Century Fund have all recommended changing school boards into education policy boards or children and youth coordinating boards, improving relationships with local government, improving involvement in school boards and board elections, and setting state-established performance criteria to hold boards accountable. Kentucky, West Virginia, and Massachusetts have enacted laws that modify the responsibilities of local school boards. The January 1994 issue of *Phi Delta Kappan* dedicated an entire section to school board reform and school governance. More than twenty-five different recommendations for changing school boards are contained within this single issue.

The volatility of the school board reform movement was demonstrated during a heated disagreement and debate between Michael Kirst, professor at Stanford University and a reform advocate, and Thomas Shannon, executive director of the National School Boards Association, at the 1993 AASA annual conference in Orlando.

Kirst suggested that school boards must relinquish a number of responsibilities so that they can perform better in policy making and visioning for schools. Boards should hire superintendents, establish district plans, determine funding priorities, set staff development policies, approve major construction projects, and develop curricular framework, he argued. They should not preside over grievances, approve competitive bidding contracts and payments, make personnel decisions, or generally micromanage schools. In his *Phi Delta Kappan* article (Kirst, 1994), he said: "While it is impossible to separate policy and administration in general terms, the change to education policy boards, as proposed by the IEL [Institute for Educational Leadership] study, would precisely define the limits and appropriate focus for the future role of the local school board" (p. 381). Regardless, the smart superintendent always asks the board to review and comment on major new ideas or initiatives, even if these changes do not require a vote from the board.

Shannon accused Kirst and other reformers of trying to make school boards scapegoats for educational failures. He said that boards encourage improvements, but neither the funds nor the public is there to support needed changes. He argued that Kirst's reform proposals would undercut representative governance of public education by eroding school board power. Shannon asked, "Does the public want a substantial part of a district's decisions made by the superintendent in the privacy of his or her executive office, or with the superintendent and the board in the bright light of a public room?" His article in the same issue of *Phi Delta Kappan* expressed concern about some of these reforms in that "they divert public attention from the real problems of educating youth in America today. . . ." Later in the article, Shannon went on to say, "Diminishing the policy-making authority of local school boards by expanding the power of individual school administrators or local school councils that are accountable to nobody simply won't be countenanced. Nor will burying education policy making in the musty cellars of municipal bureaucracies" (pp. 388–390).

Clearly, everyone agrees that deteriorating relationships between board members and superintendents must be turned around; the debate rages over how that can be done. In the meanwhile, the jobs of superintendents are becoming more difficult as their support is dwindling. A number of training programs for both superintendents and school board members are beginning to appear in some districts and states. The AASA and NSBA have both started addressing this difficult issue concertedly. In the meanwhile, it remains a major cause of school district instability.

There is a need to develop other means to improve the relationships between school board members and superintendents, for example, creation of a strong induction and development program for board members. School districts where such programs exist have experienced smoother relations between superintendent and board members. Attending the national meetings of the AASA, the Association for Supervision and Curriculum Development, and the National School Boards Association is certainly an important element of this development. Some states have developed statewide programs for board development.

Larry Zenke comments:

> One very effective program which has been initiated within this state [Florida] is the Master Board Training Program offered by the state's School Boards Association. Many of the school boards and superintendents across the state have participated in this program with success. Not only is the opportunity provided for school board members and their superintendents to get out of town together for a number of days over a period of a year, but there is the opportunity to develop communication with other school board members and superintendents through this training activity. I believe that such professional development programs for school board members and superintendents can help to provide a smoother working relationship between school boards and their

superintendents and among school board members themselves. Such improved communication and building of trust levels should enhance the efforts of school boards and superintendents to provide direction for school districts, and should as a result increase the average tenure of superintendents.

With continuous rapid turnover of the top leadership of our schools, little ongoing continuous program improvement can be expected. More efforts such as the program developed by our state's School Boards Association must be implemented in other states, perhaps through the assistance of the National School Boards Association and the American Association of School Administrators.

Chapter Seven

| **Coping with Daily Crises**

A high percentage of the superintendents facing a questionable future have experienced a "critical incident" that foretold the end of their effectiveness in the position. These incidents irreparably damage the superintendent's ability to carry out his or her duties. Critical incidents can make a superintendent vulnerable to extreme pressures that, at best, bring in conflict and demand extensive time commitments, and at worst result in loss of employment and ineffective schools. Superintendents are becoming increasingly aware of how important to their future as leaders it is to handle critical incidents properly. Superintendents have been threatened with termination after incidents as benign as a powerful individual's not getting preferential treatment for his or her children, or the superintendent's arguing against a proposal made by a religious group. A number of these incidents can be described as red-flag issues, ones holding great potential for repercussion regardless of the decision that is made.

Critical incidents that traditionally are red flags center on incompetent teachers, sexual harassment, sex education, student expulsion, inclusion, cultural and racial diversity, values education, school closings, and educational reform. Regardless of tenure, superintendents need to be prepared for whatever incident occurs. Sometimes, however, the central character in the drama—the superintendent—becomes a casualty of the situation no matter what is done. A superintendent who fell victim to furor over falling test scores, deceptive debating techniques, a critical incident with an employee, and finally (of course) deteriorating relations with the board sighed: "You get tired of those cycles, and that happens. You've got lots of other pressures, you know, getting things done, and frankly, when you spend more time dealing with problems than you do planning for the future . . . you lose some of the enthusiasm, the fire in the belly."

On a daily basis, superintendents face budget deficits, problems in academics, desegregation, communication problems, vacancies in key positions, and skepticism. This is routine. At the same time, their energy and attention are constantly being diverted toward critical incidents that breathe life or death into their position. And beyond all this, there are often clashes among strong-willed people who have legitimate differences in their points of view. Superintendents suggest that "people fight like hell over some obscure incident and ignore the need to improve schools." Those who do not believe the system has treated someone fairly will demand, and sometimes fight for, what they think is proper treatment. This siege mentality does not produce conditions for either effective schools or effective superintendents, and it requires a great deal of time. The superintendent of the Columbus (Ohio) public schools, Larry Mixon, reflected on critical incidents:

> At first, I did not recognize the critical nature of the incidents that I faced. As time passed, I began to develop a better instinct for recognizing seemingly small problems as potential time bombs. The main thing that made the incidents critical in nature was that they represented impending conflicts, especially between factions in the community or groups within the school system itself. They often happen as surprises (which is one thing that no superintendent welcomes) with short deadlines for resolution. The key to handling these was to approach the potential conflict with a win-win attitude as well as leadership style that involved lots of initial listening and processing so that all of those involved felt that they were both heard and understood.

The Damage from Critical Incidents

As superintendent of schools in Montgomery, Alabama, Thomas Bobo was pulled between a major systemwide effort for school renewal and the struggle to maintain racial harmony within the Montgomery schools. The tightrope walk of maintaining harmony between the races had consumed much of his energy. Critical incidents related to racial issues constantly pulled him away from a school renewal effort that he believed in and that had a high probability of success, given proper attention. Bobo believed that the renewal effort might develop openness and understanding that could improve race relations; however, critical incidents forced him to focus on racial issues directly, while the renewal effort was placed on hold.

The key critical incidents were fueled by a finding that a higher proportion of underachieving students were black. As a result of attendance zones, there were a number of all-black schools within the community. The incidents evolved around the belief in the black community that underachieving black students were being "taught white" even in all-black schools with a predominance of black teachers. Others argued that whites were being given favored treatment within the schools and that blacks were being held back. Bobo was in the midst of taking steps to improve the education of all children when the concerns of the black community began to disrupt systemwide efforts. The black community erupted and focused their anger on the superintendent. The school renewal effort was undermined by perceptions of inequity and prejudicial treatment. Bobo was well prepared to lead school renewal, but he was not sure how to improve race relations and to build confidence in the system among the black community. This soon became irrelevant as Bobo resigned the superintendency before the school renewal effort could be readdressed.

Difficult issues like racial disharmony, family life education, religious freedom, outcome-based education, global education, etc., tend to be debated in a public forum. This encourages entrenchment. Such open debate can reach a point where segments of the community declare war on one another and play power politics to forward their positions. Often the most vocal elements in our communities are given initial attention, while the silent majority quietly seethe over the directions being taken. The system responds to dogmatism and crusaders whose sense of mission and zeal shut out the beliefs of the majority of the community.

Typically, conflict begins to escalate in a second round of political turbulence that is not as clear, in which strategies are often planned behind closed doors. At this point, the superintendent usually begins to gain an understanding of where he or she stands along the political spectrum. If the superintendent is included in the political process, and information about community politics is shared, he or she can maintain political clout and remain effective. If the superintendent is left out, he or she will be blindsided, uninformed, and unsupported to the point of losing all effectiveness, regardless of past or present successes. Superintendents are seen as being in the eye of the storm; they can become isolated if the power structures withdraw and distance themselves. They can no longer maintain public confidence and order, and their effectiveness is seriously jeopardized.

When a critical incident isolates the superintendent, he or she often responds blindly, sometimes misjudging the direction, scale, or nature of differing positions. This blindness results in either underestimation or exaggeration of the conditions surrounding the issue, or even misunderstanding of the issue itself. Labels are often used to explain away what is not understood: *racist, liberal, conservative, religious right, radical left, competent, incompetent,* etc. Some participants incorrectly believe that labels provide insulation and make organizational life simpler, because they emphasize the differences and bring the opposition together, often around a narrow interest. However, labels are sure death for a superintendent because they belie the complexity of human character and increase misunderstanding among people. Labels serve as barriers to communication, as misunderstanding and mistrust become part of the superintendent's every effort to improve schools.

Other critical incidents may occur when persons within the school district try to expose and embellish the superintendent's flaws. In extreme cases, this actually begins before the superintendent ever arrives in the community. Critical incidents in previous districts, long since resolved, or a long-past but embarrassing family issue, may find its way into the press, years after the fact. The slightest indiscretion related to loose, agitated, or ill-advised behavior can mark the beginning of the end of the superintendent's career. An otherwise clean record with the blemish of a one-time mishandling of a critical incident in which the superintendent was blindsided can mean extreme scrutiny and inability to recover. Sometimes when critical issues do not exist, they are manufactured and connected to half-truths and innuendo. The pressure becomes so great that the easiest way out is simply to resign rather than submit to emotional and political trauma.

Employee Misconduct

A straightforward issue that can become a critical incident seriously damaging a superintendent's tenure is allegation of misconduct made against an employee of the school district. Mishandling of such allegations can cause tensions regardless of which side is in error. Superintendents can be held accountable for creating a general atmosphere that is seen to tolerate inappropriate behavior. Superintendents may fail to recognize the seriousness of misconduct reports, or they may fail to report the allegations quickly enough, possibly to take time to complete an internal investigation first. This delay is often interpreted as a cover-up or an attempt to hide serious allegations. On the other hand, if the superintendent suspends a popular employee who is later found to be innocent of all accusations, he or she can be in serious trouble. Community members and colleagues supporting the employee then express a lack of confidence in the superintendent.

These problems often develop while the superintendent is unaware of shifting attitudes and values in the community. In a number of cases, 1970s attitudes about child abuse or sexual harassment have gotten superintendents in trouble in the 1990s. For example, a superintendent was fired for his handling of sexual misconduct accusations made against a teacher in the school district. In justifying his actions in investigating the matter internally and not reporting it to police or other authorities, the superintendent said: "No one that I know of . . . was at that time advocating that every comment or allegation that came to an educator's attention—no matter how casual or improbable—was to be considered 'reason to believe' that there was an urgent need to refer the matter to the Department of Social Services." He consistently investigated all allegations internally with the help of a special assistant. The special assistant's investigation in this case did not support the student's allegation of abuse. The teacher denied any wrongdoing. The student's parents later reported the matter to the police, and the teacher pleaded guilty to a misdemeanor charge.

In another case of reported misconduct, the same superintendent placed another teacher on temporary suspension and the teacher, a coach who acknowledged having sexual relations with a seventeen-year-old student, was later allowed to resign. The coach was tried and sent to prison for having sexual relations with a female student. The superintendent was admonished for not reporting this complaint. Community outrage intensified, and it was not long thereafter that the superintendent was asked to resign.

Treating sexual harassment too lightly almost certainly leads to escalation and undesirable consequences for all concerned. When not handled properly, these cases affect morale, turnover, and reputations, and they can lead to costly lawsuits. Such were the consequences in another unusual case involving a female student in Minnesota. School officials did not respond quickly enough to her complaint that defamatory graffiti about her was written on a bathroom wall. The student sued the school district. The lawsuit created a stir not only within the district but throughout the state. The litigation resulted in Minnesota's adopting some of the strongest regulations on sexual harassment in a school environment—but not without a high cost to all those directly involved in the case.

A superintendent should never assume that in such cases nothing needs to be done. They should be handled so as to protect the rights of all parties and follow all relevant laws. The practice begins with a clear, written policy; it requires reporting all claims and thoroughly investigating them. There is, however, a likelihood that regardless of what is done or whether the party involved is innocent, everyone associated or connected with the case will have a lifelong blemish in the eyes of the community.

Student Misconduct

Statistics and surveys show that crime and violence have become an intrinsic part of the youth culture. A 1995 poll of a national violence prevention program suggested that one in nine secondary students stayed home or cut classes because of crime and violence. One in eight said they were earning lower grades as a result, and one in three said they had been involved in or seen a fight in which weapons were displayed. As a result, superintendents are now employing paging systems and detector devices in their schools. Larger segments of school district budgets are earmarked for purchasing equipment to ensure the safety of students and staff. Teachers across the nation are now asking for telephone lines not only for their computers but also for safety purposes. Television security systems are also on the rise in public schools. These security systems are needed to protect both the people in our schools and ever-more expensive equipment.

Incidents of violence and gang activity can land superintendents in a critical situation. The violence problem is compounded when drugs are involved. Superintendents may be unaware of the street activity of students attending the schools within their districts. Such activity often remains highly confidential because of a lack of communication among schools, police, social services, and the courts. As a result, superintendents often misread the behavior of students. They see conflict and aggressive behavior as discrete incidents and overlook gang patterns that might be developing. This blindness can result in a superintendent's looking as if he or she is out of touch or covering up critical incidents. Superintendents are often caught unawares by such incidents, not realizing what is going on until it is too late. By the time they come to understand the situation, the community has already lost confidence in the superintendent and withdrawn its support.

An example of a superintendent's failing to read a situation occurred in a middle-class suburb of a city of approximately five hundred thousand people. The superintendent investigated a case in which a high school student had supposedly been beaten by a group of eight to ten other students. The victim, the son of a prominent banker in the community, had gone to the hospital, where he was treated for minor cuts and bruises and then released. The superintendent talked to the boy's parents, who were not overly concerned and said the problem was with one of their son's friends who had previously dated a girl their son was now dating. The principal talked to both boys, who verified the story the parents provided. The police pressed no charges, although disciplinary action was taken by the principal. A week later, a prominent citizen in the community asked a school board member about gang violence at the local high school. The board member was not aware of the fight the previous week or of any other gang behavior. The superintendent was asked at a board meeting to explain the situation, including any problems with gangs. The superintendent said that he had investigated the matter and that it was a minor incident and not gang-related. He was unaware of any gang activity in the schools or community.

On Friday of the following week, a major gang fight broke out between two groups within the high school. Rumors had spread that a member of one gang was dating a girl that the leader of another gang had dated. The gang leaders fought and war was declared between the groups. The police arrested eighteen students from local high schools, collecting bats, metal rakes, and a knife used during the fights. A reporter following up the police report wrote that the superintendent had tried to cover up previous gang problems at the school and had kept the school board "in the dark" regarding the matter. Relations between the superintendent and the school board and community began to worsen.

Although problems with gangs seem to be on the decline nationally, superintendents have had trouble in dealing with these problems where they occurred. Educators usually lack the knowledge base and resources to deal effectively with gangs and gang activity. Catherine Conly writes:

> Despite unanimous agreement that gangs exist, there is little consensus about how they should be defined. The debate over definitions is not trivial, since definitions inevitably affect programmatic responses. Definitions serve as the foundation for a school or community's response and influence the types and extent of resources applied.
>
> Indeed, the success or failure of attempts to address gangs is likely to rest in part on the consensus that participants reach about the nature of the situation and the best way to address it [1993, p. 46].

Successful approaches often bridge punishment and prevention with positive, proactive alternatives to gangs, reinforcing social networks such as the family, school, and community. The success of a program to reduce the appeal of gangs rests upon its ability to develop skills that help students resist involvement in the first place by providing effective alternatives and support structures. In the case discussed, the superintendent failed to address the issue proactively and therefore was ultimately accused of adding to the problem by not recognizing its existence. The superintendent lost credibility and never really recovered from the incident.

Consolidating Schools

Failing to develop understanding and support for the consolidation of schools among those with an interest can lead to very difficult times. Information must be provided in such a way that it helps people work collaboratively to understand the need for the change. Collaboration is bolstered when information and research regarding the decision being made is understood, discussed, and shared by all those who are trying to improve the educational system. Effective superintendents engage participants in a process of continuous improvement and value their input. Enough people need to be involved so that everyone realizes that many interests are important in the process and that they need to think inclusively.

The role of the superintendent is to see that useful information is made available to all interested parties. This can be a difficult task for central administrative staff, but it should not be overlooked, resisted, or minimized. The superintendent and staff members provide the needed information so that participants truly understand and appreciate the decision made. With this information, participants have an opportunity—even if sometimes chaotic—to gain an understanding of the complexity of the issue. When people do not have all the information, they don't understand the decision made by those who do have the information and thus resist and counterattack.

Carol Peck, superintendent of Alhambra School District No. 68 in Phoenix, offers a common example. Two of Alhambra's elementary schools (K–8) had low enrollments in the junior high grades. Along with some central administrative staff and board members, Peck completed an intensive study of the problem and concluded that it was not cost-effective to continue providing a comprehensive junior high program at each facility. The schools were one mile apart. A great deal of their research pointed to the need to combine the schools' seventh and eighth grades at one school. Although board members did not have any of the information regarding the decision to consolidate, they did see the need for this action. After a decision was made to offer these two grades in only one of the schools, parents voiced their concerns very strongly. The community split because both attendance areas wanted the seventh and eighth grades at their school. Parents' concerns did not go away, and pressure mounted to block this plan. The pressure was so great that the superintendent and board considered going back to the inefficient status quo. A number of school board members were angry that neither they nor the community were kept well informed on the making of the decision.

As a result, a number of informal community leaders (from the school not selected) were invited to consider the information used to make the decision. Asked to suggest ideas to help obtain support for the proposal, they made several suggestions, including renaming the receiving school so it would carry a new identification. Most of these suggestions, including the renaming, were followed. The informal leaders became supporters of the plan and worked within their communities to obtain support for the school board's decision. This support helped over time. Resistance began to abate, but not without some harm, in both communities, to the prestige of the board and the superintendent.

Looking back, Peck reflected: "What I learned from this situation is that parents, teachers, administrators, and community members need to be involved from the very beginning, especially when change is a likely outcome. I would have formed a task force, including several strong community leaders, to help examine the situation and propose solutions to the problem." A year later, in discussing the benefit of keeping community members well informed and involving them in important decisions, she said, "I know these ideas work because when people are involved in developing a plan of excellence, monitoring the plan of excellence, and recognizing accomplishments as the plan is implemented, those involved are empowered to work even harder and to take risks. The success of this approach is evident by the feedback on our surveys and by our improved student achievement." If superintendents are not prepared to share information with those who will be affected by decisions, they soon find themselves feeling a great deal of heat from community resistance. Conversely, if they are willing to share and discuss information with concerned parties, they establish the needed support for successful implementation of improvement efforts.

The Conflicts Ahead

We need to move away from *planning* the future and begin providing the information that will allow it to *evolve*. As Margaret Wheatley suggests:

> Instead of strategic planning, we need to focus on strategic intent, or creating intentionality about what we are trying to do as a community of people who care about education. . . . We can't become a learning organization unless we are willing to learn from one another and from our experiences. We need to have information flowing through the system. It can't be stopped because of roles, politics, or status. It can't be limited to faculty and/or administration. Information has to flow among everyone who cares about education—including parents and community groups. This information sharing will create quite different relationships" [quoted in Steinberger, 1995, p. 16].

School superintendents can never be quite sure where or when a critical incident will occur. Showing good judgment, taking quick control of the situation, and communicating effectively are absolutely critical in determining how well the superintendent survives the incident. The most effective way to handle a critical incident is to make sure it doesn't happen in the first place. When one does occur, it is essential that it be recognized quickly and that the school and/or district respond rapidly, giving it high priority.

There are a number of steps that require the superintendent's attention. Hopefully, crisis policy, a crisis control center, and a designated spokesperson (namely the superintendent or public relations officer) are already in place for such situations. It is essential that the superintendent take charge by addressing the situation immediately. The first step is to lay out the investigation and reporting procedures. Secondly, a crisis team should define the circumstances, identify the problem, pinpoint perceptions, rank options, and construct the most effective approach to resolve the crisis. Often it is prudent to consult legal counsel and act decisively. The spokesperson should communicate openly and honestly as long as the incident is still critical. Special emphasis may need to be placed on rebuilding, recovery, and healing; however, the goal is to get past the crisis and maintain focus on the school district's vision (Norton, Webb, Dlugosh, and Sybouts, 1996; Meyers, 1986).

Of course, some situations are always considered critical incidents: accidents; injury or death of schoolchildren or staff; fire; major disagreements that appear as headline news; violation of federal, state, or local codes; criminal behavior by students or staff; and accusations regarding the handling of funds. The superintendent's future effectiveness in the school district and community depends on how well he or she handles *every* critical incident, whether one as straightforward as these or less so.

Chapter Eight

The Personal and Professional Toll

In all organizations, chief executive officers make many personal sacrifices. This is certainly true of school superintendents as well. When one chooses to become a superintendent of schools, one should recognize the decision as not only a professional one but a lifestyle choice as well. Previous chapters have discussed many of the professional challenges that superintendents face. This chapter focuses on the demands made of the superintendent's personal life.

Understanding the Demands of the Job

Almost all the participants in this study mentioned the personal toll that the job takes on them. At the same time, they were quick to point out that the rewards and satisfactions are also great. Mary Nebgen, superintendent of the Washoe County School District in Reno, captures this sentiment: "Although there are problems in the superintendency as it presently exists in the United States, I hope that the book will also emphasize the fulfilling opportunities that we as superintendents have to change the lives of a huge number of students for the better. Although some days it seems that our impact is small, over the long run—if we can hang in there for the long run—we can make substantial differences in our educational systems." Similar statements came from the great majority of superintendents participating in this study.

Fulfillment does not mean, however, that the job does not require significant personal sacrifice from those who select this important position. *Executive Educator* magazine commissioned an

"Exclusive National Survey of School Executives," conducted by a research team from Xavier University (Booth and others, 1994). The nine hundred school executives who participated suggested that "school reform" was added to the job description in the 1980s. At the same time, the number of hours necessary to complete the workday satisfactorily was boosted. Slightly more than 80 percent of the respondents reported that they work more than fifty hours a week, and almost one-third reported that they work sixty hours per week or more.

Regarding these long workdays, superintendents seem to catch the most flak from their spouses, with 38 percent reporting that their spouses complain about the hours they work. Leslie Johnson, superintendent of the Hinds County Public Schools in Raymond, Mississippi, said that "the greatest toll that a superintendency takes on a family is the amount of time that the job takes away from family life. Not only does a superintendent put in an eight-to-ten-hour regular day's work, he is also expected to take an active role in professional, civic, and church organizations and activities. Added to these responsibilities is the time away from home for professional travel both in and out of state." As in our survey, almost half of the superintendents reported that the job places too heavy a demand on them. Yet more than 71 percent reported high job satisfaction; only 8 percent were seriously dissatisfied with the job.

Superintendents report that the toll on one's health and personal life is very high and can destroy "the fire in the belly" for the job if one is not very careful. As one superintendent told us, "You can give, give, give until you have no more to give." Perhaps this type of toll is what inspired Sam Keen to suggest that certain job descriptions should require a caution label: "Excessive work may be hazardous to the health of your body and spirit." He continues:

> But there is still something unsaid, something that forces me to ask questions about my life that are, perhaps, tragic: In working so much, have I done violence to my being? How often, doing work that is good, have I betrayed what is better in myself and abandoned what is best for those I love? How many hours would have been better spent in walking in silence in the woods or wrestling with my children? Two decades ago, near the end of what was a good but troubled marriage, my wife asked me: "Would you be willing to be less efficient?" That question haunts me [Keen, 1991, p. 67].

What is most disturbing is that the brightest, most dynamic, and most effective superintendents tend to get caught up the most. The superintendent often makes real contributions to the community and schools, but at a price to self and family. The drain is compounded when the superintendent's efforts and successes are not repaid in kind. Donald Draayer, superintendent of Minnetonka School District No. 276 in Minnesota, shares some of his feelings about the sacrifices he often made as a school superintendent:

> One of my greatest regrets after twenty-one years in the superintendency is missing the recitals and concerts in which my children performed because I had a school board meeting or other professional obligations to fulfill. The very theme I often spoke to in public meetings to parents centered on time with children. I often felt hypocritical because the superintendency is filled with breakfast meetings, full workdays, and evening meetings. On those rare occasions when there is no evening meeting, the paperwork which is backed up keeps one glued to a desk or the computer or both. Thus, I feel there has been considerable family sacrifice growing out of the superintendency.
>
> My children, who are now adults, go with me to various public events in Minnesota, for example, the state fair, an orchestra concert, or a picnic in the park. They always comment that there is never a time when they are with me when someone doesn't come up to say hello or I reach out my hand in recognition of someone I know. They express understanding of the whys and wherefores of this public recognition but also reflect some regret that we rarely have personal time that is uninterrupted unless we leave the school district and the metropolitan area.

Finding the Passion

A number of recent studies suggest that fewer people are interested in the superintendency for both personal and professional reasons, and this trend will pose a critical problem in the near future (Hall and Difforett, 1992). Other studies (Daresh and Playko, 1992) argue the opposite, that people will remain interested in the superintendency as a career option because one enjoys a high degree of control and authority in this position. Obviously, there are no clear-cut answers on the condition of the American superintendency. However, even Daresh and Playko note the concern among educators over the personal toll this position takes: "for example, people appear to have lost interest in the superintendency because, in their minds, it is a job that requires too high a personal investment on the part of the individual. There are too many night meetings, confrontations with community pressure groups and teacher associations, lunches with civic groups, and negative discussions with school boards. The typical view of the superintendency is that it is a job filled with stress, anxiety, loss of personal time, and conflict" (p. 9). These views are based on what central office administrators have observed to be the case. Daresh and Playko contend that it is important to create an improved image of the superintendency, as well as to provide improved in-service preparation.

A person who desires to move up to the next rung of the ladder leading to the position of the superintendent wants to have a broader, more positive impact on the lives of children. However, some who finally reach this position seem to lose their energy, ideals, and direction and find that the position saps their vitality. One highly successful superintendent summarized his feelings by saying, "It isn't fun anymore." The long-term interference with the opportunity to satisfy personal needs and desires can lead to as much distress and exhaustion as can the prolonged activity beyond one's physical, mental, or energy level.

Superintendent Security

As an example of this merger of job and life is the concern, every time the telephone rings at night, that the call is going to bring news of a problem within the school district. Superintendents feel that they can't ever get away for some peace and quiet. Obviously, finding opportunities to withdraw from work responsibilities and conversation are critically important. This point is well characterized by Peter Negroni, superintendent of schools in Springfield, Massachusetts, who describes the kind of evening telephone calls that can be particularly disheartening for superintendents and their families: "As a superintendent who is of Puerto Rican background, and who had the charge to desegregate our schools based on a court order, I initially—and still, after five years—receive hate mail and telephone calls in the middle of the night derogatorily alluding to my ethnic background. One individual has even taken a telephone line that people can call to hear messages which usually focus on me."

The news media sometimes stir up the community over a difficult occurrence or a controversial plan or decision. Superintendents—and sometimes even members of their families—are asked to explain and defend their character and competence as much as the decision itself. A growing number of talk-radio hosts nationwide are making education a pet issue and pumping up the volume on school politics. A talk show host in Fort Wayne, Indiana, is given at least some blame for the resignation of the Fort Wayne superintendent of schools. The host explained his actions: "I fear for where public education is going. . . . And without people getting involved, the so-called education experts—the people I like to call 'educrats'—are going to take over." The superintendent described the personal attacks as "fairly relentless." Such attacks are occurring in a large number of American school districts over issues as divergent as suspending an honor student for bringing mace to school on the one hand and deleting an item in the school's budget on the other. What is an academic issue for the superintendent ends up as a social, economic, religious, or political issue in which children seem irrelevant. What is broadcast or put in print can end up adversely affecting superintendents, their families and friends, school board members, and ultimately American education.

Two superintendents were shot to death by disgruntled people in the early 1990s. Joe Piasecki in Chelsea, Michigan, and Jim Adams in Lee County, Florida, were killed during their workday. Certainly, such occurrences are—thank goodness—extreme cases. Superintendents do, however, recognize that they are highly visible in a society that seems to include a growing number of angry and violent people. Former superintendent Shirl Gilbert, who replaced Jim Adams in Indianapolis after Adams moved to Florida, said, "Those of us who do this job feel we are public servants. We don't expect to become the victim of an angry, hostile citizen with a gun."

In a survey of superintendents conducted in 1994 by the Coalition for American Children, almost half of the respondents reported that there was "somewhat" to "much more" violence and disruptive behavior in schools than five years earlier. Superintendents reported that "scarce resources" were increasingly allocated to school security, and more time was being spent on dealing with disruption and violence as frustrating effects of this phenomenon. A worsening breakdown in social relations is creating general distrust, despair, stress, and hostility, which in turn is leading to increased violence. The walls of differences that people are building around themselves, along with the stress they are feeling, are creating mass paranoia and cynicism, which result in inconsiderate and aggressive behavior. These behaviors are inevitably flowing into the schools, creating anxiety and fear among students, staff members, and administrators, including superintendents. The general mood is best described as fear of attack—verbal, psychological, physical, and economic. Educators have moved from nurturing others to protecting themselves and their students.

Joseph Kirchoff, superintendent of schools in West Delaware County, Iowa, described the aftereffects of difficulties that a sixteen-year-old was experiencing. The student returned to school after he had been dismissed, entered the principal's office, and began shooting. He injured an adult who was standing in the office and frightened staff members, administrators, and students who were nearby. The school staff's reaction to the incident was to be expected after an incident like this: they expressed how absolutely terrifying crime is when it's in your own backyard.

The effects of local crime on students, parents, staff members, administrators, and the community are immeasurable. The school staff in West Delaware County became afraid of the places where they worked. They were concerned when leaving their schools. They were not sure of their safety inside or outside the school building and had danger in the back of their minds. They began to have concern about how sick their community and families were and wondered how they could have any impact for the better. The superintendent worked with crisis teams to try to allay the fears of staff members, students, and parents. He also spent time dealing with families, courts, police, and others to resolve the incident and ensure that similar situations would not occur in the future.

Volumes could be produced documenting case studies of schools affected by community violence, which has erupted in every state. This runs the gamut: deflated tires and damaged automobiles, pressure on spouses and children, psychological and physical abuse. Certainly the problem is more pronounced in our urban centers, but it has affected all types of communities. The problem is that we don't live as a nation; we live as people in communities. Superintendents who heed the call to improve their communities and schools are facing a very hostile, factionalized, often disorderly and disloyal crowd. As public servants, they are wrapped in the same cloak of distrust as our politicians. Georgia Gov. Zell Miller echoes the sentiment of most governors: "We're not going to rest until students can learn and teachers can teach in a safe environment." Superintendents are wondering where the resources will come from to combat this and many other serious problems that the schools and communities confront.

Sources of Problems

The difficulty of the job is reflected in the 1993–94 status and opinion survey of AASA members asked to comment on problems they face as school administrators. Here are the top-ranking problems:

- School finances
- Cost reduction
- Budget cuts
- Covering growing responsibilities with less staff and resources
- Addressing pressures to continuously improve the curriculum and conditions for learning (Glass, 1992, p. 36)

One cannot survive in the superintendency or any other administrative post without the support of others. This places considerable pressure on superintendents to be perceived well by the various groups with whom they come into contact. The point is made by Ruben Ingram, past superintendent of the Fountain Valley (California) School District: "While the formal authority in California comes from the contract with the board and the statutes in the state education code, the informal authority certainly came from professional respect. I used to advise young administrators that I could protect them to a degree. It was up to them to generate the support of their community, parents, students, colleagues, district and board. I used to joke that 'everybody is voting on each of us every day.'"

Problems can develop through no fault of the superintendent's own. People can use their position to try to damage that of the superintendent, to gain power at the superintendent's expense. Political forces aligned against the superintendent can be substantial. As a result of their efforts, superintendents feel that their own work is compromised and less than complete. Relations become strained as such practices continue.

It is politically wise to provide the same information to all board members at the same time. This practice helps to prevent the ramifications of being perceived as playing favorites with one individual or one group. The superintendent must be seen as dealing with all entities within the school system and community fairly and equitably. If one person obtains information earlier than another, the former can be better prepared or more knowledgeable than others and use that to his or her advantage to gain respect and win favor at the expense of others. This problem sometimes occurs among board members when one member tries to secure information individually. The result is mistrust among all the others.

Fountain Valley Superintendent Ingram provides an example from his past experience: "The most frustrating situation I encountered was a board member who refused to disclose where she was getting her information. Ultimately, I discovered it was coming from a high-level administrator. After a lengthy investigation, and [conferring with] legal counsel, I recommended dismissal of the administrator. The board approved it 5–0." Protecting oneself against subversive activities can create unpleasant conditions, but these activities are most damaging in that they misdirect the efforts of the superintendent, strain relationships, and result in less effective educational results. A desire to counter political forces is not what motivated most superintendents to enter into the superintendency. Ingram reflected that "at the end of my career as superintendent, it seemed that the job was nothing but politics. Maybe that is why there is so much turnover in the position. The longer one is in the position, the more one's attention gets drawn to politics. I would have stayed another five to ten years if I could have concentrated on education and instructional issues alone."

Personal Attacks

Another area that can destroy a superintendent's desire for the work is totally unjustified personal attack. This can come as criticism from people who do not have a thorough perspective on or understanding of an issue. These attacks usually crop up during debate on a controversial issue, such as redistricting. John Whritner, superintendent of the Greenwich, Connecticut, schools, says of personal attacks

> when they do happen, I try to bite my tongue and remember that such things have happened before, that they are emotional and not really directed at my family pedigree or my intelligence level, and that they will be forgotten once the issue is resolved. Such attacks can be understood and tolerated if they seldom occur, but if they become a regular occurrence, they must be stopped. To be successful at stopping such attacks, the superintendent needs the leader of the board or any other group to set the proper tone. Without that, it is very difficult to eliminate unwarranted attacks.

This situation is the most stressful one for the superintendent's family to face: hearing criticism of a spouse or parent that they know to be unwarranted.

The living-in-a-fishbowl aspect of the superintendency is very difficult for family members, particularly when the superintendent is being chastised publicly. The spouse knows that he or she sometimes has a hidden responsibility: the job of the superintendent may depend on how the spouse carries himself or herself. Family members can be closely scrutinized, especially when their spouse or parent is under attack. However, this is not the only point where the personal and professional lives of superintendents commingle. The pressure that stems from knowing the job is uncertain beyond the three or so years of the contract is also stressful. The superintendent's benefits and financial future are seldom clear and can change with every election and mishap at school.

This uncertainty causes the family of a superintendent to feel vulnerable and isolated. Attacks and negative evaluations can affect the spouse's work performance as well, and the long hours don't allow a lot of time to discuss important issues. Superintendent Nebgen of Reno says: "I don't have a personal life. This job consumes about twenty-five hours a day. Between early-morning meetings and late-night meetings, there is very little time to spend with anyone else. My husband and I write each other notes during the week to keep updated on what's going on in each other's lives."

Family Sacrifice

Many other types of family sacrifices go along with the superintendency. For example, the superintendent normally begins his or her career in a small, relatively rural district. Advancement means a move in many cases, as candidates seek their first superintendency. This change can be very disruptive and stressful to families that must pull up roots and live in an area that is not like what they are used to.

Case Study: Raising Sheep

Raymond Lauk, superintendent of Cerro Gordo Community Unit School District 100 in Illinois, provides a delightful example of this uprooting situation—delightful because both Lauk and his wife are very happy where they now live and work, although they had a number of concerns when they first arrived.

Perhaps the greatest personal sacrifice my family and I made was accepting my job [my first superintendency] in a community and a region in the state which really does not mesh with our personal lifestyle. Wanting desperately to get my first superintendency, I accepted a job in rural downstate Illinois. I grew up in the Chicago suburbs, and my wife is from Rio de Janeiro. Between working and writing a dissertation, my days and nights are filled. However, for my wife, who stays at home with our two young children, this lifestyle is quite unsettling and uncomfortable.

During our first visit to the district, we looked for a house, and we were trying to decide whether to accept the position. Before returning home, we stopped at a restaurant for coffee. The owners of the restaurant were parents who lived in the school district. Through our conversation, it was revealed that I was

considering taking the superintendency and that we were looking for a house either in the small district (clearly the preference,
though not the demand of the board of education) or in the
neighboring city with a population of one hundred thousand
people. The well-intentioned woman highly recommended that
we live in the district because we could buy a small farm and my
wife could raise sheep. Raise sheep! My wife was raised on the
beaches of Copacabana and Ipanema, and now she will raise
sheep! We accepted the job and bought a house in the neighboring city. We are not raising sheep.

Lauk's story raises the issue of the superintendent's job causing his or her family to lose control of highly personal decisions.
All aspects of public life, and many aspects of private life, are
always subject to the intense examination and judgment of the
press and public. The school board and others may try to tell the
superintendent's family where they can and cannot live, whom
they should associate with, how they should dress, where they
should travel, and how they should spend their social time. This
problem can be compounded by the tendency of the press to
snoop into one's personal life and make controversial issues out
of nothing.

Citizens often stereotype superintendents, expecting them to
behave in certain ways and practice certain traits that go along with
the stereotype. The press can use differences between reality and
stereotypes to place ideas in the community's mind that are based
more on personal than professional issues. This scrutiny can cause
a pervasive tension to mark the personal lives of the superintendent and family. In a pluralistic society, a superintendent's (and
family's) values inevitably are in conflict with those of some seg-
ment or segments of the community. If these conflicts are perpetually elaborated in the fishbowl atmosphere, tension becomes a
part of life. The problems seem to be intensified when traditional
community beliefs are challenged. Most superintendents find
themselves in trouble when they are out of step with the social,
civic, and public expectations of the community in which they
practice, because they need the public's support and trust. The superintendent and his or her family must be willing to endure public scrutiny at every turn.

Time Pressures

Because one's personal and professional time becomes so precious, superintendents often have difficulty coping with marginal activities that require their time. At work, this time wasting is particularly a problem when it is based primarily on distrust and a need for control. It is difficult to proceed with one's work when questions become repetitive and the answers never satisfy the audience. Past superintendent Robert Wentz tells us that one troubling sign is "when it takes three or four tries in order to get an important issue passed by the board." In some school districts, the procedures themselves place an excessively high demand on the superintendent's time. Says John Whritner, superintendent of the Greenwich, Connecticut, schools: "Our budget process lasts eighteen months. It goes from administration to the board to a Board of Estimate and Taxation (and their committees) and to a Representative Town Meeting (with their committees). At each stage, we are being questioned and second-guessed on why certain items are included or not included. This often takes me away from dealing with important educational issues. There is always the implied sense that whatever we do can be done with fewer administrators, and I often agree but note that we need administrators to develop responses to all the crazy requests."

These conditions are becoming more prevalent as the role of the superintendent changes from expert to facilitator and information provider. Willingness to communicate openly has consistently been described as one of the most important attributes of the superintendent. So to identify what is and what is not a waste of time becomes a very difficult and treacherous judgment call. In fact, one of the primary reasons given for superintendent turnover is lack of open or extensive communication. Also very high on the list are personnel and public relations, which often require that a significant amount of time be devoted to communication if relations are to remain open and positive.

Without an effective approach to time management, the job places an extremely heavy demand on superintendents. This results in their wearing down and losing enthusiasm for the job. There is never enough time in the day, and that can be frustrating. This means the superintendent can seldom waste time yet expect to succeed in his or her position. Conversely, the overwhelming preoccupation with the importance of time makes everyone nervous about never wasting a minute of the superintendent's time.

A chronic and severe sense of time urgency has proved to be very unhealthy. Some superintendents have experienced major health problems related to balancing time pressures. As with everything else in their lives, superintendents seem to walk a very delicate tightrope. They must establish priorities and schedule their activities accordingly. This means there are always persons who feel their needs are not being attended to as quickly as possible. These people seldom understand the "absolute musts" and "most important" activities that the superintendent may be addressing.

Superintendents can get into as much difficulty from cluttering their schedules and trying to meet with everyone as they can by not meeting with enough people. This is especially true when they cannot find sufficient time to satisfactorily complete their schedules—when they're forced to rush through business, communicate with a sense of stress, and not be well-prepared for meetings. This is usually an early sign of the job no longer being enjoyable. You cannot be in high gear all the time and enjoy the work. Being able to say no is important, even if there are always repercussions.

Constant interruptions, particularly for superintendents with a busy schedule, can quickly have a detrimental effect on even the most tenured veterans. Keeping people's conversations on target, succinct, and clear is critically important. Refraining from repetitive information, quickly discerning the point of the communication, and shifting work responsibilities to others are key long-term survival techniques.

Survival Skills

Superintendents need to be generically healthy to be able to last in the role. George Garcia, superintendent of Tucson Unified School District No. 1, suggests that superintendents who are able to cope

> have a good understanding of human nature, have a good sense of humor, and accept the facts that all things can be resolved with

time and hard work and that no one solution exists for any particular problem. If you don't achieve your objective, you always have another opportunity tomorrow or next week, or next month or next year. Life goes on and it's best if you go with it instead of against it. . . . I also know that if I don't wait for the people I lead or give them alternative routes to get to the same end, I will never achieve my vision for my organization.

Although many have attempted to describe common characteristics of superintendents, there does not seem to be a single personal profile for those who cope best with the position. What seems to be important is that the superintendent recognize the stressors of the job and find a specific coping mechanism for dealing with the stress. Superintendents use a number of different approaches; what seems important is to schedule into one's routine time to use stress reducers.

For the stress that is part of the job, one primary reducer is talking with trusted colleagues, fellow superintendents, and family members. It is very important to have someone with whom one can discuss emotions and concerns about the situations being faced. That someone must be a trusted colleague, family member, or friend who can be counted on not to repeat such conversations. It is important to develop a few strong, trusting relationships with colleagues, other superintendents, and family members who can provide perspective—and a source of positive energy, inspiration, and direction—when one is facing difficult issues and times, or coping with the irritations and disappointments of the job. The need for support is important in the early years of the superintendency, but it is often mentioned by seasoned superintendents as well. Brian Benzel, superintendent of the Edmonds School District in Lynnwood, Washington, stresses this: "I use my immediate colleagues, especially the deputy superintendent and my administrative assistant, to be my listening ears. I find it easier to search out and apply successful strategies when I've 'vented' in confidence with trusted colleagues. My wife (an elementary principal in a neighboring district) also is a valuable listener and understands the context of most of the issues I'm confronting."

Meeting and sharing with superintendents and administrators from other districts has often been cited as a very important way to avoid stress and burnout. This sharing among peers includes activities such as attending professional meetings, conferring with colleagues, and trading ideas across districts. These activities help superintendents gain perspective, expand approaches, and explore new options.

Leaders need an opportunity to get together and discuss what it means to be a leader. History has shown that those who are successful have significant targets to achieve. Superintendents can sometimes lose sight of why they entered the education profession as a result of the buffeting they experience. That is why it is important to revisit our "roots" to regain clarity of purpose and direction. This is greatly enhanced through opportunities to dialogue with other professionals in the field. The exchange of ideas, strategies, and coping mechanisms that have personal meaning is a valuable opportunity for practicing superintendents. The benefit of such association is limited if there is little discussion about how one is faring in his or her work. It is also important for superintendents to smell the roses: to seek balance between talking about serious concerns and frivolous, entertaining conversation, even levity.

Superintendents also mention benefits from meeting and developing associations with people outside of education. This reaching out provides opportunities to gain different perspectives on the world. The important thing is to see what is going on in one's professional life from a new vantage point, so one can gain greater clarity before proceeding. Superintendents also know the importance of reading material both within and outside the profession to gain knowledge, understanding, and perspective.

A similar strategy is to schedule time to get away from the day-to-day routine, to give oneself time to reflect. This is often difficult in organizations whose successes are based on ambition, responsiveness, activity, productivity, long hours, and hard work. However, it is neither effective nor healthy to work hard and be on the go constantly. Periodically and consciously, experienced superintendents pull away from the day-in, day-out work of the superintendency for more reflection. Superintendent Leslie Johnson has found that such reflective activity can occur by "setting aside one day out of the week when I am not committed to meetings. This day affords me a number of options. I might use it to catch up on work that has had to be put aside during the week, or I might spend part of the day meeting informally with members of my staff to brainstorm. This noncommitted time will not appear in the normal course of a superintendent's week—it takes a concerted effort to arrange the time."

Johnson goes on to suggest that sometimes such reflections occur at seminars, conferences, and weekends away from the routine. He notes that "attending professional meetings, conferring with colleagues, sharing ideas—all help me to continue to expand my knowledge and to explore new options for my district. Meeting and sharing with superintendents and administrators from other districts and states is a natural high for me and a good preventive for burnout." Superintendents often find they are facing the same challenges and ups-and-downs that are being experienced in other school districts. This discovery can help provide perspective and the realization that problems being faced are not uniquely "mine or caused by me." However, most fundamental is the need to take private time to relax and do activities you particularly enjoy.

One of the pleasures many superintendents gain from their work is visiting classrooms and being involved in programs that focus on students. Mary Nebgen says: "As a superintendent, a lot of my time is spent visiting schools and talking to teachers and students. Maybe this helps to avoid burnout, because it reminds you what it's all about. When I see the quality of instruction that's taking place in the classrooms, the wonderful things that teachers are doing with students, it just encourages me to continue." Almost all superintendents who participated in our survey mentioned improvement in student performance or strong student achievement as being an important source of job satisfaction.

Many of the superintendents also mentioned the significant "charge" they got from watching people employed in the district improve their performance. Of course, these outcomes go hand in hand, but the satisfaction is no less when the achievement is by a staff member. One of the most enjoyable aspects of the job is to observe the successes of people whom one has empowered in their positions. Guiding staff, supporting them, and facilitating their successful efforts consistently gives superintendents a great deal of pride and pleasure. It is most rewarding to see principals rally and unite staff members to improve student achievement.

The complexity and stress of the superintendency can sometimes overshadow, blur, and rigidify one's actions if time is not taken to put everything in proper perspective. It is a job in which one can lose direction, wear out, and damage one's health when that perspective begins to fade. It is not the *activity* in the superintendency that is important so much as the *satisfying results* of the work. Too strong a focus on activity can result in pointless effort, compulsion, frantic pace, and misdirection, which quickly destroy even the strongest optimism. Activity can be used to avoid reflection and to hide from the truth. Most superintendents avoid this pitfall by taking time to reflect, create tranquility, and develop perspective. These personal attributes allow superintendents both to avoid distress and to improve their performance.

Part Three

Responses and Remedies

Chapter Nine

Building Community Alliances

Establishing positive and supportive relationships within the community is like putting money in the bank. Accordingly, superintendents must know the core values embodied in the community and understand the political power base. What are the underlying concerns of the community, and how might initiatives affect these concerns? What real limits exist that must be pushed back to improve the system? How can public trust, confidence, participation, and support be gained during the chaos of transformation and renewal?

The challenge of the superintendency is not to provide solutions. It is to facilitate a process by which discordant voices, disparate interests, and conflicting points of view can work for the best interest of the community and school system. Effective superintendents have a clear understanding of the community and its power structures. Armed with this understanding, superintendents can implement and improve programs while they explore concerns. They neutralize incidents, using them to their advantage to provide new direction and momentum. The new direction should be clearly articulated by people inside and outside the school system; those people then become a base of support for needed initiatives.

The experienced superintendent has learned that differences of view do not disappear by being suppressed. The health of the organization depends on dealing openly with the conflicting views that exist both within and outside the organization. Plans and directions must grow out of the clash of opposing views, as a mutually shared vision for the organization evolves. How effectively the superintendent can deal with the clashes in developing the vision determines how well the organization and community will align in achieving the vision. As Jane Boston, director of Stanford Cross-Cultural Education, states it: "Deeply held beliefs and values have incredible durability. What distinguishes the forum of competing interests in a democracy from anarchy and chaos is the commitment from participants to seek the common good. . . . They, as we, may not achieve this ideal. I, however, rest easier knowing that they are talking, listening, and struggling together with difficult issues across vast differences" (Boston, 1994, p. 39).

Facilitating and Supporting

We are in a whole new era, one that challenges the ways we have done things and the roles that we have had in the past. The superintendency needs to be redefined as a role that is constantly bringing diverse interests together to shape a new future. Everyone in education has the potential to provide leadership; the role of the superintendent is to provide general direction and facilitate this leadership. The superintendent needs to be able to bring out the best in people. This role requires sensitivity to the skills, knowledge, and experience that internal and external members of the school community have to offer, and the ability to orchestrate those talents in furthering the interests of children. The superintendent can bring everyone's power to the table for the common good.

Superintendents must be very patient to allow support to develop. They can succeed only if they have the support of the community, the staff and school employees, and—perhaps most important—a strong majority of the power elite and school board. According to Greenwich Superintendent John Whritner, Connecticut's 1995 Superintendent of the Year, the only way to obtain community support is through credibility:

> If you have it, you are well perceived by the community, you are able to weather difficult issues and people, and you have gone miles in achieving positive public relations. A large part of this comes from being perceived as honest and competent by the general population.

I believe that I have positive public relations because I have credibility with most people in the community. I am part of the community, serving on many bodies and getting to know many of the people who have little contact with the schools but who help form other peoples' opinions. I try to send personal notes when they should be legitimately sent. I try to be visible in schools and community. I meet regularly with town leaders. I accept defeats fairly graciously. I am persistent in requests when I believe they are necessary. I alternate with the board in being the lightning rod for controversy. I pick my battles and try to decide early on which ones are worth giving up chips.

As Whritner suggests, it is very important that the superintendent be visible on behalf of the schools, seen everywhere in the district and in the community. This visibility is best achieved by being very active in community organizations and serving on their boards; making many presentations to service clubs, the chamber of commerce, and other groups; and going to all the schools, especially to attend special school, neighborhood, and community events. Credibility, however, is more than presence; it is keeping your promises, building trust by following through on what you say, and closing the gaps in understanding between you and others.

A certain amount of stereotyping occurs with the superintendency. People assign attributes to you that they believe superintendents have or that they have experienced with other superintendents. The only way to break down these preconceived notions is to let people know and see who you really are. Superintendent Brian Benzel of Lynnwood, Washington, found that

> As my children have grown up and I am less visible in attending school affairs as a parent, I'm increasingly viewed as an older authority figure. Younger parents tend to have more stereotypes based on their media-induced perception of how institutional leaders act. This condition means I need to make conscious efforts to meet with parents and talk with them in both formal and informal settings.
>
> One strategy I use is to hold six or seven parent meetings a year to talk with anyone who wants to come visit. Invitations are extended throughout the parent organizations at each school. This avenue gives me some access to the ever-changing parents' group. I

also attend principal meetings on a regular basis and receive direct and indirect indicators that we have a healthy climate within the district. Principals tell me they feel supported, and we have frequent conversations about complex, tough issues. Position authority is sometimes evident, but we work hard to support each other in collegial fashion. I also visit schools weekly and seek the same kind of interaction with staff at the school level. Finally, I conduct a survey of staff every other spring [in which I ask them] "What can I do better?" and "What do you like about what I do?" The survey results reflect a view that I work hard, am honest and open, committed to excellence, and generally approachable. I get lots of satisfaction when a fellow district worker compliments me or another district person to others in the community. For example, a teacher recently told me her doctor (a critic of the district and suspicious of me) asked her what I was like. She reported positive comments and defended our work in school reform and improvement. This kind of confidence is invaluable to building an effective learning organization.

Omaha Superintendent Norbert Schuerman views gaining the support of community groups as one of the most important skills for future superintendents: "The most important activities of the superintendent are coalition building; handling special interest groups; being able to acquire the support of people; being able to respond professionally to all the bashing public schools receive; and being able to both develop and defend a first-class K–12 public education program."

Handling Challenges Effectively

When first confronting challenges, it is essential to listen and not become defensive. Communication follows a progression: from listening and sharing to gaining awareness of each other's positions, motivations, and desired outcomes; then to obtaining reinforcement for ideas and directions; finally to building a commitment for the needed actions. Once there is an agreed-upon, attainable plan of action, the school system must follow through on it and keep key people informed every step of the way. The results of the community's shared work should be accessible to the local citizenry through television interviews, newspaper interviews, radio talk shows, letters to the editor, and invitations to influential community participants to appear at school and other public meetings. A sense of community is developed by supporting the value of working together throughout the superintendent's tenure. This collaboration helps build both perspective and confidence—and, perhaps most important, a sense of community.

Communication is very different from disseminating information. Communication means two-way activity: community surveys, focus-group discussions, town hall meetings, advisory teams made up of opinion leaders, vertical teams, and so on. Superintendents Peter Negroni and John Murphy provide examples of these types of communication systems.

Case Study: Building the Coalitions

During his first two years as superintendent of the Springfield, Massachusetts, public schools, Peter Negroni established formal partnerships with both traditional and nontraditional groups. "Parents formed a citywide support group called the Springfield Parent Advisory Network," he reports:

Businesses joined forces with the school system and individual schools as members of the school-centered decision making teams and as tutors and providers of incentives for improved education. Social service agencies joined the schools in providing on-site services and in facilitating an integrated services model for students and families. The religious community joined the schools in focusing on key issues of racism and violence.

Other city departments have also come to see that they and the schools are connected. I meet on a regular basis with parents and community groups, who often bring information, a distinct point of view, and/or a concern that needs to be addressed. The superintendent also must visit the school sites, observing and talking to teachers, administrators, and students.

According to Negroni, an effective central office administrative team is essential if the superintendent is to become an effective educational leader. Such a team requires competent, energetic, self-directed leaders who share the school division's vision. The Springfield public schools have school-centered decision making

teams composed of the principal, teachers, parents, a business/
community person, and students in the secondary schools. Each
person on the team has an equal role. All decisions are reached
through consensus. Negroni has received support from the political structure, business, parents, and educators for implementing
the shared vision for the schools. This show of support does not
mean that he does not still receive hate mail and telephone calls in
the middle of the night from disgruntled members of the community who hope to change the direction that the schools are taking.
However, it does mean that there is a much more balanced level of
support and that the interests of a narrow group of sometimes almost fanatic people do not dominate the school agenda.

Case Study: Winning Public Support

John Murphy, former superintendent of schools in Charlotte-
Mecklenburg, North Carolina, is one of many superintendents who
stress the importance of involving a diverse public in planning, advocating, and implementing continuous improvement efforts.
Once the public feels disenfranchised, school improvement dies
and the superintendent's tenure is cut short. This happens because
educational issues quite often become political issues, and educators are questioned about everything unless they keep the community informed. A superintendent must be both a community leader
and a government leader; the roles are conjoined.

Murphy called on his seven years of experience as superintendent in Prince George's County, Maryland, to make changes in
Charlotte-Mecklenburg. He created magnet schools as a desegregation tool. He tried a year-round school, increased testing, school
performance goals, strict accountability standards, and other ideas.
However, he learned something about communication and community support for innovation that he brought with him to Charlotte. He placed winning public support for the schools agenda as a
top priority in his efforts in Charlotte-Mecklenburg.

Murphy reflects:

We made the political leaders partners in school reform. At the
same time that the panel on world-class schools was meeting, we
gave the larger community a say-so in the deliberation. (The
world-class schools panel of nationally known educators met to

study Charlotte's system and to make recommendations on lasting reform.) Everything was up for grabs. Nothing—no policy, structure, organization, no program—was off limits. We sought and received input from nearly ten thousand people. We started with four day-long community forums: one for principals and teachers, representing all 113 schools; one for parents and concerned citizens; one for business and civic leaders; and one for more than two hundred high school students. The opinion-gathering activities culminated in a community summit, sponsored by *The Charlotte Observer* and the chamber of commerce, attended by some two thousand people, including a host of state and local political leaders.

Following the summit, the school system documented its progress in a program entitled "The Charlotte Process: Reclaiming the Legacy."

Murphy won support and high marks for his reform efforts but, unfortunately, much less support for his personality and style. Credibility issues began to surface as well as human relations concerns. Murphy did not seem to fit the image of a superintendent that public-opinion makers held, or their expectations regarding appropriate behavior. The programs developed were implemented and widely supported; however, he himself did not receive the same level of support, and he chose to resign. His successor was asked to support and expand upon the programs that had been implemented.

The Religious Right: An Example

In his research on educational change, Michael Fullan says "There is no question that the problems of reform are insurmountable without a dramatic increase in the number of alliances practicing positive politics" (1993b, p. 350). The secret for superintendent success beyond the year 2000 will be to have an effective and broad-based system of communication, one that builds a coalition of advocates for the improvements being made. Effective communication will be the lifeline for the schools.

Some groups that have clashed over the proper place of religion in public education are now committed to the idea of finding common ground. As one prominent example, after years of often bitter controversy representatives of eighteen major education and religious organizations came together to sign a statement of "Principles on Religious Liberty, Public Education, and the Future of American Democracy." Among the signatories were the Freedom Forum First Amendment Center at Vanderbilt University, the Association for Supervision and Curriculum Development (ASCD), the National Association of Evangelicals, Citizens for Excellence in Education, the National School Boards Association (NSBA), the Christian Coalition, People for the American Way, the National Association of Secondary School Principals, the American Association of School Administrators (AASA), and the National Congress of Parents and Teachers. The statement (Exhibit 9.1) sets forth six principles that form the "civic ground rules for addressing conflicts in public education."

The statement "symbolizes the determination of the endorsing organizations to look beyond very real differences of purpose and philosophy for the sake of our common concern about the public education of America's children" (Carter, 1995, p. 1). These efforts to establish a framework for dialogue about school reform, educational responsibilities, and religious rights grew out of strong concerns about the future of education, but also out of the potential erosion of democratic principles resulting from increasingly volatile confrontations between educators and some religious groups. Teachers cannot teach, and students cannot learn, in an atmosphere of mistrust between churches, families, and schools. School boards and superintendents cannot concentrate on developing and implementing the best educational policy when critical time, energy, and resources are diverted by controversy and acrimony.

Public schools serve many constituencies: students; parents; teachers; administrators; business leaders; racial, ethnic and religious groups; as well as the community at large. It is often very difficult to reconcile the conflicting demands and needs of these interest groups in the public schools. The democratic process, which requires due regard for the rights of dissenters, must resolve these disagreements. This does not mean that any group must compromise its own mission or abandon its principles. But it does ask that all individuals and organizations that are truly concerned about ensuring the best possible public education for all children

Exhibit 9.1. Principles on Religious Liberty, Public Education, and the Future of American Democracy.

1. *Religious liberty for all*
   Religious liberty is an inalienable right of every person.

2. *The meaning of citizenship*
   Citizenship in a diverse society means living with our deepest differences and committing ourselves to work for public policies that are in the best interests of all individuals, families, communities, and our nation.

3. *Public schools belong to all citizens*
   Public schools must model the democratic process and constitutional principles in the development of policies and curricula.

4. *The relationship between religious liberty and public schools*
   Public schools may not inculcate nor inhibit religion. They must be places where religion and religious conviction are treated with fairness and respect.

5. *The relationship between parents and schools*
   Parents are recognized as having the primary responsibility for the upbringing of their children, including education.

6. *The conduct of public disputes*
   Civil debate, the cornerstone of a true democracy, is vital to the success of any effort to improve and reform America's public schools.

Source: Haynes, 1994.

abandon the mind-set of mistrust and the rhetoric of divisiveness. "Public education must be sensitive to, and open to, the concerns of religious-minded parents who sometimes feel they are less than welcome," said U.S. Secretary of Education Richard Riley. "But at the same time, religious-minded Americans must be willing to build bridges, to respect the freedom of conscience of other Americans, and to not see public education as their enemy" (Riley, 1994). In spelling out responsible participation, the AASA's Seeking Common Ground for Improvement of Public Education Task Force, a collaboration of AASA with the Regional Laboratory for Educational Improvement of the Northeast and Islands identified nine principles to serve as fundamental ground rules. They appear in Appendix B.

Public schools are the keepers of the nation's conscience. The leadership of America, including education leaders, must strengthen our resolve to find a common vision for the common good. Our public schools are indispensable to our nation's future and its well-being. The public schools bring American youth together and enculturate them. This is the consistent stream of inclusiveness that has led to effective citizenship.

Collaboration, Coalition, and Alliance

The continuous improvement process is being delegated to the school, where principals and teachers are expected to respond to the needs and demographics of their own communities. The superintendent must provide direction and control for the schools, while facilitating the active participation of those inside and outside the system. The superintendent should focus his or her attention on the flow of information/communication, representation of disparate ideologies, incorporation of value and belief systems, management of interest and pressure groups, oversight of internal affairs, administrative control, and resource allocation. All of this activity occurs under the watchful eye of the school board—which doesn't always recognize external pressures on the superintendent.

This call for leadership, as well as for management, is coming at the same time that future success demands that schools break out of old patterns and adopt new attitudes, skills, behaviors, and approaches to education. John Murphy pulled together groups to identify what it would take to transform the school district into "world class" schools. This process ended with the development of a covenant for education, "The Charlotte Process: Reclaiming the Legacy." Charlotte is considered a true success story by almost all measures of metropolitan development, and the Charlotte-Mecklenburg school district is given significant credit in this turnaround.

The resulting reforms are examples of changes that require adoption of new attitudes. They shake the system at its foundation. The nature of the deliberations and conclusions is captured in a single statement by panel member Patricia Graham: "For 150 years, American schools kept the pedagogy constant and let the results vary; for the future, we must vary the pedagogy and produce high levels of accomplishment for all. In other words, we must raise standards and then vary the means—not the ends—of education in ways that respect the particular differences of children."

Charlotte's private-sector pay, adjusted for inflation, has increased more than 11 percent, while many other southern metropolitan communities have experienced pay decreases over this same period. The city has been extraordinarily successful in rallying support behind the Charlotte region and marketing it to the world. Education was instrumental in this process. Some of the ideas that have come out of the compacts entitled "Reclaiming the Legacy" and "The Legacy: Next Steps" are magnet schools, year-round schools, increased testing, school performance and strict accountability standards, group or collective accountability (principal responsibility), and schools for children with behavior problems (improved cultures for students who want to learn). Murphy states, "Disorder isn't all bad. Uniformity is the bane of true reform. In the quantum world, order emerges from disorder. It is in this new, apparently disordered world that the American schools of tomorrow are being invented. That's a good thing. Insist on order and uniformity, and we doom ourselves to more of the same. Good ideas turn dogmatic and produce one best instructional formula, one best curriculum, and one best test. Spontaneity, flexibility, and common sense take flight." In cases like these, where major value systems and patterns of operation are being changed, progress is usually measured in years, not days or months. Concerns are rife both within and outside the school system, and information, communication, and collaboration are absolutely essential to the success of the project. This process takes time, and the superintendent must be supportive of it.

To provide needed community information, the performance assessment system must also be addressed. Assessments and evaluations are conducted to answer a wide range of questions about student development and performance, educator skills and performance, curriculum effectiveness and processes, quality of textbooks and curricular materials, etc. The difficult decisions in accountability relate to narrowing assessments and evaluations to a manageable set that provides the most useful information. The benefit of narrowing assessment by focusing it on instruction is that we learn about pupils' accomplishments and instructors' successes.

This assessment can be expanded to include elements of the curriculum as well. An ineffective curriculum can sink the most competent instructional approach, and vice versa.

John Murphy implemented a controversial system that he describes as "group or collective accountability." He made the school the center of the assessment model and held the principal responsible for the performance of that school. This concept is supported by the principles of Total Quality Management and the teachings of W. Edwards Deming. Deming often stated that when an organization is not performing well, it is always the responsibility of management and seldom, if ever, the responsibility of the frontline worker. The results of the Charlotte-Mecklenburg school assessments are published in the newspaper, and if a principal cannot improve low performance he or she is replaced with someone able to obtain satisfactory performance.

The principal is supported in making needed changes within the school to ensure it meets community expectations. However, if improvements do not occur in a reasonable period, he or she is removed from that principalship. Holding principals responsible to the community for school success has been determined by the North Carolina Department of Education as quite effective, and it is being considered as a state policy for all school districts. In reflecting on the importance of accountability and performance assessments, Murphy contends that:

> Evaluation and reward systems in America's public schools are out of whack. Whether a matter of oversight or reluctance to change, public education is an enterprise in which competence and incompetence are largely ignored, both noted but not distinguished from one another. The best employees are paid the same as the worst. Whether you do a good job educating students or a bad job, nothing different happens to you either way. In fact, there is little attempt to figure out who is and is not doing a good job for the students in their charge.
>
> Most school districts hold tight to a compliance mentality. The bulk of incentives respond to following the rules. Few urge or reward risk taking, improved schooling, or high academic results for students. Until the day we as a profession join the modern world

and move to a well-conceived, outcome-based evaluation and profit-sharing system, major results will evade us. Redefining learning in this nation requires redefining accountability and assessment—both for students and for staff. To improve performance we must create mechanisms that reward improvement.

Murphy was considered quite successful in developing a vision for a premier urban, integrated school district. During his tenure discipline in the schools improved, accountability was strengthened, test scores improved, and overall evaluation by various groups showed remarkable progress. However, ideas like those above run against decades of tradition and are quite controversial. The battles in Murphy's case were exacerbated by his personality and the way he irritated those involved in the precarious coalitions formed within the city. A series of small problems began to break down Murphy's support base. The fifty or so principals who had been removed from their positions began exerting political influence against Murphy. Other issues included his making a statement that "parents should serve jail terms and pay fines when their children misbehave"; insufficient numbers of women in top administrative positions; a controversial school bond issue; a small amount of school district money used for Murphy's dental work; and a barrage of criticism in the media.

Despite objective evidence that suggested Murphy's accomplishments within the school district were overwhelmingly positive, the Community County Commissioners and Mecklenburg voters turned against him. Consequently, Murphy announced he would leave the superintendency when his contract expired in June 1996. In response thereto, an ironic "call" went up in Charlotte-Mecklenburg for a superintendent who would support existing reforms, push for needed new ones, and work cooperatively with the various political coalitions within the community.

Alliances are required to accomplish significant educational improvement (examples occur in places like Charlotte-Mecklenburg; San Diego; St. Charles Parish, Louisiana; Cincinnati; and Allentown, Pennsylvania). Those inside and outside the organization resist and fear innovations they don't understand. The role of the superintendent becomes one of ensuring that everyone is informed and heard, and that as many participants as possible are involved in the process. Joan Kowal, past superintendent of schools in Volusia County, Florida, found that:

> Changing the status quo is more than changing procedures and policies. Changing what is, and what has been, means redefining relationships, reshaping attitudes, and shifting, ever so gently, our behaviors. It requires consensus and coalition building. It obligates superintendents to align beliefs and practices while encouraging everyone else to do the same. It demands high and clearly defined expectations.
>
> Our human capacity to accomplish great things, to make a difference in the lives of students, increases exponentially when we combine our knowledge, talents, and energies for a common purpose. The positive power of numbers is evidenced in our organizational teaming and networking. Systemic staff and community development is at the very heart of our success in school renewal.
>
> School improvement is difficult because change is difficult. Authentic school improvement requires commitment, trust, and focus from everyone involved in the process. . . . Effective communication is a lifeline between schools and communities, supporting our central vision and sustaining the belief that education is everyone's responsibility. The level of its success is evidenced by the extent to which education becomes a community obsession.

This new focus for the superintendency goes beyond the traditional role defined in terms of financial responsibilities, climate building, curriculum development, staff and personnel decisions, and other matters more internal to the school organization. These responsibilities are being decentralized to the schools themselves. The superintendent is taking on the role of a statesperson who builds coalitions to support needed educational improvement.

The Superintendent as Statesperson and Facilitator

The superintendent provides a sense of interconnectedness and ensures that no group that is needed to support public education feels it is not a full partner in the process. This is a new role for the superintendent, one for which he or she is not always prepared.

Superintendents sometimes ignore the political pressures of conflicting interests, believing that they are educators, not politicians. Resistance to this changing role can also take the form of excessive professionalism, in which degrees and training in education are held to be more important than responsiveness to the community.

In such cases, superintendents see their role as that of an expert maintaining order and control. They do not want any waves of reform to disturb the firmly maintained calmness in the educational waters, particularly waves generated outside the education establishment. They do not want to have to justify the direction that the schools are taking or to work through the long process of developing community understanding, participation, and support. Such superintendents are ill-prepared and unmotivated to open up the process and to deal with the temporary confusion and ambiguity that can result. They are afraid of losing control of planning the future of education and are concerned about how the community will respond to broader participation in the planning process.

For these superintendents, the existing professional model is one of maintaining control and clarity, protecting education from external influences, holding the existing system together, and smoothing the waters of turbulence. Such superintendents have a stake in protecting existing roles, layers, boundaries, and programs, which often gets interpreted as maintaining the existing system and remaining disconnected. This attitude can result in a circle-the-wagons approach to protecting the schools from unwelcome interference or conflicting views. These superintendents emphasize protecting the views of the vested authorities in power. As experts, they make problems simpler to ensure that people are not overburdened, overwhelmed, or frustrated. However, some use expertise to discourage broader participation or decision making.

The challenge to superintendents comes in the need to keep all interested participants informed, to support participation without allowing endless debate, to communicate core values, to create purposeful deliberation, to set and keep ground rules, to respond to new and changing demands, to set specific and attainable achievements, to clearly communicate the vision that evolves, and to help celebrate victories and successes. The system supports the flow of information among everyone who cares about education.

In this way, the superintendent creates an environment that allows numerous interested parties to focus their energies on improving the lives of children. The existing school system is challenged and questioned, and if it cannot respond it is forced to reconfigure itself to better suit the environment. This change occurs as the organization is constantly interacting with the environment in a boundaryless, natural system. This is what a community is all about.

Without the knowledge and understanding of a diverse group of participants, very little educational improvement can take place. In tackling the difficult issues confronting the Washington, D.C., schools, Superintendent Franklin Smith found that

> the superintendent's ability to communicate effectively with all groups—within the community and within the school system—helps to clarify issues, ease concerns, and articulate expectations. If he or she is able to remain student-focused and build coalitions among parents, school staff, central office staff, and community members, it is certainly advantageous.

> The ability to build broad-based coalitions around a vision of education is one of the most important skills a superintendent can possess. It can dilute the effectiveness of special interest groups and the parochial concerns of board members. It can also ensure the support of school system personnel, parents, and community members. In a job that offers little stability and security, successfully appealing to a wider audience can mean the difference between employment and unemployment.

> My authority to bring about major change depends, in large part, on my ability to work cooperatively. I am able to initiate and implement some changes independently. But I have found that unilateral decisions are sometimes detrimental to forward progress. In order to be implemented successfully, change often depends on acceptance by a majority of the stakeholders.

The stimulus for change, as well as the base for job security, is broadened, as more groups take on legitimate roles in the educational process. Although superintendents have the proper authority to implement change, the real power to do so comes from the support of stakeholders: the community, school board, teachers, business leaders, taxpayers, parents, chamber of commerce members, city government workers, etc. Without the support of the entire community (the village), most superintendents suggest, it is wise to leave well enough alone. Support is built through continuous dialogue, and a shared vision about where the schools need to be. Superintendents prepare all interest groups, build trust among them, and bring them into the conversation, so that the system can be responsive to a dynamic set of educational needs. This is how superintendents build a broader, more stable foundation from which to work; this is how they build community.

Cultivating diverse participation helps to keep any one group from manipulating the issues behind the scene. At the same time, it does not overburden any particular group with the responsibility for improving the condition of children's lives. Leaders can also get a better handle on what citizens think and what the big issues are within the community. Separate agendas are more likely to exist if groups are not brought together—and separate agendas fracture efforts to improve schools and communities. Success depends on individual groups' gaining an understanding of one another's positions and coming to a shared vision for the schools. This shared vision requires a clear understanding of what schools can and can't do. Ramon Cortines, past chancellor of the New York City schools, says that "superintendents are fortunate when their boards, their parents, educators, and the general citizenry understand one another and the goals and accomplishments of the system." In fact, superintendents have responsibilities to ensure that this happens. This common understanding builds bridges of trust and respect among our diverse citizenry. This is how citizens become better acquainted and enhance their knowledge as they develop a vision for the public school system.

Successful superintendents think in terms of linking schools to broader systems of support. They describe their work as the mobilization of support for their schools (Mitchell and Seach). They attract supporters from a broad cross-section of the community. Some superintendents express the belief that alliance and coalition building is needed at this time "because public confidence has been lost, not because school performance is objectively below legitimate expectations" (Mitchell and Seach, 1991, p. 30).

Broad-Based Participation

Efforts to involve local teachers, parents, and community members in the planning process have proven to be quite successful when measured in terms of student outcomes (McEvoy, 1986; McNeil, 1988; Cunningham and Gresso, 1993). The superintendent is responsible for orchestrating this continuous process of school improvement. He or she must ensure that participants clearly understand their roles and the reasons they are working together, and that they be provided appropriate infrastructures through which meaningful improvement can occur. Because of the diversity of viewpoints represented, this process is not easy, and it can be very time-consuming, especially if the superintendent and principals are unable to "read" the majority deliberation and provide appropriate leadership. Lew Rhodes states: "I see that relationships—especially between stakeholders—are more important than the boundaries of a system. We must focus on the nature of these relationships and identify which relationships are more meaningful. The currency of the relationships is the information exchanged; and the purpose of the system should drive the exchange" (personal communication, Dec. 15, 1995).

The energy and commitment that grow out of the resulting "democratic discourse" can be focused by the superintendent and principals to move school improvement goals forward. Those involved learn how to work together as a community and come to recognize the importance of communication, decision making, and commitment to the shared vision for an improved school system. This commitment provides the advantages of a supportive structure for implementing school improvement, exchanging ideas, helping one another, providing resources, and making use of a broad range of knowledge and experience. Today, a central focus for our nation's superintendents is acquiring and honing the skills of building culture, coalitions, and alliances; interprofessional collaboration; political insight; multiple constituencies; shared visions; communication; and the process we call community.

Chapter Ten

Developing District Capacity

The concept of education as a "response system" emerged from an invitational seminar hosted by the AASA and Northern Telecom at the Aspen Institute in Maryland (American Association of School Administrators, 1994). The paradigm provides important insights into the role of the superintendent in today's environment. Margaret Wheatley, a participant at the conference, suggested that there are only answers that fit the moment; therefore, superintendents must help the system adapt to its dynamic nature and continuously find solutions to fit that moment in time. Her thinking is very similar to W. Edwards Deming's work (1986; American Association of School Administrators, 1993c) on the importance of continuous improvement in organizational success and viability. Wheatley told participants: "We find it by creating a relationship-rich environment—that is also rich in information—where people can focus on what needs to get done. They have some simple rules of interaction, which I would call values or principles, shared purpose, and that's all. In comes a crisis or opportunity, and people organize around it. . . . This is the fluid, boundaryless organization of the future" (American Association of School Administrators, 1994, p. 3).

Superintendents often view the first crack in the smooth functioning of a school with great anxiety. They sense it is a trigger to the need for clamping down, controlling all the pieces, quickly resolving concerns, and calling on political allies to circle the wagons. There is a natural desire to protect the delivery system; the normal response is to restore the old order, rather than to risk the perils of allowing a new order of things to evolve. In this way, superintendents manage from a position of fear. Unfortunately, fear causes superintendents to stifle the life-enhancing response that motivates the search for a better way of doing things. The messy process of muddling through to a better way can be viewed as failure, instability, and incompetence, a signal of weakness—and, to political enemies of the superintendent, a time for attack. When the school district operates on the response-system paradigm, these fears have less foundation.

Instead of trying to reduce turmoil and chaos, the superintendent should try to hold the organization within this natural state of evolution until a critical mass of employees gains an understanding of what must be done. This is not easy, because the variance between present practice and the evolving ideal creates a disequilibrium among those who want to stick with what has worked well in the past. Many systems pour all their energies into conserving past successes, maintaining efficiency and stability, resisting risks, and maintaining the delivery system. A dynamic responsive system, by contrast, requires flexibility, creativity, development of potential, sharing, inspirational progress, and risk taking. Moving from the tried-and-true to a new response to changing educational expectations requires a period of confusion, learning, and inefficiency—thus disequilibrium. This is a bitter pill to swallow, and some mistakenly believe that the quicker it is taken, that is, the sooner a new solution is attempted, the quicker the equilibrium can be reestablished. But quick solutions mean not everyone can be involved, learning does not occur, information is ignored, resistance must be defeated, and new ideas must be "sold." Some suggest it is better not to take the pill at all and to try to maintain the status quo, a risky solution in itself. Another form of maintenance is to change superintendents rather than deal with the complex, messy issue of changing the system.

Successful innovation requires a superintendent who understands the need for creating order out of chaos but who does not allow employees or communities to short-circuit the needed process of continuous communication, deliberation, and improvement. As Wheatley states it,

> People have a great resistance to stuff they don't know. We have a
> great fear of complexity because we can't control it. And, in that

fear, we lose the ability to work with chaos, because chaos is the source of creativity. Chaos is not a permanent state, but I'm convinced now that it is a necessary precondition to get to a breakthrough—what people call "breakthrough thinking" or "out of the box" or any of that terminology. You must pass through a stage in which you realize that your idea for the organization doesn't work. And that is so uncomfortable that people retreat from it. . . . It's the same thing that happens in a natural system. When confronted with information that doesn't fit, a natural system falls apart so it can either die or reconfigure itself. If it reconfigures itself, it will be better suited to its environment [cited in Brown, 1993, p. 20].

It is difficult to accept information that is disturbing or doesn't fit because it challenges existing views of reality. Yet it is just this information that ultimately allows organizations to make quantum leaps.

Continuous Improvement: An Example

People are terrified about moving into a new, somewhat ambiguous future. Deming suggested that administrators are the people most terrified of change. When a teacher was asked, "Why aren't you making the needed improvements within your school?" she responded, "We are waiting until the administrators die." One must understand the information and needs of the future in order to be responsive to them. One must be willing to experiment with first this, then that, in a messy, ambiguous process of innovation. This experimentation requires the ability to admit one was wrong so one can find what is right and really make a difference. Jennifer James, a noted cultural anthropologist, is fond of saying, "You must plow the fields of your past, so you can plant new seeds." The superintendent must help the organization deal with the pain and loss that occur during the chaos of changing the status quo, moving forward, developing a vision, and making the transition to what needs to exist.

Societally, we are in a period of denial and anger, and the superintendent is often the one asked to pay the price. School boards and communities must understand that better education comes only through the pain of confronting the complexities of American life and experimenting with new approaches to promoting more successful student learning. Transformational leaders do not create the shifts, however; they create the culture that supports staff responsiveness. When the culture is strong, symmetry always emerges. Transformational leaders do not *create* order for the organization; they align their organizations with the natural order of things, allowing inherent order and harmony to emerge out of changing circumstances.

Case Study: Successes and Difficulties in Responding

By 1989, Gary Wright, then superintendent of schools in the Lindbergh School District, a suburb of St. Louis, felt pressure to come to closure in order for the schools to move forward. He had come to the Lindbergh School District in 1980 and was quickly caught up in a massive desegregation case. It originally involved the St. Louis schools, but the suburban school districts were soon involved in litigation. In a little over two years, Lindbergh schools were transformed from less than one percent to almost 20 percent minority representation. This was followed by years of economic slowdown and massive budget cuts with staff reductions that included fifty teachers. There was a large decease in student enrollment, and five schools were closed. (Additionally, the tax levy aimed at raising funds to renovate existing buildings and update facilities was defeated in 1988.)

After five hectic years on the job, Wright began to create a decentralized, responsive system for school improvement and transformed the Lindbergh School District into a model for the state and nation. "The district had been quite effective in getting teachers and principals to identify general issues to be addressed," he said at the time; "however, an impatience has developed regarding the need to find a better way to address the issues identified. It is time that we develop and implement school improvement plans." Impatience to improve schools was expressed by teachers, parents, community, and board members as a concern for "the quality of education that Lindbergh children were receiving."

Wright was concerned, however, that the process of improving the schools might be moving too fast. He was concerned that implementing plans at this point might discourage conversations that were occurring, muffle differing viewpoints that were emerging, and reduce diversity among the individuals involved in the process

of improving schools. He could see a richness of viewpoint develop
ing both within and outside the school system; however, at the
same time he sensed a feeling of turmoil that was beginning to become a concern for all those involved. The deterministic, existing
view of schooling was being challenged by a greater number of people who had no idea what a new school would look like. In a way,
people were now living in two worlds, one of which was no longer
satisfactory and the other not yet known. Superintendent Wright
was concerned that people in the schools and community who had
just begun to move up the learning curve might be forced to respond before they were ready. He knew the school district had experienced years of difficulty, and he wanted to ensure that there
was broad support for innovative plans and that local school efforts
would result in carefully controlled experimentation.

The system was no longer exhibiting the quiet, smooth functioning that human beings treasure. Discussion was occurring in a
very public forum. Although much of the dialogue was productive,
Wright was under a great deal of pressure regarding control of the
situation. He created a formal structure through which school improvement recommendations were to be made. He decided to develop a centralized support group, as well as developmental teams
within each of the schools: "We are developing a district support
group that will, in turn, develop school teams that will make
schools better for students and teachers. We need to keep everyone
informed of what we are doing, and we must make sure that team
members have the skill and knowledge necessary to be effective.
The district support team is there to provide services to the
schools."

Several factors seemed to be blocking the progress of these
teams. First, there was discomfort with the uncertainty about future
directions and the time needed to develop concrete school improvement plans. Second, the multiple perspectives regarding the directions the schools should take were creating conflict and confusion.
Third, there was a concern that the consensus required to successfully support an implementation plan might not naturally evolve.
Fourth, administrators feared that participants did not have the
skills and knowledge they needed to develop school improvement
plans. By far the most significant threat to school improvement,
however, was the overall narrow focus on maintaining the present
delivery system, tinkering with the existing paradigm, and the related resentment and resistance to change. Strong pressure was

being exerted to end the transition by returning to the past. While the superintendent was trying to allay fears, critics were putting even greater pressure on the time restrictions for making needed changes. Instead of showing patience and allowing time for needed improvements to evolve and spread throughout the district, a small but vocal group pushed for a quick, centralized fix for the schools. The fear of the unknown was pushing against the decentralized, responsive approach to school improvement being promoted by the superintendent.

Morale within the school district began to decline as turmoil, confusion, and misunderstanding embroiled the process of developing improvement. People inside and outside the schools began to express doubts about the whole process and whether the school district would ever recover. One heard comments such as "The system is out of control." It was difficult to convince those who had a role in education that this was an important time for inquiry, clarification, and experimentation.

Regarding such a process, Margaret Wheatley says, "We'd better create support for the process of experimentation, and thinking together, and working it out, and making mistakes, and getting it wrong as well as right, and changing all the time" (Brown, 1993, p. 17). Wright saw this as a very important period of inquiry and learning; he was attempting to convince those involved that this was a natural part of the learning and development process.

Planning teams discussed ideas from such approaches as effective schools (Ron Edmonds), comprehensive schools (William Bennett), community service schools (Ernest Boyer), and essential schools (Ted Sizer). This activity was not intended to provide solutions to the pressing problem of building a clear vision for an ideal school, but to raise consciousness of improvement efforts under way in other districts. Because the teams had done training activities and made school visitations, they were now being viewed by others as an elite group. As a result of envy, collegiality within schools began to disintegrate and enthusiasm started to falter. It became more difficult to encourage teachers to be open, take risks, experiment, develop themselves, and remain open-minded. The media began to sensationalize problems rather than focus on the difficult effort under way to improve the schools. Lack of finances and a major effort to pass a school tax levy were diverting resources and time from the improvement process. Momentum was faltering. Progress was being challenged every inch of the way, but the superintendent was serving as the driving force and holding all the pieces together; the needed critical mass was developing. This was probably most evident in the passing of the tax levy that had been defeated in 1988, the first one that had passed in over twenty years.

The development of school improvement in the Lindbergh School District was a difficult process. The fear and resistance created by change and the unknown were difficult to deal with, and support systems were hard to maintain. There was continuous tension between a desire to build mutually shared visions, allow experimentation, and provide support for successful innovation, and a desire to press ahead with a tightly controlled systemwide model. Exposing one's ideas to the scrutiny of others and of discussing new issues and approaches was more difficult than first expected. The complexity of time constraints and the logistics of getting people together to discuss important issues of school reform made the task very difficult under existing structures.

Wright had created powerful momentum for change and districtwide linkages among schools to support school improvement. Just when it appeared that significant headway was being made, the school district became strapped for money again. The superintendent was asked to cut more money from the district's budget; once again the turmoil was recharged. Everything the district was doing and planning was back under the microscope. The questions were endless; everything that had been resolved was revisited with "Why are you doing this?" and "How can you cut money out of that?" Many people were aware of Wright's outstanding performance in very difficult times and his ability to continue moving the district forward. As a result, two years before his contract was to end, he was offered another position with a foundation. Wright decided that it was a good time to leave the superintendency and do something else with his professional life.

Marilyn Cohn, from Washington University, who worked with the Lindbergh School District, says, "These are exciting times in education, because major changes that are highly valued by most teachers and teacher educators are being initiated. Unfortunately, the forces against change in bureaucratic organizations are formidable, and therefore the track record for substantive and long-lasting change in schools is a poor one. In order to maximize the chances for eventually achieving and sustaining meaningful change, we must study the most interesting and promising school improvement efforts and determine what are the factors that contribute to or impede their success." A person must be willing to devote a considerable part of his or her life to tackling the school improvement process. Being forewarned of the difficulties is the best way to be forearmed to deal with the heavy demands of this turbulent process.

Differentiating Crises and Noncrises

Research tells us that continuous improvement and responsiveness are organic and dynamic, not linear and systemic (Fullan and Stiegelbauer, 1991; Cunningham and Gresso, 1993; Wheatley, 1992; and Covey, 1989). There is no objective reality during the change process, except for the core values and culture of the organization. The focus should be on what the organization is and what it would look like in an ideal state. The organization does not try to become something it is not. Its energy is focused on being the best at whatever it is about. The organization knows what it's good at, what it wants to and needs to be doing, and the principles that must guide it. The transformation to the future depends on the visions, values, and guiding principles that provide alignment and stability in this process. Once these conditions exist, school divisions can give individuals within the organization the autonomy to really make a difference.

True crises may arise within the school district; they require swift and firm action. A genuine crisis such as complaints that principals within the district are condoning and even promoting "teaching the tests," so that their schools will look good on testing data requires an immediate response, if the schools are to maintain their credibility. Although it is often best to involve people in decision making, unforeseen crises and critical incidents need immediate action, for which involvement may not be possible or desirable. Superintendents must have an emergency plan ready for such crisis situations.

When superintendents have their feet to the fire in a noncrisis situation, they should not respond as if it were a crisis. Releasing test scores showing that students are not doing nearly as well in history as they are in science and mathematics is not an immediate crisis. The information may be disappointing and create some chaos, but this turmoil should be managed so as to develop understanding, involvement, and commitment to improving the situation. This takes time. Bureaucratic, structured, and governed school systems may restrict self-renewal, because they take a crisis-response approach that reduces or eliminates the organization's capacity to connect, communicate, and respond. Wheatley talks of "A universe rich in processes that support growth and coherence. . . . Nothing happens in a quantum world without something encountering something else. Nothing is independent of the relationships that occur" (Wheatley, 1992, p. 17). According to Wheatley, the interactions themselves allow the organization to reform and ultimately stabilize favorably—allowing the organization to revitalize itself.

Protecting Participants

Superintendents in the twenty-first century will be expected to promote interconnectedness, facilitate information flow and response, and provide leadership for the resulting transformations. Responding to dialogue leads to continuously improved schools and ultimately improved student learning. Improvement occurs when the pioneers are turned loose and allowed to blaze a trail for their less-adventuresome colleagues.

The culture is best supported with credibility, conviction, and gratitude. Instead of superintendents coming in with their own game plan, they must help those having a legitimate role to play to develop vision for change, in collaboration with others and in response to definitions of local needs. The superintendent promotes open exchange of ideas and encourages others to act in concert rather than at cross-purposes.

Superintendents must stand for important values and place students first in all that they do. They must prepare others for the difficulties, the time required, and the support needed throughout the change process. Steady progress becomes the watchword, moving from milestone to milestone. They give credit, support risk takers, encourage the spread of success, and constantly engage everyone in the improvement process. The goal should be stability, consistency, and steady progress, not instant results.

Irvin Blumer, superintendent of the Newton Public Schools in Massachusetts, expounds the importance of core values to this process:

> The role of the superintendent is to help create a community of learners within the schools. That requires developing ownership for three or four core values that are central to the entire school system and that become owned by all facets of the school system. All members of the school community are involved in the decision-making process as it relates to core values. . . .
>
> Everyone understands that the "core values" cannot be violated. Because the understanding around core values is so powerful, the only decisions that cannot be shared are decisions that would detract from the core values that bind the community together. At the same time, the school system has a common set of beliefs that bind it together, making it a "system."
>
> The issue about how much resistance one faces and how to deal with it is intimately connected to the concept of core values. Do all members of the school community understand the basic values of the schools and do they own them? If the answer to that is yes, then people have a better framework from which to enter into a discussion about what changes are needed and why. While anxiety may not be lessened, the fact that people have an understanding and ownership concerning beliefs makes the resistance much lower. If during the change process you remember that it is not a straight-line projection and that there will be setbacks as you move ahead, and you articulate that up front and clearly, change occurs more smoothly.
>
> Excellence is built in, because core values and professionalism require a commitment to high standards and expectations, and a belief that all children can learn and learning can be a rigorous experience for all children. Within that context, there should be no defectors, and it is everyone's responsibility to ensure that this belief is translated into action. The degree of success around that might vary, but the commitment cannot vary in any way.

The common mission and shared core values create alignment and support for the process of democratic deliberation, planning, and experimentation. They provide a basis on which participants can come together in a shared plan for an improved future. The superintendent is responsible for ensuring that what is being done is congruent with the core values of the schools. This value system serves as the glue that allows diverse groups to work together to significantly improve education. Larry Mixon, superintendent of the Columbus Public Schools in Ohio, says:

> This is why many are drawn to "quick fixes," changes of rules, regulations, policies, and missions that are perceptible but only give the illusion of true change. The difficulty then starts with trying to figure out how one begins a "cultural change" within an organization that builds the foundation upon which true instructional change will occur. The most difficult part of school improvement efforts is to keep individuals all pointed in the same direction over an extended period of time. For this to happen, it is important to develop systemwide values, a district mission, and goals to support that mission, upon which all can agree. Thus, the typical things that get in the way of change efforts—such as frequent changes in leadership, political "turfism," vested interests, fear of the unknown—all can be overcome if you have common values, mission, and goals. Leadership in change efforts, to be effective, must demonstrate that it is committed to the process over time. It must focus on the development of excellence in a total quality environment where everyone works together in the spirit of slow, daily, gradual improvement.

Educational improvement will require new kinds of leadership. We need leaders to create conversations, to change the levels and kinds of discourse going on in and around schools, and to stimulate inquiry, questioning, problem solving, and a focus on learning for everyone in the system, not just students. This is the challenge of the contemporary superintendency.

Old Questions, New Answers

How can educators increase both excellence and equity in schools to ensure success for all learners? How can teachers and administrators collaborate to make curriculum and instruction more relevant and actively engaging for students? What kinds of enhanced training and support will educators need to bring about substantive and productive renewal?

These questions are not new ones. What is new, however, is the response crafted by many superintendents. In Newtonville, Massachusetts, for example, Superintendent Blumer operates with four core values: (1) centrality of the classroom, (2) respect for human differences, (3) belief in collegial behavior, and (4) belief in the importance of communication. Because of the power of these core values, the only decisions that cannot be shared in the Newton public schools are those that could undermine the values binding the community together. Beyond that, decision making exists at the school level, closest to children, where it belongs. Superintendent Beatriz Reyna-Curry in San Elizario, Texas, also believes that schools must agree on certain outcomes for all students, as well as on some expectations of behavior between the staff and their organization. She contends that no schools should be allowed to "do their own thing" to the detriment of students; however, within its guiding principles the school must be more responsive to the needs of students and the communities in which they live.

Superintendents must respond to the demands of their external constituencies while encouraging staff members to be innovative and to focus on improving teaching and learning. "When an organization faces a variety of stakeholders, all of whom insist on having a voice," says Michael Fullan, "the choice is whether such involvement will occur as mutually isolated influences working randomly or at cross-purposes—or whether it will be developed through joint initiatives" (1993b, p. 161). Fullan indicates that when organizations collaborate, they engage in an act of shared creation.

Former Chancellor Ramon Cortines believes that in a large school district such as New York City there are many schools that would have almost instant success with school-based leadership, given the quality of existing leaders, their focus on teaching and learning, the extensive and welcome involvement of parents, and the professionalism of staff members. But, he quickly adds, there are many other schools that would flounder because of deficiencies in these areas. Therefore, in New York City and probably most other locations, targeted technical assistance from the district and other collaborative entities is necessary to support the continuous improvement process. Unless school districts provide adequate training and support for people engaged in these reform efforts, they will not likely achieve success for all students.

Reinventing the Central Office

When school districts decentralize their operations or undergo systemic reform, the responsibilities of people in the central office are bound to change. There is considerable ambivalence in the reactions of central office personnel to restructuring efforts, especially those involving decentralization of decision making to the school level (Murphy, 1993a; Fullan, 1993b). Others declare that there is an absence of a clearly defended role for district offices. Chief executive officers in local education feel themselves to be caught in the middle between state authority and local autonomy (Crowson, 1988; see also Murphy, 1993b). Decentralization has brought significant changes in the role of superintendents, central office administrators, and supervisory staff. The central office must come to see itself not as a regulator or initiator but as a service provider. The function of the central office must be to assure that individual schools have what they need to be successful.

Pajak (1989) cites a 1989 study that found that central office supervisors traditionally have been viewed as a support arm of the school district serving in a "backstage role." Supervisors now view themselves as developers of professional talent throughout the school district. They function as leaders of leaders. When John Murphy was superintendent in Prince George's County, Maryland, he "wanted central office not to be the one that handed down mandates from on high but to turn that around and say we're really here to help." Similarly, John Middleton, former superintendent in Columbus, Ohio, proposed systemic change that involved various community constituencies in collaborative planning, rigorous staff development, and a collaborative decision-making process in schools for the academic benefit of all students. In so doing, each superintendent shifted the locus of control from the central office to the schools. An emphasis on students, the "mantra" of both superintendents, promised progress by providing a focus that transcended individual and institutional self-interest. This emphasis promoted collaboration and improved learning opportunities for students.

Teachers best understand the needs, demographics, and abilities of their students. Glickman, Gordon, and Ross-Gordon conclude: "The tragedy in this [mandated approaches] view of curriculum and teachers is the loss of a powerful vehicle for creating an instructional dialogue in a school or district, which could enhance teachers' individual and collective thinking about instruction and consequently improve systemwide and schoolwide instruction. Most teachers, when trusted, when given time and money, and when given the assistance, choice, and responsibility to develop curricula, will make extraordinarily sound decisions about what students should be taught. Often, their decisions will be far superior to those made in district central offices, state departments, or commercial publishing firms" (1995, p. 389).

Central office staff members must take on new roles as supporters and enablers of work taking place in the schools. They must focus on helping schools achieve their improvement goals. As Fred Wood, dean of education at the University of Oklahoma, put it, "the central office's role becomes one of facilitating and supporting and making sure there is implementation of change." Central office supervisors are likely to fade into the sunset from many school district central offices or be eliminated abruptly unless their roles shift from leading to helping in school district restructuring. School districts thrive to the extent that a broad base of professional talent is developed over time to respond to emerging visions of improved education. The forging of the future thus becomes a quest for human resource development, and the central office can become a major force in that effort.

Staff development efforts are initiated by all supervisory groups, not just by the traditional central office staff development department. Job-embedded staff development requires superintendents, assistant superintendents, curriculum supervisors, principals, and teacher leaders to see themselves as teachers of adults and to view the development of others, within and outside of education, as one of their most important responsibilities. Individuals who perform these roles are increasingly held accountable for their performance as planners and implementers of various forms of professional development and renewal. Staff development is no longer to be viewed as something done by someone in the central office; instead, it is seen as a critical function listed in the job descriptions of many district employees (Sparks, 1994). Staff development programs emphasize the new knowledge and skills needed for partnership and collaborative efforts both within and outside the organization.

In Edmonton, Alberta, the two hundred schools now control more than 80 percent of the districtwide capital and operating budget. However, the central office plays a critical role in staff development. Schools continue to rely on districtwide staff developers for expertise. Central office staff developers help Edmonton's schools shape their own staff development activities by serving as staff development resource brokers. This role sometimes involves linking schools that have excellent track records with schools in need of assistance, thus helping struggling schools uncover resources that already exist within the district (in terms of skills, experience, and expertise). Michael Strembitsky, former superintendent of schools in Edmonton, reports that staff development activity has greatly increased under decentralization. He estimates that it has more than doubled!

A reconceptualized central office can help individuals at the school level acquire the skills they need to make decentralization yield positive results in the classroom. One of the most important roles the superintendent and central office can play in a climate of decentralization is to "ensure that quality decisions are made at the school site, and that the processes used to make those decisions are designed to ensure quality" (Schlechty, 1993, p. 23). Staff development is essential if a responsive approach is being taken.

New Perspectives, New Possibilities, New Knowledge

We are living in the new reality created by emerging technology—a world in which we are now electronically, instantaneously connected. The result is a speed and unpredictability of change and a level of complexity never before dreamed of. Success is now dependent on educational leaders' ability to create new knowledge together with colleagues at both the central office and school sites. Central office personnel must embody the best in current practice and research. More than any other body of workers within a school system, they should be informed about the latest research in educational trends literature and the latest successes in practice. In turn, they should make efforts to articulate this body of information to schools in such a way that school staffs can understand and use this data.

Central office educational leaders must engage in mutual inquiry, discovery, and learning. Together, they must create learning communities to illuminate the knowledge needed in the new millennium. Consequently, the role of the superintendent is changing to that of enabler/facilitator—which includes serving as the organizer and facilitator of information rather than the source of knowledge. One of many critical support activities is to educate staff and community members on technology and its capability to improve communication.

In *The Smarter Organization,* Michael McGill and John Slocum, Jr., write: "Smarter organizations are different in every way. A smart organization is distinguished by the leadership, communications, and decision-making processes that it uses to learn from its experience. The learning organization can alter the very way in which it processes its experiences. . . . This continuous process is reflected in the characteristics of all learning organizations: openness, systemic thinking, creativity, personal efficacy, and empathy" (1994, p. 12). Continuous learning organizations succeed because they capture ego energy—the energy of people who are developing and growing for their own reasons—and connect it to the power of communication technology. A workforce that learns is flexible, adaptive, and self-regenerating.

Smart organizations must learn with, from, and for their clients. They must overcome anxiety and resistance to the technology that can assist in this process. They must model the learning process and skills and dispositions, and facilitate their clients' learning while the work of school reform is being accomplished. Analogous to individual learning, an organization's learning (such as a school district's learning) is defined as increasing its capacity to take effective action, or, as Peter Senge, suggests "to create the results its members truly desire" (Senge, 1990, p. 3).

The new central office's primary role is to stimulate local school-based action by formulating a general direction for the schools, assisting the schools in gathering and feeding back performance data, and supporting local school-based needs. The superintendent's role is to ensure that the efforts of local schools are supported by the central office, the school board, and the political power structure. Superintendents are in the best position to create networks of support for reform with external agencies and other school districts.

In 1992, Diana Lam was named superintendent for the Dubuque (Iowa) Community School district. During her two years there, she established an early learning center and an intermediate center, computerized the district's administrative services, and developed a comprehensive internal and external communication system. Now in San Antonio, Lam continues her quest to develop school systems into true learning organizations: environments where continuous learning is the top priority for students and adults. To that end, she is leading the San Antonio Independent School District in efforts to obtain grants for the development and implementation of a professional development infrastructure. The "teacher board" she has created is opening lines of communication among staff members, while she also makes herself readily available to parents and community leaders.

Superintendent Lam's focus on service to the students is also reflected in efforts to restructure the district organization to support school-based decision making, streamlined communication, and improved staffing in the schools. The new "organizational web" represents a dramatic departure from the traditional top-down administrative structure. Clear policies must strike a balance between autonomy for schools and support and control at the district level. Lam says "there can be no long-term rethinking of schools if there is not a long-term rethinking of the central policies and support structures provided to schools." Glickman suggests the primary role of school districts is to coordinate and provide support and assistance to schools by

- Defining the district's core beliefs about teaching and learning
- Defining the goals and objectives (outcomes) of an educated student
- Providing the money, technical services, and human consulta tion to allow the school to figure out how to get the job done
- Providing information and identifying common needs
- Coordinating and linking resources (1993, p. 12)

Creating learning communities is not a logical, linear process. In fact, it can be chaotic, as some superintendents can attest. Peter Kline and Bernard Saunders (1995) believe there are ten steps to becoming a learning organization:

1. *Assess your learning culture.* An organization must know where it is and where it is going.
2. *Promote the positive.* People must feel connected to their associates in a positive way.
3. *Make the workplace safe for thinking.* The organization must create an environment that encourages, incubates, or creates a "greenhouse" for new ideas.
4. *Reward risk taking.* It is an integral part of any learning.
5. *Help people become resources for one another.* Synergistic sharing promotes complex patterns of interaction that strengthen the organization.
6. *Put learning power to work.* The commitment made by the organization to the individual's development is repaid with increased innovation.
7. *Map out the vision.* Create opportunities for employees to "see themselves" as successful contributors.
8. *Bring the vision to life.* Kinesthetic modeling is a powerful method that explores ideas by modeling them.
9. *Connect the systems.* Develop a systemic understanding of the relationship among all members or teams. This helps people see and take pride in each individual's contribution.
10. *Get the show on the road.* At the beginning, people need encouragement, not criticism (1995, p. 20).

To engage the full range of their "intelligences," educators must engage in processes and activities that disrupt their normal thought processes, creating a bit of chaos from which to draw new wisdom. This mental disruption is creativity in motion; it brings knowledge into being that has not existed before. Education leaders in central offices that are helping organizations need to accelerate and intensify the experience of learning through exposure to new practices and the current research. Mjokowski says that "generalist competencies and dispositions will need to be combined with an array of specialist skills which reside in teams of variably talented people who work flexibly to respond to diverse needs. Discipline and program boundaries will need to be highly permeable" (1995, p. 53). Sustainable success requires the capacity for ongoing learning and continuous transformation.

Dismantling Central Authority

Since 1993, school reform leaders from Chicago, Denver, New York, Seattle, Philadelphia, and Los Angeles—all engaged in systemic reform—have come together to form the Cross City Campaign for Urban School Reform. This coalition of leaders released a report entitled *Reinventing Central Office: A Primer for Successful Schools* (Hallett, 1995), which calls for a radical shift of authority and funds from the central office to local schools. Despite more than a decade of education reform, this report recommends dismantling centralized authority. School-based restructuring shifts the focus from improvement, or doing what we do now better, to reconceptualizing and reinventing schools and the roles and responsibilities of teachers, administrators, students, and parents.

Cross City's report outlines a strategy for improving schools by decentralizing funds, authority, and accountability. It identifies the functions that should still be carried out centrally to ensure fairness and citywide excellence. In the report's vision, "central office departments are entrepreneurial, competing with other vendors to provide services. By existing only to serve school needs, departments that perform useful services quickly and cost-effectively continue to grow" (Hallett, 1995, p. 20). School districts exist primarily to support the development of effective schools for all children.

The Cross City Campaign envisions that the central office will remain the site for important functions such as goals and standards, equity, assistance, budget, information, emergency funds, legal assistance, personnel, and competitive services. (These are explained further in Appendix C.) Hallett also maintains that "if we want schools that are accountable for student achievement . . . we've got to give them the authority to do their job and remove the ineffective command and control bureaucracies."

Service Centers for Schools

Central office personnel, like their peers at the school level, are simply "faced with new roles, which are more complex, less clear, and require new skills on their part" (Fullan, 1993b). The new roles also reaffirm the importance of district assistance in local school improvement efforts (Murphy and Hallinger, 1993).

In May 1992, J. Michael Brandt, superintendent in Cincinnati, Ohio, reduced the number of central office administrators from 127 to 62. His streamlining was accompanied by a flattening of the organizational structure. Specifically, several layers of the bureaucracy, including the district's area superintendents and the entire department of administration, curriculum, and instruction were eliminated (Gursky, 1992, p. 13). Another example of massive changes occurred once again, with the advent of a new superintendent in Prince George's county, Maryland, whose stated plan is to decentralize operations even beyond the changes initiated by John Murphy, the former superintendent. This intent has prompted a mandate for central office supervisors to spend more time in schools and less time on central office tasks. The role of the central office supervisors in staff development, however, remains largely unchanged—the expectation being that they will continue to take the leadership in designing, conducting, and coordinating staff development training for the large-scale changes in curriculum, instruction, assessment, and school organization that the new wave of restructuring will bring.

This growing trend for central offices to function as service centers for *schools*—rather than centers for monitoring and control—can be seen in the restructuring of school districts in Kentucky (Murphy, 1993a). Three important themes in the new role for superintendents and central office staff emerged from a study of 176 superintendents under the Kentucky Education Reform Act (KERA): (1) developing community, (2) coaching from the sidelines, and (3) providing facilitation and support.

In helping support transformational reforms, the function of central office personnel changes from attempting to ensure uniformity across schools to orchestrating diversity to ensure that the common educational goals of the system are met. Central office personnel are spending less time initiating projects and more time responding to school requests, acting as liaisons between the building and the central office, and acting as brokers of central office services (Hirsh and Sparks, 1991). These changes are having a profound effect on the superintendent's role. The one dimension that has not changed with the decentralization focus is the propensity of the public and school boards to hold the superintendent accountable even for school-based and decentralized decision making.

Now, as at no other time, society demands excellent leaders. And there has never been a more urgent need to confidently and successfully lead school districts. But the deceptive simplicity of this statement disguises the paradox of leadership: while turbulent times demand the strongest and best leaders, the change process requires broadening the base and decentralization to achieve the new education paradigm. This means that superintendents are held responsible for massive changes developed and implemented through local school and community efforts. The superintendent's role becomes one of providing direction, developing and nurturing people involved, facilitating and supporting their work, providing needed resources, and ultimately assuring accountability for appropriate student achievement.

Chapter Eleven

Motivating Systemic Change

The entire education community must start helping its publics to understand the complexities of the problems facing schools and to appreciate that, even with hard work, solving them will be slow, incremental, difficult, and costly. The idea of rapid reform has powerful appeal. But reform requires a lot from educators, particularly superintendents—far more than they can possibly manage if others don't help them with the core dilemmas they face. To lead school systems, which reflect society far more than they shape it, is hard enough when shared values, mutual respect, and civility prevail; it is nearly impossible when they don't.

Superintendents across the United States are recognizing that the education system needs fundamental changes to keep pace with an increasingly complex global society. Yet the deeper we get into the process of change, the more confused we can become. The language that educators use when talking about change in schools provides a clue to the source of the problem: terms such as *restructure, reform, redesign, reorganize, repair.* They all imply that change involves moving from one "steady state" to another. The language of a system longing for equilibrium suggests that what is important is changing the "structure," "organization," or "design" of the school . . . that is, finding a single, long-term solution to school system concerns.

To be systemic, change must be based on a different set of assumptions. Changing the mental models that individuals in schools use to interact with one another (the governing ideas) is more important than changing structure. As superintendents change the mental models that they use to interact with others, they change what they organize their energy around, and the necessary changes in structure follow. Everything in the universe is in a constant state of change—but we profess to be surprised by change! Beverly Anderson's matrix showing a continuum of systemic change (Table 11.1) can help stakeholders rise above singular views to a more systemic perspective of how changes occur. Superintendents are not working to *reform* schools; rather, they are working to *continuously improve* them. They typically move from milestone to milestone in the hope of ensuring that schools are always getting better. This work calls for a shift to a completely new paradigm of public education.

Understanding Human Systems

Among the challenges facing education leaders is to learn how to manage systems and how to use planning to create a new future. Peter Senge says "The new future is understanding human systems by exploring the nature of systems and learning to manage them so that the needs of people are better served" (1995, p. 2). According to Jerry Patterson, former superintendent in Appleton, Wisconsin, "a system is a collection of parts that interact to function purposefully as a whole" (1993, p. 67). Most systems reside within larger systems. In schools, as we begin to engage people in the school improvement process, our mental models must change. Our beliefs and perceptions often limit what we consider possible. But planning is a reflective process and keeps us open to new possibilities. It enables us to remain flexible.

A key to the ongoing effectiveness of any organization is ability to renew itself, to seek and find better ways of fulfilling its mission and responding to change. The challenge to superintendents is to elicit sustained focus and effort in an enterprise notorious for climbing on every passing bandwagon. This problem can be avoided only if education leaders recognize that one of their fundamental responsibilities is to help create a systemwide commitment to continuous improvement of teaching and learning; "This perpetual disquiet, this constant search for a better way, is the

Table 11.1. The Continuum of Systemic Change.

Elements of Change	Maintenance of Old System	Awareness	Exploration
Vision	Vision reflects: • Learning based on seat time • Teaching as lecture • Mandates and inputs • Education system separate from social service systems	• Multiple stakeholders realize need to change • Strategic plans call for funda-mental changes	• Stakeholder groups promote new ideas for parts of system • New examples debated • Growing numbers and types of stakeholders drawn together
Public and Political Support	• Support taken for granted • Only a concern when finances are needed • Public informed, not engaged	• Policymakers, media discuss need for changes • Public forums on change	• Task forces formed • Leaders speak on some issues • Minor resource allocations • Public involved in redefining learning outcomes
Networking	• Networking seen as insignificant • Partnerships are one-shot, supplemental	• Networking valued • A critical mass of teachers explore joining networks • Realization that partnerships need to be longer-term, integral	• Networks (including electronic) share information • Schools, districts, and states join networks • School leaders contact potential partners

Transition	Emergence of New Infrastructure	Predominance of New System
• Emerging consensus • Old components shed • Need for linkages understood	• Vision includes student outcomes, system structure, underlying beliefs • Continual refinement of vision, expanded involvement	• Belief that all students can learn at higher levels • Learning is achieving and applying knowledge • Education connected to social services
• Public debate • Leaders campaign for change • Resistant groups vocal • More resources allocated • Diversity recognized	• Ongoing task forces • Resources are ongoing; emphasis on meeting diverse student needs • Public engaged in change	• Public, political, business involvement essential • Allocation of resources based on new vision
• Networks recognized as long-term features • Debates on how to support ongoing networks • Disenfranchised groups use networks for empowerment	• Networks accepted practice; major source of new knowledge • Empowerment issues debated • Multiple partners support vision	• Resources allocated for networks • Networks serve as major communication channels • Power is shared

Table 11.1. The Continuum of Systemic Change, cont'd.

Elements of Change	Maintenance of Old System	Awareness	Exploration
Teaching and Learning Changes	Emphasis on: • Standard curriculum • Delivery of information • Standardized tests • Raising scores	• Recognition that current research is not used in teaching, and that education problems are due to broad social, economic, technological changes	• Resources committed to learning new teaching methods; multiyear commitments • New modes of assessment explored • Outcomes are defined
Administrative Roles and Responsibilities	Responsibilities seen as: • Diminishing conflict • Emphasizing standardization, rules • Providing information • Top-down decison making	• Administrators recognize need to change roles • New roles, responsibilities discussed • Media attention on innovative leaders	• Site-based decision making piloted • Professional development focuses on new roles • Bureaucracy questioned • Some resources allocated to learning outcomes
Policy Alignment	Policy emphasizes: • Textbook selection • Standardized teaching, tests • Comparisons among schools on student achievement • Hierarchical structure	• Experimentation promoted • Recognition that standardized tests don't measure all learning outcomes; low achievement may be due to conditions beyond teaching	• New assessments explored • Policies defining graduation based on demonstrated learning piloted • Curriculums emphasize higher learning for all

Transition	Emergence of New Infrastructure	Predominance of New System
• Teachers, schools, districts try new approaches • Teachers given time to plan • **Recognition of change needed and resources required** • Changes assessed	• Assessments encourage improvement, recognize uneven progress • Graduation based on outcomes • Teaching engages students • Ongoing teacher development	In most schools: • Student learning is active • Assessments are focused on outcomes • Teacher and administrator preparation uses outcomes
• Methods developed to distribute decision making • Emphasis on outcomes to be achieved; flexibility in how • Resources for ongoing teacher professional development	• Administrators hired using new criteria • Site-based decision making • School-community councils • Teachers responsible for instructional decisions	Administrators: • Encourage rethinking, improvement, innovation • Allocate resources to support student learning • Use site-based management
• Task forces define learning outcomes • Schools have latitude to redesign teaching and learning • Recognition that policies need review	• Exit outcomes developed, emphasize complex learning • Multiple means of assessment • Major review of policy • Education and social service policies connected	Policy supports: • Ongoing improvement • High student standards • Learning outcomes • Flexible instruction • Alternative assessment

Source: Anderson, 1993.

essence of a renewing organization" (DuFour and Eaker, 1992, p. 37). Regardless of how long a superintendent remains in a school district, his or her work is never completed, because the school system still needs to evolve within a supportive educational culture.

Macher (1992) believes the most valuable learning occurs when teams of employees from different departments, job functions, and authority levels meet to share their various perspectives and analyze together how to improve the system. This is a matrix-type organizational schema in which employees are configured in ways that are best for students. But what conditions are needed for continuous learning to occur? Macher notes that learning occurs best when people feel free to break from tradition, to try out new ideas.

What are the implications for school improvement? What are the catalysts that enhance the process? From the perspective of the school as a learning organization, are people organized to learn from what they are doing? Does the culture of the school support reflective study of what is occurring to promote improvements? Effective educational leaders recognize the influence that the local culture has in effecting school improvement. Therefore, to change schools, superintendents must work with the attitudes and norms of the school community (Prince, 1989).

School improvement results when school cultures are reformed, and changed practice grows from the conscious choice to improve. This is a different way of thinking about school improvement; it creates a process rather than imposing a solution. After all, schools improve as the concepts people hold dear change. It's also important to note, says Joyce, "that responsibility for school renewal is a joint effort at both the school and the district level" (1993, p. 43). He acknowledges that maintaining the organization while learning new ways of working together is a delicate process: "The organization has to keep going while changing, and some of the things that are accomplished regularly have to continue" (p. 44). But significant changes cannot occur unless there is a willingness to invest in and support teachers and principals. The development of human resources must be at the heart of school improvement. Schools will not change unless the people working within those schools change. Accordingly, superintendents must provide leadership in changing how professional staff time is regarded, organized, and used.

Pointing the Compass

Schooling assumes all students can give meaning to a complex and fragmented array of academic courses, and that all students recognize or are able to construct a congruence between schooling and their lives. However, many students are struggling in their academic programs and in their social behavior in the schools. Still others are highly talented but not challenged to their fullest potential (Wang and Reynolds, 1995).

Uppermost in superintendents' minds today is finding how best to meet the needs of the changing population of students, who are affected as never before by the realities of shifting demographics, advancing technology, and the demands of an uncertain future. School districts are highly complex human organizations, and the work of superintendents is equally complex. Often the general public does not fully understand how the role of the superintendent is shaped by changes taking place in society and in the population. In Fairfax County, Virginia, changes in ethnic composition are accelerating. In 1987, minorities made up 21.6 percent of Fairfax's student body; they now make up 28 percent of the system's 140,000 students. "The demographic forecast, which predicts that the number of minority students will soon nearly equal that of white students, reflects trends that already have begun transforming Fairfax classrooms" (Nguyen, 1995, p. V2.1). Nguyen also reported that "by the year 2003, the schools' white population will decline from 72 percent, and the black population will increase to 14 percent, from 10 percent; and the number of Hispanic students will more than double to 16 percent" (p. V2.2).

It is predicted that Fairfax County students will be poorer and more ethnically diverse in the next fifteen years. Also, the school population will be far outnumbered by the county's senior citizens. "That's not the image people have of Fairfax County," noted school superintendent Robert Spillane. A demographic forecast predicts that by the year 2010, the county will have three times as many retired or elderly residents as school children. That statistic likely will mean even more competition for county dollars and services, as well as far fewer people with a direct connection to the schools.

Schools must be better able to meet the needs of the diverse student populations that they will serve in the future. This implies working more closely with other service agencies. Donald Ingwerson's twelve years as superintendent in the Jefferson County, Kentucky, public schools gave him a deep appreciation of the importance of coordinating the work of all child support and advocacy groups. During his tenure as superintendent, nearly 750 collaborative agreements were established, pledging that agencies dealing with child abuse, homelessness, and so forth would meet regularly. Agencies from the city and county, the economic development groups, the chamber of commerce, the schools, the Metro United Way, the Private Industry Council, and the university meet regularly to collaborate on behalf of youth who need services. The role of superintendents in the reform process, Ingwerson believes, is as leaders who "point the compass."

During his first two years as superintendent in Springfield, Massachusetts, Peter Negroni established formal partnerships with traditional and nontraditional groups. Parents formed a citywide support group called the Springfield Parent Advisory Network. Businesspeople joined forces with the school system as tutors and providers of incentives for improved attendance. Social service agencies joined the schools in providing on-site services and in facilitating an integrated services model for students and families. In addition, other city departments have come together to ensure that they are connected to the schools.

Schools increasingly recognize the need for deeper parent involvement but are sometimes discouraged because it seems there's no one out there to work with. Partnerships with community organizations can contribute to the solution, as when schools join forces with others in the community to help strengthen family support services. All of these partnerships help strengthen the bonds between parents and the schools, as schools become outposts of civility and centers of lifelong learning, rather than impersonal institutions. Schools of this sort help students shield their academic performance from the pressures of negative outside influences or life circumstances.

Capacity to Improve

Society's expectations of schooling call for a transformation of the core business: to provide powerful, authentic, and rigorous learning for students. Such fundamental change in schools is difficult to accomplish. In the private sector, when a company loses touch with its clients, gets fuzzy about its mission, fails to respond to changing market conditions, cannot use new knowledge, cannot raise quality, or becomes overly bureaucratic—when it suffers any *one* of these problems—it requires major change. Both W. Edwards Deming and Margaret Wheatley warn us that short-term solutions and tinkering at the margins waste valuable resources and short-circuit the improvement process. The same is true with our education system. The people are performing well, sometimes heroically; but the system is not.

In the District of Columbia, Superintendent Franklin Smith is working with the community and school personnel to transform the city's schools. The school district is becoming more customer-driven, a concept that is slowly breaking the cycle of inefficient educational delivery. Smith's agenda is ambitious. Yet from his first day in D.C.—after six years in the top spot in the Dayton, Ohio, schools—circumstances have forced him to pursue that agenda while swinging the budget axe. Such is the dilemma superintendents face today. As he revisits policies and procedures, the D.C. schools are moving from a centralized to a decentralized system. This change does not mean, however, that they have eliminated all the roadblocks to more effectively managing education and streamlining the educational delivery system. There are other hopeful signs. Teachers' morale has improved, despite a budget crisis. And the school system is devoting more effort to teacher training under Smith's leadership than in many years. He says he's resigned to the fact that being effective entails receiving more criticism than gratitude. He has a simple motto: "If you've done your best, you've done all that you can do."

Compelling Visions: Motivating and Empowering

Core values drive the school district. They are the shared understandings and beliefs that should determine all action and behavior. Consequently, it is vital that these core values be identified, clearly articulated, and communicated to all stakeholders. Here are some examples of core values:

- Developing as lifelong learners
- Becoming active, contributing members of a global society
- Being technologically literate
- Believing that all students "can" and "will" learn
- Understanding that schooling represents preparation for life
- Respecting human differences

These core values provide the impetus that moves the school district toward its shared vision. Because core values are shared and valued as norms in the district, they provide a checklist against which decisions can be assessed.

Fullan (1993a) believes that all members of a self-renewing organization, not just the leaders, need to have a clear vision of what they are about. Without a sense of purpose, they have no screen through which to filter what is significant from what is not. A case in point: in 1991, the Effective Schools Process in Columbus, Ohio, involved various community constituents in collaborative planning, rigorous staff development, and a collaborative decision-making process in schools for the academic benefit of all students. This collaborative decision making led to the development of a school mission and the use of school databases to develop individual school improvement plans. The former superintendent of schools, John Middleton, made it clear that the change agenda depended on collaboration among school staff, parents, and the community. The change process required flexibility, enthusiasm, resilience, teamwork, and high levels of communication; the result was a clearly defined and focused mission. It was essential that the entire community buy into the mission before comprehensive change could occur.

Self-renewing organizations recognize that the problems facing them are too difficult for any one group to solve. They know they must draw in their stakeholders and collaborate with others who share their values. With collaboration come new opportunities for learning. "Alliances, partnerships, consortia, and collaboration," Fullan asserts, "all connote joint agreements and action over a period of time in which all parties learn to work differently and achieve qualitatively different results" (1993b, pp. 349–350).

However, values and mission are not enough. The superintendent must lead the schools in developing a clear vision of curriculum, instruction, and student achievement connections. The goal of the planning effort should be to frame a specific description of their ideal school, a description to guide all of the action that follows. The vision also provides an opportunity to develop alignment, which is so critical to individual contributions to the organization. Superintendents must also be able to transform ideas into action, to help schools become places of learning that make a difference in the lives of children. The superintendent must engage others in the action and enable them to visualize their ideal schools.

Superintendents must be passionate and powerful in pushing for innovation and change. Successful superintendents recognize that the power of a clear vision of excellence can be more effective than the power of authority. Transformational learning is a process of discovery and deep reflection that leads to profound shifts in direction, behaviors, values, beliefs, and operating assumptions. It leads to a reordering of our worldview and our daily activity. The resulting changes are dramatic, sweeping, and systemic.

Improving School Performance

In the past, both Blumberg (1985) and Cuban (1988) concluded that the managerial and political role, not the instructional role, dominated superintendents' behavior. Their exploration of superintendents' work found that curriculum, instruction, and staff development rarely arose in a prominent way. Other studies have suggested that most superintendents concentrate more on managing people and human resources than do many leaders of other enterprises. But while the logistical and administrative functions of schools remain important, instructional leadership by superintendents is critical to their new leadership role. Peter Negroni of Springfield, Massachusetts, concurs that superintendents must embrace educational leadership, which supersedes the daily minutiae of events and demands. Concomitantly, the district organization must support this evolving role of the superintendent as educational leader. Otherwise, contends Superintendent Joe Work of Little Axe Public Schools I-70 in Norman, Oklahoma, the superintendent's role can easily be forced into political "hackism" and crisis management. In short, "improvement must focus instruction: instructional leadership, organization and implementation of instructional services, teacher development, and expectations and monitoring of student performance. . . ." (Levine and Eubanks, 1991, p. 202).

Today, school districts are confronted with the need for monumental change in how they deliver services and the results generated by those services. Alton Crews, director of the Southern Regional Education Board Leadership Academy, contends that "Our schools aren't worse than they used to be. They are better than they have ever been—at doing what they've always done. But what schools have always done is not what we need them to do today." The belief that schools can be improved without changing is one of the more intractable community beliefs that superintendents must overcome in their efforts to bring about meaningful school improvement.

Because change may mean as much as eight years of doing the "right" things consistently and persistently, sustained improvement requires serious long-term support and encouragement. Fullan (1993b) offers that "Schools and districts cannot now manage innovation and never will be able to without radically redesigning their approach to learning and sustained improvement. Schools cannot redesign themselves. Individual schools can become highly innovative for short periods of time without the district, but they cannot stay innovative without district action to establish the conditions for continuous and long-term improvement" (p. 209).

People bring about change. Therefore, to improve schools a district must invest in people, support people, and develop people (Schlechty, 1990). Schooling cannot be significantly improved without helping teachers enhance their effectiveness. It is also impossible to legislate excellence. Regulations cannot substitute for nor create the vision, shared values, personal commitment, and culture that make up the soul of an excellent school district. When individuals work in isolation, without a shared purpose or common vision of the ideal school, the schools in the district do not improve.

The relationship between the district and the schools is an important one in sustaining the efforts of individual schools. The district must provide overall vision for the schools and clear articulation among the various levels of people within the district. The central office can help coordinate these activities and provide efficiency of scale.

In an ever-changing world, schools must embrace new knowledge about teaching and learning. They must adequately prepare students from diverse and often difficult circumstances for full participation in a democratic society. American schools are faced with many difficulties in designing these changes. First, they are required to provide equal educational opportunity for all students. At the same time, they are expected to offer a differentiated education to students so that varying abilities, learning styles, and motivational levels can be accommodated. All of these students are also expected to be prepared to function in the highly technological and diverse society of the twenty-first century. These needs can be met only through a process that makes teachers members of learning communities that are dedicated to the continuous search for better ways of teaching and learning.

For far too long, staff development programs have not brought about substantially different teacher behaviors. Many of these programs were superficial, one-shot opportunities that had minimal impact. Professional development should become the bridge between where educators are and where they need to be to meet the new challenges of guiding all students in achieving higher standards of learning. Equitable access to such professional development opportunities is imperative.

If instruction and organization for collective action are to be realized, staff members must be oriented toward visions of improvement and organized to forge synergistic communities that solve problems collectively (Joyce, 1993; Joyce, Hersh, and McKibbon, 1983; Joyce and Showers, 1987). Under the guidance of a new superintendent, an underfunded and uninspired rural New England school district galvanized community support for school improvement and completely revitalized its program through collaborative decision making. Teachers, committees, and administrative teams all made goal setting and achievement part of the school culture. Similarly, Harry Eastridge, superintendent of Cuyahoga County Schools (Valley View, Ohio), has established a "workshop mentality" for his staff, where the cornerstone to enhancing school improvement is studying and using research about effective school practices and instructional alternatives. Quite simply, if the educational leader nurtures opportunities for staff members to share experiences, synthesize the results, and work as a team, the likelihood is great the team will be successful in improving schools.

Clearly, the fate of public education depends, as never before, on superintendents' ability to anticipate and envision a totally new system of education. In this new paradigm, superintendents are leaders with creative insight into the new millennium; they are prepared to invent new school systems capable of preparing all students for life in the learning society. But significant improvement in school performance will not occur unless superintendents assume strong, passionate leadership in instruction. The complexity of the emerging curricular changes requires superintendents to focus the district's time and resources on school improvement. How students think and learn, and how schools can best serve all students, become the key questions for the twenty-first century. Therefore, superintendents must possess and project a clear sense of priorities and strong advocacy for high expectations for all students.

The Charter School Phenomenon

Quite simply, the tide of change has swelled so dramatically that superintendents sometimes feel the waves have overwhelmed them. To make this point, let's look at and develop one issue: charter schools.

Educators hear the term *charter school* often, but what exactly is a charter school? Conceived as public schools that provide public education with public funds, they exercise the contractual autonomy of a not-for-profit educational entity. The concept of charter schools was initiated to preserve the idea of the common school while addressing the current emphasis on improvement and accountability. As an autonomous unit, charter schools are usually exempt from many state regulations, and many experts believe that this freedom encourages innovation. Charter schools follow current policy thinking in that accountability for outcomes is enforced at the top, but responsibility for meeting outcomes, with freedom to determine curriculum, is at the local level, resting with those individuals perceived to be in the best position for decision making about practice.

While private school choice remains a contentious issue, the idea of charter schools is gaining momentum in state legislatures throughout the nation. Statistics suggest that as of early 1995, nearly half the states have either authorized charter schools or are considering legislation to authorize these innovations. This newest alternative may have great impact on the structure and functioning of public schools in the long term by allowing greater opportunities for local communities to be able to innovate and experiment with new approaches.

The idea of charter schools has attracted support on many different fronts because it is viewed by reformers as combining school-based decision making, choice, and innovation. According to Bierlein and Mulholland (1994), "charter schools, more than most reforms, force educators to question the wisdom of conventional practices and may create the dynamics that will foster change within the entire school system" (p. 34). Theoretically, charter schools are supposed to be publicly funded seedbeds of innovation and experimentation—which is why they are granted waivers from certain state and school district regulations.

The charter idea also creates opportunity for dramatically different schools and incentives for superintendents to change schools within their districts. However, under charter school legislation, local school boards and district offices may find their roles and responsibilities significantly changed. Some of the leadership challenges charter schools pose for superintendents are that:

- They require new relationships between school boards and schools
- They utilize true site-based decision making
- They provide new roles for teachers (Bierlein and Mulholland, 1994, p. 34)

Certainly, one can view charter schools as threatening the balance between governmental control and individual action. But it can also be seen, just as defensibly, as bringing a public institution under more local democratic control. There are many questions yet to be answered regarding the efficacy of charter schools, but many educators believe that they represent a bold reform attempt that holds great promise. For that reason, Joseph Schneider, AASA senior associate executive director, advises superintendents "to embrace charter schools as one way to spur innovation in their districts." He adds that "two hundred charters have been approved nationwide, though not all are operational" (quoted in Marx, 1996).

Charter schools may represent a compelling intermediate reform, heralding the possibility of radical innovation and wholesale overhaul of public schools. As superintendents struggle to reform public education, they cannot ignore the rapidly escalating outcry for school improvement. Robert Peterkin, former superintendent of the Milwaukee schools and presently director of the Urban Superintendents Program at the Harvard Graduate School of Education, describes superintendents' charge thusly: "We must plan extensive programmatic offerings of high quality within the public sector as the linchpin of our reform efforts, and those initiatives must be coupled with equity of access for all students."

Clearly, the picture of charter schools is not yet in focus. Several issues remain to be resolved: support for innovation and support for start-up activities, both financial and educational; management training for organizers; creative use of credentialed and noncredentialed staff; and parental support. The potential outcomes need to be weighed in the context of what is best for American education, which mandates that a free education be provided to all children.

For groups who negotiate and contract for charter schools, the advantages outweigh the negative aspects. There are great advantages in freedom to innovate, freedom to provide teachers with the professional development they need and deserve, and freedom from many local and state restrictions. For those who wish to bring the American school system into the twenty-first century, charter schools may provide an opportunity to experiment within existing public schools. The key point is to provide communities and school personnel the opportunity and freedom to experiment and implement new and improved approaches to teaching and learning.

Part Four

New Directions and Responsibilities

Chapter Twelve

Creating Innovative Schools

Superintendents help staff members within the school district to become aware of the latest thinking about effective practice. This is no easy task, considering the array of educational issues and approaches that are constantly being debated and considered to have merit.

Superintendents help shape the debate and discussion both formally and informally. They can distribute readings on certain topics, or sponsor visits by principals, supervisors, teachers, and community members to schools whose practices are similar to the ones the superintendent and board would like the staff to consider. The mission and goals of the district can help define more narrowly what topics might be considered for staff development; they can provide focus for the staff. Staff development activities can be organized around key themes for the school district. Staff members can be selected who support, and have expertise in, key areas that the school system is trying to implement.

The bully pulpit is perhaps the strongest power the superintendent has in this area. The voice of the superintendent is heard in many ways: articles in newspapers; speeches before civic, community, professional, and educational groups; classroom visits where ideas are exchanged. Central office administrators and principals can also serve as catalysts for desired discussion, if they support the overall direction the district is considering and are equal partners on important planning teams. Data can also be used strategically to build support for needed conversations in desired areas. George Garcia, superintendent of Tucson Unified School

District 1, in Arizona, finds that "the role of the large city superintendent is primarily to provide direction and chart the vision created from the voices below, nurture the people who implement the vision daily, and reward all those who help others achieve it or who achieve it themselves. The organization must be in step with the community's expectations."

In providing direction, education leaders need to be well versed in the many possibilities for improving schools and addressing current issues, if they are to provide appropriate direction and focus. The main sources of this knowledge are reading and discussion. Summer institutes, such as those at Harvard and Columbia universities, provide an excellent way to stay current. Perhaps the best source of information about creative, new, successful efforts is professional associations such as the American Association of School Administrators (AASA), the Association for Supervision and Curriculum Development (ASCD), the National School Boards Association (NSBA), and others. Regional and state superintendents often meet to discuss new ideas and invite presenters to discuss the latest research and successful practice.

Vision as a Driving Force

Self-renewing organizations recognize that the problems they face are too difficult for any one group to solve. They realize they must draw in their stakeholders and collaborate with others who share their values. Fullan says it's easier to advocate change when we think that others need to change than it is to consider the possibility that *we* must do the changing (1993a). He found that changes initiated in the past tended to promote self-image over substantive attempts at real improvement. The tongue-in-cheek attitude is that it is acceptable to develop innovations as long as they aren't implemented. Berman and McLaughlin (1978) describe this as the superintendent's "illusion of change" approach. Certainly this approach has symbolic value and may be necessary for political survival, but educational assessment suggests it is not enough.

A focus on mandates and/or problems is not conducive to innovation. Getting rid of what is wrong is not the same as getting things right. Worse, a sense of inadequacy develops as educators spend their careers correcting problems rather than creating an ideal school and working to actualize it. Problems create constant turbulence as they shift and fade, and others surface. Setting new outcomes and raising expectations without a parallel effort to improve curriculum and instruction ends with equally poor results.

Models based on visionary approaches that have active initiation at the grassroots level, strong staff development, strong advocacy, a clear shared vision, support for experimentation, a long-term perspective, and respect for research and previous successes have had the greatest impact on school improvement (Cunningham and Gresso, 1993; McLaughlin, 1990; Lezotte, 1988; Goodlad, 1984). Change efforts work best when they are focused on creating a clear description of an improved school rather than on solving problems that exist within the school. The problem-solving, and to some extent mandated, approaches to change create a group dynamic of defensiveness, power struggle, mistrust, and a sense of inadequacy, which are not conducive to the efforts required to reform schools (Cunningham and Gresso, 1993).

Many successful superintendents no longer discuss problems. There are too many, and there would be little benefit in discussing them anyway. As it is, problems have supported far too much of the literature in the field of education and tend to be the major focus of discussion in committees and communities. This focus on problems has certainly not improved education, and most observers would agree that it has done harm to the needed reform process.

Peter Senge suggests that schools are really not very good places for student learning. He is concerned about fragmentation in the process and the inability of schools to capture the imagination and commitment of students. He believes that there is not enough focus on thinking skills, learning skills, and ways to use knowledge productively. "We say school is about learning," Senge notes, "but by and large, schooling has traditionally been about people memorizing a lot of stuff that they really don't care too much about, and the whole approach is quite fragmented. Really deep learning is a process that inevitably is driven by the learner, not by someone else. And it always involves moving back and forth between a domain of thinking and a domain of action. So having a student sit passively taking in information is hardly a very good model for learning; it is just what we're used to" (O'Neil, 1995b, p. 20). As true as this may be, it only provides direction in its future orientation and in its understanding of present conditions. A clear vision is needed along with a clear understanding of what presently exists—where we are and where we want to be.

The challenge to superintendents is to build school systems that are capable of rethinking and recreating schools as institutions that will be responsive to human needs in the twenty-first century. This effort takes time and will not be successful if important steps, such as gaining understanding among the relevant players, are rushed or skipped. Moving too quickly eventually leads to block-ages. There is a delicate balance here, ironically, in that people can get so impatient and frustrated by ambiguity that they lose interest or direction and blame the leader. Effective leaders must help participants through each of the stages by responding before energy and interest dissipate.

Creating Next-Generation Schools and Citizens

The creation of an ideal twenty-first-century school ultimately depends on the ability of the staff to visualize what that school looks like. The vision should provide a clear description of an ideal school, a vivid and comprehensive description of a desired future. Vision converts knowledge, experience, and success into a reality that is clearly understood and achievable. Vision provides the bridge between useful knowledge and purposeful, coordinated action.

According to Peter Senge (1990), organizational success results from encouraging and supporting staff members to achieve those things that they understand and that are most important to them. Therefore, it is critically important that staff members be aware of the latest successes both within and outside the school district. It is also important that staff members participate in what Senge describes as team learning, so they are all operating on the same information or knowledge base.

The demand is for the development of a compelling vision spelling out educational outcomes that articulate what students are to know and be able to do, and how they can best learn to know and do it. To this end, superintendents help their staff members acquire the latest knowledge about learning, teaching, and school-ing. This learning process ensures that educators have the most recent knowledge as they help rework and revise curriculum content, instructional methods, and the roles of teachers. Continuous improvement is built on lessons learned from the failures and successes of the past and a vision of what would be ideal for the future.

Effective school districts do not ask questions about where they are, but rather about where they want to be. Naisbitt and Aburdene found that "once we accept the challenge of reinventing education, we are free to stop justifying our failures and move ahead to the creative part, which asks, 'Where do I go from here?' Educators are aligned with and dedicated to the pursuit of an ideal for an improved school" (1985, p. 35). The superintendent's challenge is to provide the information needed to answer this question in a way that best fits staff and student needs. In a study of eighty-one superintendents, Laraine Roberts found that there was unanimous agreement about "the importance of developing an open, information-based organization in which staff could act responsibly and knowingly because of access to relevant information, staff and community opinions, and other data" (1991, p. 10).

The Culture of Innovation

Research tells us that substantial educational reform grows in the hearts and minds of those who are employed within the organization. It emerges as a set of values and norms and a vision for the organization that is shared by the people who work in that culture. John Goodlad (1984) says, "The ambiance of each school differs. These differences appear to have more to do with the quality of life and indeed, the quality of education in schools than do the explicit curriculum and the methods of teaching" (p. 28). Thus, the personal dedication of individuals within a school makes a classroom, a school, and sometimes even an entire school district display real greatness.

Excellent schools develop as individuals within the organization form and try out new ideas. Educators have the ability and freedom to test ideas, and, if successful, they are active in the efforts to institutionalize them. This is how innovation and ultimately excellence grow. Carl P. Glickman states: "People need to understand that these programs work not because they are so meticulously crafted and engineered but because the faculty in these schools will not let

them fail. . . . I shudder when I think of a superintendent or principal trying to implement, in a top-down manner, a program developed through grassroots participation" (1990, p. 73).

In this way, educators continuously form and re-form education to meet the needs of a new generation of schools. The culture
of improvement provides very stable building blocks that breed a
sense of success and confidence for cumulative innovation. In fact,
Paul Berman and Milbrey W. McLaughlin found that "mutual
adaptation was the only process leading to teacher change; in other
words, teachers changed as they (and only they) worked to modify a project's design to suit their particular school or classroom"
(1978, pp. 8–9).

The vision is inspiring, clear, and challenging. More precisely,
it is the link between dreams and action. Gary Awkerman defines
the visionary approach as "Any collective effort of stakeholders to
focus their planning exclusively on creating a best future for a complete system" (1991, p. 205). Matthew Miles and Karen Seashore-
Louis (1990) concluded: "Our findings were that broad, enabling,
passionate, shared images of what the school should become do
much to guide successful improvement" (p. 59). Fullan and Miles
(1992) state: "To achieve collective power, we must develop personal power and assure that it is aligned with a shared vision for an
ideal school. Effective work cultures will encourage their employees to develop themselves fully, assume ownership, and accept
accountability. The effective school supports confidence and experimentation. Leaders help their subordinates develop the
courage to take responsibility, to apply their full ability and skill,
and to see that schools achieve greatness" (p. 748).

Progress occurs when we increase the number of people who
believe in and use new materials, new behaviors, new practices,
and new beliefs. According to Ernest Boyer (cited in Cunningham
and Gresso, 1993), past president of the Carnegie Foundation for
the Advancement of Teaching, "The only way we're going to get
from where we are to where we want to be is through staff development . . . when you talk about school improvement, you're talking people improvement" (p. 173).

Development and transference become basic values, expectations, and practices of the culture. Extensive sharing of knowledge
is modeled by all those within the organization. The leader's role

is to sustain increased development of all the staff while helping each individual see how that development might be used to benefit the entire organization. School improvement is based on the premise that nothing changes if the people within the organization do not change. The culture places an expectation on employees that they will transfer new behavior to the improvement of student learning. Implementation provides an opportunity for each person to continue his or her development through the lessons learned as the plans are continuously improved.

Deming (1986), Juran (1988), Crosby (1988), and other total quality management (TQM) experts found that employees automatically make needed improvements if you simply provide the data as to where they are in regard to where they want to be. The absence of measures of performance quality results in larger, longer, and more serious errors in performance. Knowledge regarding the quality of performance requires accurate and timely data about actual performance of students in relation to the desired expectations. Effective schools use various measures of performance to help achieve their own vision of excellence. Teachers make decisions regarding possible improvements very pragmatically. Unless the system provides measures of results for verification of new innovations and improvements, then continuous improvement of their performance is highly unlikely (Berman and McLaughlin, 1978). Thomas R. Gursky (1986) found that "If the use of new practices is to be sustained and changes are to endure, teachers must receive regular feedback on the effects of these changes on student learning. . . . Whatever the student learning outcome employed, it is critically important to plan some procedure by which teachers can receive regular feedback on that outcome to access the effects of their efforts" (pp. 5–12).

Possible New Directions for Visionary Schools

Superintendents across the nation are being called on to prepare their schools to meet the challenges ahead. This means they must have ideas about what improved schools look like, and they must ensure that their staffs do as well. What are some of the possible components that superintendents and school districts should work on to develop twenty-first-century schools?

In a study conducted to identify themes that superintendents might find helpful in transforming schools, Lunenburg (1992) found what he described as ten fundamental common themes that are essential in any "work on restructuring the content of schooling" (p. 37):

1. *Heterogeneous grouping:* All of the recent documents call for ending tracking and reducing ability grouping (Adler, 1982; Boyer, 1983; Goodlad, 1984; National Association of State Boards of Education, 1988; Sizer, 1984, 1992).

2. *Cooperative learning:* This concept has worked very effectively with at-risk students. Students will engage in far less competitive learning. In heterogeneous groups, they will work democratically and collaboratively.

3. *High expectations for all:* All students, if motivated and provided adequate opportunities, can learn important, challenging, and interesting content. Important knowledge is no longer for an elite. It is for all students, regardless of their social circumstances or career aspirations.

4. *Responsiveness to student diversity:* Superintendents should view the increasing cultural, linguistic, and socioeconomic diversity of the student population as an opportunity as well as a challenge. Curriculum content and pedagogical approaches must build on and be respectful of the diversity.

5. *Emphasis on active learning:* Students will spend far more time— sometimes individually, often in groups—doing, experimenting, and discovering knowledge and understanding for themselves.

6. *Essential curriculum:* Schools should select the most important concepts and skills to emphasize, so that they can concentrate on the quality of understanding rather than on the quantity of information presented. And students will acquire the tools to add to their knowledge independently.

7. *Authentic assessment:* The type of assessment employed will be determined by the learning measured. This means there will be increased use of performance as a means of assessment. Educators as well as students will be held accountable for what students can do, instead of relying solely on standardized test results.

8. *Technology as a tool:* Computers, videodiscs, distance learning, Internet, and other state-of-the-art technologies will be used as resources to enhance learning.
9. *Time as a learning resource:* School time will be organized around learning, instead of the other way around. Teacher and administrator needs will be secondary to the needs of the learners. The typical fifty-minute, seven-period school day may need to be restructured to fit the curriculum.
10. *Diverse pedagogy:* Educators will employ more diverse and balanced kinds of teaching and learning experiences to implement curricula. This diverse pedagogy will require new kinds of teacher training and staff development for teachers and administrators (American Association for the Advancement of Science, 1989; Connolly and Vilardi, 1989; National Council of Teachers of Mathematics, 1989).

These are some of the general themes that provide guidance as educators work together to improve schools.

The curriculum must nurture understanding, teachers must help children look at things in multiple ways, and assessment must measure both knowledge and skills (thus it must include performance-based components). Many reform advocates contend that learning has value and meaning beyond the instructional context. Thus, the curriculum needs to combine rigor and relevance if we are to prepare students to take on meaningful roles in the modern world.

Curriculum

The traditional emphasis on acquiring knowledge and skills is giving way to greater emphasis on intelligent thinking and the application of knowledge as needed within a specific context to promote personal and social transformation. The most recent directions are to focus on what Benjamin Bloom (1956) describes as higher levels of learning: analysis (examining parts to make the whole clearer), synthesis (putting parts together in new ways to create transformations), and evaluation (judging the value of results).

Three broad-based curriculum approaches are now being examined (Glickman, Gordon, Ross-Gordon, 1995, pp. 374–375).

The *traditional discipline-based curriculum* focuses on a strict interpretation of the discipline within separate subjects in separate time blocks. The *interdisciplinary curriculum* (sometimes called integrated curriculum) uses a common theme to connect traditional disciplines such as science, mathematics, social studies, language arts, art, physical education, etc. The focus is on discovering relationships and making applications across content areas. The *transdisciplinary curriculum* is organized around common themes, skills, problems, or visions in such a way that traditional disciplines no longer serve to categorize content. Learning activities are actually built around important topics, and class schedules become totally subsidiary as they are synthesized in creative new ways. This approach integrates contemporary issues as the curriculum becomes a dynamic, continually evolving structure.

Howard Gardner (1993a) emphasizes the importance of teaching for understanding and developing the ability to apply knowledge, concepts, etc., to new situations. The curriculum should provide students with opportunities to test ideas, explore relevance, develop multiple perspectives, and evaluate results. This new approach, sometimes called the constructivist approach, is more closely aligned with normal daily life, where we are constantly called on to cross discipline lines. We must teach students to think across disciplines, Gardner insists. Joan Grady, senior program associate with the Midcontinent Regional Education Laboratory in Aurora, Colorado, says, "When planning interdisciplinary curriculum, teachers should be sure to make it meaningful to the kids. Teachers should tap into local issues. If students can see the relevance in their own lives, they will put more effort into their schoolwork." She suggests a number of successful examples: coming up with recommendations to encourage either ranching or mining, finding causes of poor-quality drinking water and suggesting solutions, promoting Europe/American trade, or global citizenry. The students study a new theme with a new faculty team every semester through graduation.

These approaches take much more planning time and require the support of administrators and the local community. A study by two UCLA researchers of an interdisciplinary curriculum in twenty-nine Los Angeles schools found that students in the program wrote better, had a stronger grasp of abstract concepts, and had fewer absences and dropouts than their peers in more traditional schools.

Joel Barker, of Infinity Limited, Inc., and Barbara Barnes, director of the Ecology, Futures, and Global (EFG) Curriculum Collaborative, are developing a new transdisciplinary curriculum for "preparing our children for the twenty-first century." Schools in eighteen states, Canada, and the United Kingdom are utilizing the EFG "architecture." Assessment data from Chattanooga, Tennessee, showed better-than-average growth in all subjects with exceptional improvements in attendance, social studies, and science. A major theme of this approach is the development of pathways to competence and the commitment to stick with students until they learn what they need to know (K–competence). The curriculum takes on a constructivist, thematic approach, allowing students to go along at their own pace. Information is taught when needed for the student's specific instructional project. There are three major themes:

1. *Ecological (relation with nature).* The focus is on who we are, with overall stress on the concepts of life. All of the sciences participate in projects within this theme. The goal is for students to understand their role within an ecosystem and the positive or negative effects they can have on it.

2. *Futures (relation with time).* The focus is on where we are, why we are here, and where we want to go. Subjects incorporated into this theme include physical education, philosophy, history, music, economics, anticipation tools, nutrition, psychology, studio arts, innovation, and science fiction. Community service is often included as an important part of these projects. The goal for students is to understand the relationship between past, present, and future actions, and feel empowered to affect, adapt to, and respond to change.

3. *Global (citizens of the twenty-first century).* The focus is on who we are and how we fit into the world in which we live. This is where students develop knowledge of culture, fluency of language, and understanding how they fit into civilization. Subjects incorporated into this theme are language, history, religion, anthropology, geography, political science, world literature, and sociology. Interaction with people in diverse locations, as well as foreign travel, is encouraged as part of this theme. The goal for students is to gain a broad knowledge of the world's cultures, deep knowledge of one's own culture, and a language other than their own.

Everything taught is always connected to and made relevant by meaning, context, and use. Core values in this program include mathematics, reading, information acquisition and management, teamwork, values clarification, analytical systems, project planning, and thought presentation.

Assessment is completed through demonstrations; paper-and-pencil tests are seldom used. Student assessment is conducted through the use of portfolios, which typically contain products, peer assessment, reports, exhibitions, demonstrations, and juried presentations. All projects include a description of the relevant competency along with a rubric clearly describing both expectations and how the outcomes will be evaluated. Computer resources are integrated with other resources to individualize activity, build skills, pace activity, and allow for both group and individual activity. Narrative report cards are provided to monitor student progress.

Educational Standards and Assessment

Over the past three decades, there has been a major focus on establishment of standards and assessment of student performance. Diane Ravitch of the U.S. Department of Education suggests that

"the Department of Education is supporting systemwide reform in the states based on standards. We are funding the development by states of K–12 curriculum frameworks based upon high standards in mathematics and science, and we plan also to do so in history, English, geography, the arts, and foreign languages. . . .

But standards will only have this effect when a school, community, or state not only embraces high standards but also takes the necessary steps to realign curriculum, textbooks, assessments, and teacher training and education to them—so that the whole school or education system is consciously directing its energies toward the same goal" [1992, p. 27].

However, these issues are still far from being resolved, and superintendents are expected to continuously improve district and state approaches. Standards typically reflect the value judgments of those who establish them and should be set fairly high but within reach. Standards typically codify what is acceptable performance for both educators and their students. Generally, standards define what education should achieve if it is to be relevant to the needs of society. Unfortunately, some of the standards and much of the assessment to date have done very little to support the needed reform efforts—in fact, they are sometimes a blockage.

The most widely discussed reform is the potential development of national standards and a national test similar to those implemented in Great Britain in the early 1990s. An amazing number of different groups have entered this debate, and the direction it will take is still not clear. This process is controversial; Virginia did not accept federal funds that were tied to a set of federal standards. Similar debates are occurring in various states and professional associations. Kentucky is one of the increasing number of states that have mandated statewide tests at the fourth, eighth, and twelfth grades to establish whether students are meeting standards. Kentucky's new testing system is considerably more expensive than traditional multiple-choice tests. Teachers are also asked to spend uncompensated time on assembling and grading portfolio assessments. This approach has been challenged by a Rand study of Vermont's portfolio assessment program, which found troubling inconsistencies among teacher graders of portfolios.

Superintendents must keep abreast of what is going on and keep their boards and school district personnel informed about the implications of efforts to establish standards. Carol Peck, superintendent in the Alhambra school district in Phoenix, found that

> the balance between student testing and the time it takes to administer these tests frequently causes dilemmas. With new mandated state tests, the amount of time needed is a major concern of teachers. In order to resolve the conflict, a group of teachers met with administrators throughout the 1993–94 school year. The purpose of the meetings was to design a new scope and sequence, and an assessment system for reading, math, and writing. The new curriculum and assessment program were developed to lessen the instructional time used for testing and to implement a system that provided accountability with valid and reliable assessment measures.
>
> The teachers worked throughout the school year and during the summer. This year, we are in the process of implementing the curriculum and assessment, with assistance from the teachers

involved in the program development. Mathematics and reading academies were developed to assist in the implementation. Each academy included a teacher from each school who has received comprehensive staff development during the summer. The academy members provided staff development and assistance for teachers. The success in the first year of a completely new instructional program in mathematics and reading is remarkable. This program's success is related to involving teachers in curriculum and assessment decisions from the beginning of the process.

The process of meeting state-mandated assessment expectations requires time for planning and staff development, as does the creation of one's own assessment method. Regardless, education will be evaluated in relation to some standards as to whether it falls short or exceeds expectations. Assessments are used to determine levels of student achievement and performance. A superintendent must be prepared to address many assessment issues when guiding his or her district. Typical areas of expertise have included norm-referenced and criterion-referenced tests, competency tests, assessment of progress, and standardized tests. Today, however, many experts are talking about alternative approaches to assessment. As Grant Wiggins, an expert in this area, suggests, "The proof of a person's capacity is found in their ability to perform or produce, not in their ability to answer on cue." Dissatisfaction has developed with rote learning, memorization, and the low-level skills often measured by standardized tests. As a result, educators now use terms such as *authentic, performance,* and *portfolios* when describing forms of assessment. Technology is also being explored as a means by which approaches can be made efficient and practical, thus easing the burden of assessment.

These alternative approaches ask students to perform tasks that require application and communication of in-depth understanding. Alternative assessment approaches allow students to use numerous forms of activity to demonstrate their reasoning and understanding of the topic. These assessment approaches are embedded within curriculum and instruction; thus they often cause teachers to change the way they approach the teaching/learning process. As understanding of assessment techniques increases, educators are rethinking approaches in other areas, such as letter grades and report cards, communicating performance to parents and community, transportability of student performance to other schools and districts, and so on. A California superintendent says, "The results indicate that the district was successful in increasing the clarity of what it expects teachers to teach and students to learn. It has initiated the consolidation or alignment of teacher decisions regarding lesson objectives, materials, grade-level expectations, and skills tested by the assessment instrument. A pattern of teacher decision making regarding the implementation of this alignment appears to have emerged."

Initial research tends to suggest that improved assessment methods improve teaching and learning. As Lorrie Shepard reports, "The success of our assessment project supports the claims of assessment reform advocates, albeit on a much more modest and tentative scale. Performance assessments have great potential for redirecting instruction toward more challenging and appropriate learning goals. Open-ended assessment tasks not only prompted teachers to teach differently, but criteria were made explicit, and children learned more" (1995, p. 43).

Establishment of standards and assessment methodologies is very important to the development of an accountability system. Fenwick English has pointed out the importance of ensuring that curriculum, teaching, and assessment are congruent with one another. Unfortunately, an assessment can support needed reforms, or it can hold them back. English (1988) has identified a number of examples of the problems that develop when assessment, curriculum, and instruction are not aligned. The important point is that as curriculum and instruction change, so must the systems of accountability. A number of reform efforts have been abandoned because the methods of assessment were not altered to match the new curriculum and instruction. This becomes a crucial issue as reform grows more important to an increasing number of people.

The Full-Service School

Educators have long known that children don't have a fair chance to learn if they are hungry, abused, ignored, neglected, ill, afraid, or in any other form of distress. The idea behind school-linked services is to make it easier to get needed services to children and their families. The placement of social services in schools helps provide early intervention before problems become more difficult to address. According to Julia Koppich and Michael Kirst (1993),

> The concept underlying school-linked services is a rather simple one: the school becomes the "hub," or focal point, of a broad range of child- and family-oriented social services. Schools do not assume primary responsibility for these additional services, but the school acts as the organizational touch point to make services available, accessible, meaningful, and appropriate for children and their families. . . . Schools, then, the advocates contend, provide the most appropriate setting for integrating a range of services that children need to succeed. Services might actually be located at the school site, with professionals from social service agencies "outstationed" at the school. Alternatively, a case worker, familiar with a range of services, might be assigned to the school to work with children and their families, "brokering" an array of prospective service offerings [pp. 123–125].

This approach requires creation of working partnerships with health, social services, criminal justice, and other such agencies. The justification for the needed effort is a belief that none of these professionals, including educators, can achieve their desired outcomes without addressing the needs of the entire child.

Full-service schools redefine education as much larger and more inclusive, with development of integrated systems and interdependence among childcare providers. This concept received national attention in January 1991 when California Governor Pete Wilson created the cabinet-level position of secretary of child development and education and charged the new appointee with the integration of social, health, mental health, and support services in the schools.

In May 1991, Florida Gov. Lawton Chiles spoke out in favor of making schools the center for providing services to the community, keeping them open fourteen hours a day, twelve months a year. Perhaps one of the best examples of school-linked services is found at the Feinberg-Fisher Elementary School in Miami Beach. Vice President Al Gore's visit to this school in April 1993, gave it national prominence, as Gore commented, "This school has broken new ground; it's a pioneer and a model for the future."

Feinberg-Fisher is a full-service community center for students, parents, and grandparents. It provides health clinics and social services for families, day and evening vocational training for adults, and meals for senior citizens. This project has gone beyond the integration of services in that it provides help to parents to improve their lives and that of the community. Octavio Visiedo, Dade County school superintendent, said, "Feinberg-Fisher is not just an educational center; it's a hub for the community." This program is being initiated in other elementary and high schools in Dade County.

Evaluations of school-linked services to date offer some support for their success. Katherine Hooper-Briar and Hal Lawson (1994) conclude: "More than any one person or profession can, complete interprofessional collaboration and service integration require us to band together in the service of children, youth, and families. A child-focused, family-centered, community development-oriented vision thus opens new avenues for success as a new century approaches" (p. 53).

Other Critical Issues

During the next decade, superintendents will need to develop expertise in a number of areas that might be relevant to their school districts. For instance, a theme that continues to receive attention is preschool and early childhood education. Superintendent Mary Nebgen of the Washoe County School District in Reno believes that "our best hope in terms of encouraging improved student performance is to get our students earlier. Some of our students who enter school in kindergarten are already experiencing problems with self-esteem and are clearly not ready for school. We as educators will be arguing strongly for state funding of preschool during upcoming legislative sessions."

Discipline and poor behavior is another issue that has remained in the forefront for the past thirty years and will certainly be there at least in the near future. Typically, teachers respond to poor behavior by trying to control unruly children, which often exacerbates the problem and provokes a spiraling cycle of negative response, greater control, and deteriorating relationships. Learning takes a downhill course as hostility, violence, and crime increases. The approaches that seem to work best in countering this negative cycle encourage students and their parents to bond with the school. The integrated-services approach helps achieve this type of partnership. The key, however, is to help both the child and teacher better understand and deal with any problems the child is having. Success requires an improved understanding of student development and ways to help students take responsibility for their behavior and its consequences. Approaches such as assertive discipline, student empowerment, conflict resolution skills, positive reinforcement, negotiating mutual gains, and student removal provide a partial list of solutions. Teachers need to be provided support in handling children with special needs other than learning, so those students who do want to learn can have the opportunity to do so, without constant disruption.

There are a number of programs to improve schools, such as John Goodlad's School Renewal Project, Phillip Schlechty's Leadership for School Reform, Hank Levin's Accelerated Schools, Dorothy Rich's Mega Skills, Lawrence Lezotte's Total Quality Effective Schools, Mortimer Adler's Paideia Proposal, Alfred Alschuler and Stephen Myers's Global Youth Academies, Ted Sizer's Coalition Schools, and the James Comer Model, to name but a few. A number of computer and technology companies offer packaged instructional approaches for use in schools. Networks also provide opportunities to learn, develop skills, and devise reforms. Two examples are Foxfire Teacher Outreach and the National Writing Project. Networks provide teachers with the motivation to challenge existing practices and to grow professionally.

Certainly, another driving force for the reform of our schools is technology. Educators must create a technology culture for all schools. This will require massive efforts in jointly developing the needed infrastructure, operating systems, curricula and instruction, and teacher training. The key is to think *technology* and not only computers. Teachers are working to integrate networks, communications systems, and digital technology into the curriculum and instruction. Some of the key benefits are the constant availability of information, ease of access, multimedia approaches, and expanded access. Technology also provides a linkage to the world outside the walls of the schoolhouse. It will touch every aspect of our lives as we move into the new millennium, the information age.

Technology is so important to our educational future that we have made it the central focus of Chapter Thirteen.

Superintendent Reformer

A major part of the superintendent's work is to ensure that staff members are focused on student learning, aware of the latest research and successful practice, and continuously improving the learning process in their classrooms (improvement never ends). The role of educators is to design programs that prepare young people for the new century. This effort is best guided by a shared awareness of the knowledge base that supports effective and relevant student learning. Educational reformers must continuously deepen their understanding of the teaching/learning process and the needs of their students, community, state, and nation. Effective superintendents help their staff find out what is known about education and what teachers do in their schools, and connect that knowledge with a vision of what they will need to do in the future to educate twenty-first-century citizens.

Authors who totally disagree on the present condition of education do agree that there is a need for fundamental reforms in schooling—including major structural changes (Bracey, 1984, 1995; Stedman, 1995; Berliner and Biddle, 1995). There is also some agreement on the outcomes that are needed: ability to solve problems, think critically, write and speak effectively, research information, use new technologies, and listen to and understand the concerns of others. In 1994, the AASA completed a study (American Association of School Administrators, 1993a) ranking critical elements in "preparing students for the twenty-first century." In part, the top-ranked items included:

1. *Academic content* (use of math, logic, reasoning, and writing skills; functional/operational literacy; critical interpersonal skills; use of technology to assess or process information)
2. *Behaviors* (understanding honesty, integrity, the golden rule; respect for effort, the work ethic, self-discipline; respect for multiculturalism and diversity; need for individual contributions, ability to work with team members)

3. *Essential skills* (oral/written communication; critical thinking, problem solving/reasoning, analytical skills; responsibility for own actions; discipline and ethics; ability to assess one's own goals)
4. *Changes in schools* (incorporate "marketplace" technology in learning and as part of exit criteria; accommodate new technology; promote active versus passive learning; greater time for professional development, particularly in technology; clarify students' goals/standards; more time for "real world" projects; increase parental/community involvement in schools)

These are critical issues for all educators. By achieving them, schools can be changed to better meet continuously evolving outcomes.

A New Vision

According to a survey completed by the Business Coalition for Education Reform, the respondents identified "introducing new approaches to an established education infrastructure" and "overcoming a general fear of educational change" as the two most important challenges facing today's superintendents. The demand is to stop tinkering with the existing paradigm of education and to help all educators make the shift to a new paradigm of education. Administrators are being asked to create an environment for children that is conducive to learning and prepares them for a highly technological society. This requires a change in mental models from curriculum-centered to learner-centered schooling; from assigning individual tasks to collaborative work; from promoting passive learning to active learning; from printed media to technological ones; from a grade focus to an achievement focus; from a national to a global perspective; from independent efforts to combined ones; and from abstract learning to authentic learning.

Janet Barry, superintendent of the Central Kitsap School District in Silverdale, Washington, and 1996 AASA Superintendent of the Year, believes that building public confidence in education must be a top priority. She contends that building public confidence, meeting higher levels of expectation for school performance, and doing it such that citizens get a better return on their investment are all interconnected with the success of the superintendent. The superintendent must be a "teacher of teachers," providing a very positive focus on "all students' learning well," using a collaborative approach while avoiding confrontation when possible. Superintendents should work with others to "chart a course carefully and [move] toward a shared ideal for schooling." Barry suggests that innovation is highly prized in her school district, but creative new efforts must be systematically linked to the district's vision. Her school district has been recognized as being on the leading edge of technology application in education. Barry sees technology as one of the driving forces in the creation of a school system that meets the needs of twenty-first-century citizens.

Chapter Thirteen

Harnessing the Benefits of Technology

More than ever before, technology is at the forefront of a rapidly changing world. Information technology is driving change at an accelerated rate. As did their forebears, our children must become pioneers as they move into a future of change and great adventure, where technology allows them to access information from anywhere in the world in a matter of seconds, and where the roles and responsibilities of the populace present new challenges and opportunities. Some futurists predict that large systems (such as education) that do not respond to this paradigm shift are in particular danger of becoming irrelevant to the needs of the present generation and those of the future. These futurists contend that it is impossible for existing educational systems to meet the challenges of the twenty-first century without embracing the increasing power of information technologies.

Today's interactive technologies are fundamentally different from those of the past, having the potential to transform education and change society in ways that make educational reform inevitable. How smoothly this future is realized depends on the actions of students, parents, teachers, administrators, and community leaders, all of whom share responsibility for ensuring that technology is used widely in our schools.

Education leaders must ensure that technology supports the mission of schools: providing quality education to all students. Technology has the potential to reshape education, ending the disjunction between schools and their communities. It provides new ways for educators to be more accessible and accountable to parents, communities, and students. This potential presents unique challenges to superintendents.

Technology as the Key

New technologies have the potential of opening up the world to students. The initial application of computers has been in word processing, which makes writing easier for everyone, including special needs students; but this is just the tip of the iceberg. Technology can support the hands-on, interdisciplinary learning that was discussed in Chapter Twelve. Perhaps the two technologies that have the most potential, at least in the short run, are computers and distance learning communications systems. Both can access almost limitless information and knowledge. They allow for low-cost interaction among people in locations distant from one another. With these technologies, information can be easily stored, retrieved, and modified from multiple locations—even internationally. They support "real time" (online) communication and sharing of information from technology libraries or directly among individuals within the school, the state, the nation, or the world. As David Mahan, former superintendent of the St. Louis Public Schools, says:

> I think that one of the most exciting developments in the area of technology is the opportunity that is presented for students to learn from instructors who may be located throughout the country by giving lessons via technology. Opportunities for students to interact with other students across the nation via technology also present great potential. The same relationship exists for teachers and administrators to have dialogue with colleagues in other school districts relative to sharing of ideas and planning programs.
>
> Technology presents unusual opportunities for independent learning, with the availability of vast realms of learning materials that can be made accessible through new technology. From the perspective of the superintendent, technology provides data at a level of sophistication that was not available in the past. The availability of data is invaluable in making decisions relative to curriculum, students, and the community.

The potential applications of current technology in schools are very exciting: electronic books, real-time virtual simulations, digital photography, multimedia presentations, and computer-assisted (and -managed) instruction. Students will be expected to develop multimedia reports incorporating sound, words, pictures, and video. Joe Work from the Little Axe Public Schools I-70 in Norman, Oklahoma, believes that "computer satellite systems and the Internet are only the tip of the availability of technology. Soon we shall be able to access information through fiber optics, placing the world at our fingertips. The role of technology will be much more important in accessing distant information and assisting in instruction for both students and staff." Technology offers significant potential to improve both staff development and student learning.

There is an important need to integrate computer-assisted instruction with the remainder of the curriculum. Too often, students are assigned to computer laboratories to do things that have little or no relationship to the regular learning activities in their classrooms. Technology is thus seen as almost irrelevant, with no reinforcement of its application or benefits.

Computers work best when they are an integral part of the instructional program, not an unrelated sideshow. This requires school staff to decide which technology concepts should be integrated, and where in the curriculum. Teachers must learn how emerging technologies redefine teaching and learning. Superintendents can provide supervision, recognition, and resources as teachers work to change instructional delivery and integrate technology into the daily learning process. Superintendents must encourage risk taking without penalty, along with group sharing and peer demonstrations of technological applications that improve instructional outcomes.

Technology has great potential to help students become independent learners and help teachers facilitate learning. Schoolwork can be completed at diverse locations, including one's home—and that's true for teachers and administrators, too. Software programs such as Team Focus or Lotus Notes allow multiple and parallel planning by large groups. Isa Kaftal Zimmerman, superintendent of the Acton-Boxborough Regional School District in Massachusetts, believes that multimedia technology "opens learning to students so they can be interactive with the learning environment. It allows students to match their learning styles with the learning objectives, and gives students control over what they want to learn and produce. The same is true for teachers and administrators."

New Technological Visions of Schooling

Advances in technology have swept into nearly every aspect of society, with profound results. Technology is now an integral part of our lives, at home and, increasingly, at work. Although slow to assimilate these changes, schools are no exception. Technology's inroads into the classroom are erratic, however. Luther Williams of the National Science Foundation says that "education is an enterprise distinguished by its paucity of technology, and obviously that situation must change." Although the potential is present for radically different methods of teaching and learning, many teachers and administrators do not comprehend the range of technological possibilities and the implications for instruction.

Never before has technology so directly affected teaching and learning. Never before have schools been so challenged by alternative information-delivery systems. Never before have students experienced instantaneous worldwide communications in the classroom. Incorporating technology for instruction, resources, evaluation, and management requires that school cultures develop a new alertness and flexibility. Some technologies will prove beneficial; others, less so. The discerning school leader must know the difference. The discerning school organization offers training opportunities in the skills required to be technologically competent. The enterprising school district and its leadership must understand that its mission is not so much to teach as it is to create a culture—driven by technology—in which students, teachers, administrators, and parents are continuously learning.

Many American schools apply technology in the service of existing practice rather than in accomplishing new ends. New visions of schooling, however, propose instruction in which technology is a means of changing what is learned, how it is learned, how it is measured, and what the teacher does in the classroom. The report *Prisoners of Time*, by the National Education Commission on Time and Learning (1994), affirmed the conclusion that "the true promise of technology lies in the classroom" (p. 37). Technology has become a powerful catalyst for changing how students learn and teachers teach. The focus of schooling is shifting to include teaching students the processes of learning and the skills needed to obtain, manage, analyze, synthesize, and create new forms of information.

Students today have instant access to a hundred times more information than any students before them. Nicholas Negroponte, in his book *Being Digital* (1995), says there are profound implications here for the process of learning: a move, as he puts it, from atoms to bits in the classroom is a move from student passivity to active participation and exploration. Nancy Hechinger, one of the principal designers of the Edison Project, notes that technology plays multiple roles in supporting teaching and learning. Specifically, technology:

- Gives students greater access, power, and equity
- Provides connectivity that changes power (knowledge) relationships
- Provides open-ended tools for exploration and research
- Integrates all of these elements into a knowledge-building community (Hechinger, 1993)

Such a vision gives technology new roles in support of teaching and learning, enabling new directions for curriculum, and leading to new relationships among various education constituencies.

"We have produced more information in the last thirty years than in the previous five hundred," notes Raymond Farley, superintendent of the Hunterdon Central Regional High School District in New Jersey. "The body of knowledge is doubling so quickly that experts tell us that by the year 2011 it's going to double every seventy days." It is no longer sufficient to teach students how to acquire information; they must now also learn how to separate the precious metal from the dross.

In a new technology-based paradigm, teachers manage a system in which there are multiple sources of information. No longer are teachers the primary source of information for students, as their traditional role required. Rather, teachers are a resource for students, helping them find and use information, apply technologies to assess the value of that information, and apply strategies for using that information to solve problems. A former Massachusetts superintendent envisions that "the new role will be a more professional one that allows for the application of the full range of a teacher's creativity, now stifled by the need for repetitive presentations." She adds, "Planning will be a major responsibility, and teachers will be able to benefit from continuous professional growth through contact with one another, a rare luxury in the current design of schools." Teachers become lead learners and facilitators for students, who are learning how to learn in settings that, through technology, reach far beyond the schoolhouse.

Technology is always a means, not an end. Dave Hendry, of the Foundation for Advancements in Science and Education, reminds us as education leaders that it's important not to get so drawn into the complexities that we lose sight of where we want to go or what we wanted to achieve in the first place. In reality, the whirlwind of technological development often obscures the important questions superintendents need to ask:

What needs are we trying to fill?

What programs are available for meeting those needs?

What equipment is needed to run those programs, and can it be upgraded to run other programs that result from further development of technology?

Which option is the most cost-effective?

Properly used, technology can be the central agent for meaningful education reform, to the benefit of all learners. There is no single prescription for the transformation of learning experiences and how teachers meet the challenge of changing their practices, beyond embracing the concept of teacher, learner, and technology as partners in change.

What Schools Lack for the Twenty-First Century

While the private sector demands workers with the skills needed to compete in the "information society," most U.S. schools lack key technologies. They also lack teachers who are properly trained to use the equipment that is leading education into the twenty-first century. Superintendents face an important challenge in bringing schools up to appropriate standards and making technology a key part of the learning culture.

Tools

Unfortunately, many schools have not kept pace with the information revolution. While other sectors of the community have undergone a technological metamorphosis, most of education still is mired in nineteenth-century curriculum and instructional patterns. By spring 1995, there were 5.8 million computers in schools, but 50 million in homes, and the gap is growing. One in ten school computers has a CD-ROM drive, and it is likely to be a single speed. In contrast, one-third of home computers have a CD-ROM drive that runs at double speed or better (U.S. Congress, Office of Technology Assessment, 1995).

In those rare cases where educators and students have been provided adequate technology, training, and support, classrooms are bursting with new energy and higher productivity. A recent report from the Institute for Defense Analysis suggests that those who scored in the 50th percentile on various types of tests and then went through pertinent computer and videodisc-based instruction increased their scores to the 66th percentile in a short period. Students believe it provides more opportunity for creativity, more choices, and is more interesting.

Simply getting computers into America's classrooms has to be seen as just one step in our growing effort to move American education into the future. The Congressional Office of Technology Assessment reported in 1995 that there is one computer for every nine pupils in the U.S. classrooms, but students don't fully benefit from the equipment because their teachers lack technical training. The General Accounting Office, Congress's investigative arm, noted that a survey of ten thousand schools found that most schools don't have facilities to make full use of computers and video. More than half of the schools reported a lack of modems and phone lines. And one-third of the schools that reported they had enough computers complained of insufficient electrical wiring, according to the GAO report. Computers that aren't linked to internal or external networks are limited "in their access to the vast amount of electronic information available, and do not allow . . . for the interaction between students, students and teachers, or the school and the outside world," the report said.

Teachers

Most teachers are isolated in their classrooms, telephones remain rare in those rooms, and opportunities for significant professional exchange and growth are limited and often ill-designed. Only one teacher in eight has a classroom telephone; fewer than 1 percent have access to voice mail, which can make it easier to communicate with parents. Thirty-five percent of public schools have access to the Internet, but only 3 percent of classrooms, the study found. Additionally, schools have not been beneficiaries of the universal service access policies in the United States. Our schools are the most impoverished institutions in society.

Typically, schools have acquired technology piecemeal as budgets permit. Advances in technology have left many schools with a variety of components, both software and hardware, that are outmoded or result in "islands of information," data existing on different systems not readily accessible to all who need them. Are education leaders making the best use of existing technology? Are they forging appropriate linkages between the school and the workplace to ensure a match with skills following high school completion? Are they getting the most and the best from their scarce technology resources? The answer seems to be not yet. More important, teachers need more training and time to experiment with new instructional technologies and new resources, according to the Office of Technology Assessment report. Helping teachers effectively incorporate technology into the teaching and learning process may not only help students become competent technology users, but may also help them become accomplished learners overall, with skills necessary for the information age.

For our schools to catch up with the rest of society, we must take the best of whatever technology is available to our schools, teachers, and students. We must change how we view teaching and learning in the same way we have had to change how we view other areas of our lives where technology has transformed the way we do things.

The new technologies can help transform schools but only if they are used to support new models of teaching and learning. Emerging technologies can provide sustained support to teachers as they experiment with new ways of teaching and learning. If technology is simply used to automate traditional pedagogical models, it will have very little impact on schools. Conversely, if it's used to enable new models of teaching and learning (models that can't be implemented without technology), then it will have a major impact. And if it's used to enable models of instruction that extend beyond the school, into the community, into the workplace, into the family, then it will also have a tremendous impact on education and learning.

The Superintendent's Vision

The enterprising superintendent must understand that the school's mission is not so much to teach as it is to create a culture—driven by technology—in which students, teachers, administrators, and parents are continuously learning. He or she must provide leadership that ensures new visions of schooling, visions proposing instruction in which technology is a means of changing what is learned, how it is learned, how it is measured, and what the teacher does in the classroom. Such a vision of the future gives technology new roles in support of teaching and learning, enabling new directions for curriculum, and leading to new relationships among various education constituencies.

The effective superintendent must use the power of technology as a catalyst for high standards, assessment, and accountability; for professional development; for getting students active and motivated; for parent engagement; and for decentralization. Superintendents must nurture a culture that is built upon a foundation of connectivity, coherence, integrative knowledge, shared and mutually created meaning, dynamic relationships, abundant information, and the human experience itself. As education secretary Riley notes (1994), "America does not have to fear the future if we are willing to educate our young people to master the information economy."

Information-Rich Schools

Access to online computer technology makes vast amounts of information readily available to students and other users. Lack of access widens the learning gap between the advantaged and the disadvantaged. Despite this reality, the nation appears to be moving in the direction of widening the knowledge gap between the haves and the have nots. Equity, or "opportunity to learn," is a very real problem for education leaders. How can we ensure that every child has access to the technology needed to succeed? Given the inequities in funding, this issue fans people's fear of change and institutional inequity.

Lois Harrison-Jones, former superintendent of schools in Boston, called on the federal government to increase funds for telecommunications technology in all public schools. Furthermore, Harrison-Jones predicted, "As funds continue to be cut for public education . . . the gap that presently exists between students from inner-city, low-income families and their counterparts in more affluent communities is only going to widen."

According to Stempel and Kelly, "By not providing our students with basic technological tools for the twenty-first century, we are effectively holding our students hostage to our outmoded world view" (1994, p. 5). One of the quandaries of the information revolution is that those who are information poor are often unaware of it, so they are unable to participate in reform. Furthermore, in contrast to the information poor the information rich have largely determined and privatized the issues of the information revolution according to their own visions and realities. It is also suggested that unless things change, the information revolution may further aggravate the inequities that exist among "have" and "have not" schools. The use of technology in instruction, outreach, and enrichment can help level the education playing field and increase student achievement across the board.

Professional Development for New Technologies

Today, another communication revolution is occurring as information technologies reshape the way we work and live. We are accessing and using information as never before; the progress is so rapid that what is powerful today will be passé tomorrow. Educators are finding it increasingly more difficult, yet increasingly more important, to stay current in their fields and to decide what information is worth knowing.

As superintendents approach the new century, they must obviously focus on networking—technical and human—as crucial in the continuing dialogue among students, teachers, administrators, parents, and employers. The technology to support networking provides the present generation and future generations with the tools needed to live resilient and productive lives. But the issue of providing teacher training and developing new curricula to complement networks has received little study. Teachers receive less technical support than any other group of professionals. The vast majority of teachers are not able to take full advantage of the technology now available without receiving technical support. For technology in the classroom to succeed, as much time and resources must be invested in teachers as is invested in the actual hardware and software. School districts must work in partnership with state and local government, higher education, and business to implement training programs. These programs train teachers to integrate information technologies into curricula, familiarize them with these technologies, and acquaint them with the best instructional techniques. The programs should provide ongoing professional support, not just short-term help. If teachers are to become empowered managers and resource guides for the expanding world of information, they must have opportunities for professional development to assume this vital new role.

How do teachers come to employ the new technologies with a higher degree of comfort and skill? Selecting the right technology to enhance student learning is a daunting task for even the most savvy school decision maker. Mistakes are costly, both in dollars and student learning. To develop a technologically competent and literate teaching force during the new millennium, the following principles deserve superintendents' attention (McKenzie, 1993):

- The district technology, curriculum, and staff development committees should collaborate to clarify expectations for technological literacy.

- Training in new technologies should attend to the challenge of transferring use to the teacher's classroom.
- Learning new technologies should strengthen the instructional strategies identified as appropriate by the district's long-range education plan.
- Learning new technologies should offer many different options for various learning styles and levels of development.
- Learning new technologies should involve participants in the invention of classroom applications.
- Learning new technologies should involve participants in team learning, both during and after workshops.
- Learning new technologies should involve participants in experience-based opportunities, with learning resulting from doing and exploring.
- Learning new technologies should involve participants in questioning outmoded classroom paradigms.
- Staff development must consider the feelings, fears, and anxieties of the learners (pp. 78–83).

Superintendents should ensure that there is a purpose to the learning (perceived need by the teacher-learner), and it must become a part of everyday practice.

The 1995 Education Technology Survey, commissioned by the National Education Association (NEA), National Association of Secondary School Principals (NASSP), National Association of Elementary School Principals (NAESP), American Association of School Administrators (AASA), and Cable in the Classroom, surveyed one thousand teachers, media coordinators, elementary and secondary principals, and administrators about the technologies used most in classrooms and the barriers that prevent many U.S. students from using the information superhighway. The survey (Cable in the Classroom, 1995) revealed that 85 percent of the respondents used Internet and other online services. Nearly 80 percent of the educators felt that the most significant barriers, other than funding, to greater use of computers, online services, and the Internet are lack of knowledge about the various services, lack of workshops or training in using the services, lack of time to learn how to use them, and lack of access to telephone, cable, or data lines in the classroom. Lack of relevance to the curriculum and lack of motivation on the part of teachers were not major barriers to greater use of any of the electronic services. Educators' perceptions of electronic services seemed to be influenced by the extent of their training.

The goal is the effective use of information technologies to solve problems and make meaning. Superintendents must allow their thinking to cut loose from the limited paradigms and perspectives of the past and recognize that new technologies require new curricula, new instruction, and new staff development strategies. There is no doubt that a widescale introduction of information technologies to the school requires overall professional development. Formal training and retraining is expensive and time-consuming, yet essential for success. Technology is changing how we do all things, and students must be literate in its application. It provides many opportunities to greatly improve American education, and educators must be prepared to take advantage of it.

Teaching and learning with technology has emerged as one of the most important new issues in education; providing key professional development opportunities on this subject for educators is essential to improving the quality of learning for students. While many programs exist to help schools purchase computer equipment, administrators and teachers rarely receive training in how to use technology and effective computer-based teaching and learning methodologies. As James Billington, Librarian of Congress, notes so aptly, "Technology alone cannot bring literacy or solve the nation's educational problems, but if we do not use technology to make more knowledge accessible to all Americans, we will have forfeited an enormous opportunity to move this country forward."

The Information Superhighway

As our classrooms evolve to address increasingly complex demands, the implications of the Information Age become central to the continuing debate over how to improve American education. Vice President Gore coined the phrase "information superhighway" for a reality that is still somewhat in the future. The highway of digital technologies will change the face of work, schools, home life, and society. The Clinton administration, spearheaded by Gore, is calling for a data superhighway that can change how students learn and teachers teach. It has stated a clear goal of connecting every school, library, hospital, and clinic to the National Information Infrastructure (NII) by the year 2000. To do so, the White House has formed an Information Infrastructure Task Force to articulate and implement the administration's vision for the NII.

So, what exactly is the National Information Infrastructure? According to the Center for Strategic Communications (1994), it is "a broadband interactive communications network that is primarily owned, operated, and maintained by the private sector to link homes, organizations, and businesses as well as provide access to private and public information resources. It will encompass:

- Computer, televisions, telephones, radios, and personal communication devices;
- Telecommunications systems, such as the phone network and cable TV systems;
- Information resources; and
- People who service and use the system" (p. 1).

Some proponents note that the promising vision of an advanced telecommunications system infrastructure lies not only in its potential to help public and private institutions prosper and survive, but also in its capacity to improve social, educational, and economic services for the vast majority of the nation's citizens.

Unfortunately, the information superhighway is still more imagination than reality. But that doesn't mean some tangible headway hasn't already been made in the education arena. Nationally, in 1994 53 percent of approximately eighty-five thousand public schools used both networks and modems, allowing them access to outside resources. Many of our youngsters are already becoming sophisticated about how television hookups, computers, online services, and interactive ventures can enrich the learning process. A variety of activities nationwide—from distance learning services, to Internet/online network distribution and teacher training—are on the increase.

Both Frank Withrow, director of learning technologies, and Anuradha Kohls, project associate, at the Council of Chief State School Officers in Washington, D.C., contend that education's niche in the NII is lifelong distance learning (Withrow and Kohls, 1995). Clearly, distance learning is a growing piece of the mosaic of learning technologies needed to achieve the nation's education goals. In the United States, we are currently using only about 25 percent of existing installed telecommunications capacity. The movement to bring new services of an educational or so-called "edutainment" nature into the cable marketplace is also picking up speed. Educational programming is a hot button, and established cable networks as well as recent newcomers are stepping in to fill the demand.

In Vermont, the portfolios used to measure student development are being put on digital discs. Chicago public schools are combining the power of telecommunications and the Internet to train teachers in mathematics and science. Schools in Charlotte, North Carolina, are using video technology to reach into the home. Philadelphia schools are using voice technology to teach language skills to learning-disabled students. Students in the suburbs of Phoenix are completing their school lessons on computers that are linked to the Internet.

Teachers, administrators, and students are entering cyberspace and beginning to travel down the information superhighway in staggering numbers. Educators and students are networking, telneting, gophering, webbing, surfing . . . in other words, communicating with and getting information from people and places that just a few years ago were considered difficult if not impossible to access.

A case in point is Superintendent Isa Kaftal Zimmerman in the Acton-Boxborough Regional School District, Massachusetts, who uses networking daily to communicate with colleagues around the state (sometimes beyond), with parents who serve on advisory committees, and with students who are learning to use the Internet. Similarly, Superintendent Kenneth Burnley in Colorado Springs acknowledges that the age of technology is rapidly changing the world of public school administrators. He suggests the most promising technologies are enhancing their ability to access information: "the ability to contact people and resources from all over the world easily is exciting and scary for the school system."

Efficient and Friendly Technology

The information superhighway brings the world to the classroom, including material deemed inappropriate for children. As more schools bring the Internet into their classrooms, school districts are developing policies to shield students from the seamier side of the information superhighway. Many school districts now require parental consent before students can log on to the Internet. Almost all school districts that use technology have a complete set of guidelines that both students and parents must sign. In Indiana, all schools must agree to impose certain restrictions on student access to the Internet as a condition of receiving state funding for Internet connections. The Indiana department of education is allocating $10 million for grants (up to $38,000 per school) to bring schools onto the state network.

Thanks to better, user-friendly software packages, e-mail is quickly becoming the communication method of choice for busy people. The networked world has shrunk so much that a message on a listserv or bulletin board can generate messages across the world in seconds. Gone are the costs in money and time of printing, copying, mailing or faxing notes, letters, newsletters, or any other combination of correspondence or information. Unlike telephone calls, e-mail messages can be sent and answered at the convenience of the sender and recipient. Technology and the information superhighway are fundamentally changing American society, from communications to entertainment, from home to workplace. As businesses adopt new technologies aimed at gaining a competitive advantage, the average citizen is wondering if she or he will be able to understand how to use it and afford it. But what about our children and our schools? Technological and social change will transform twenty-first-century institutions from transmitters of knowledge, which characterizes education in highly stable societies, to creators of new paradigms, which is the norm in a rapidly changing society. Like any enterprise, education must be a bold and creative undertaking, preparing individuals for a changing world rather than a world of permanence.

Consequently, the present is no time for business as usual, or for education as usual. Information technology is in flux; new media are constantly emerging. One thing that distinguishes the information age from the industrial age is that the cycle time for innovation is decreasing very rapidly (for example, chip technology doubles capacity every six months while costs decrease by one-half in the same time span). Superintendents recognize you can't catch up; you must "generation skip" to stay in the game. But most technologies take several cycles or generations before yielding real benefits. School districts must therefore invest for the long haul. This is where it is critical for the superintendent and the school board to have perspective, to take the long view and monitor the results.

Information technology investment decisions are not necessarily made on the basis of currently available technology. Rather, they involve envisioning where the school district wants to be technologically, and understanding in the broadest sense what information technology is all about—in other words, how information and technology are creating the future. In leading their school districts toward using technology creatively and constructively, superintendents must (1) encourage bold thinking, (2) take the long view, (3) set the tone at the top that technology matters, (4) provide vision and encouragement, and (5) ensure that adequate resources are available. The future is now. Schools must learn to work with the telecommunications industry and government regulators to guarantee students adequate access to communications networks and reasonable rates to use them.

Emerging communications technologies are ushering in a completely new information superhighway. The ability to navigate the superhighway distinguishes high-quality institution from the hopelessly out-of-date. But while many schools are preparing to take advantage of computer networks and other technologies, most schools are basically uninformed about relevant policy developments and what they mean. The challenge for superintendents is to find a way to harness the power of these new technologies to provide comprehensive, cost-effective, accessible, and sustained service for teaching and learning. Given the pace of change, school systems must make a commitment to informational technologies.

The objective for superintendents should not be to buy into a given technology and use it to do more efficiently what the schools have always done. Educators must use technologies to achieve their primary objective of preparing students to live productively in a constantly changing world. As technology becomes more powerful and plentiful, and as societies evolve into learning communities, our schools will be caught up in the compelling forces of change.

Advanced technologies have restructured our lives and will continue to do so. Organizations, including school districts, are being flattened as communications networks crisscross the infrastructure. According to Jane Willier, "By the year 2000, at least 44 percent of workers will gather, process, retrieve, or analyze information electronically" (1995, p. 5). Power and creativity will be dispersed, decentralized, and democratized. The information superhighway, Willier says, "is still under construction, and most users are still traveling on dirt back roads. But all of that will change as communications and computer technologies converge." New technology connects people to people, and people to data, directly. Information moves faster, and this speed alters the nature of managerial authority and the superintendent's work.

Chapter Fourteen

The Superintendent of the Future

America's future is inextricably linked to the quality of its public schools, its K–12 educators, and the leadership of its superintendents. As one century nears its end and another begins, it is a most propitious time to reflect on the past and contemplate the future of public education. Our energies and resources must be channeled toward ensuring quality public school education. Our schools are the cornerstone of progress in the free world; they must be prepared for the new millennium.

This century has been one of unprecedented change. We have moved from horse and buggy transport to travel in space; from the invention of the telephone to the World Wide Web. The cumulative effects have brought about national and global interdependence and interconnectedness, which require a new worldview. A constellation of social, technological, economic, demographic, and organizational factors is changing the world within which schools operate. From these shifts, and from previously unimagined technologies, are emerging new realities, new opportunities, and new challenges for the superintendency.

Society expects citizens to deal individually and collectively with change, and education has the potential to make a significant contribution to the realization of that goal. To do so, educators must become skilled change agents, proficient in the dynamics of change.

We should feel a sense of urgency as we approach the twenty-first century. The educational and social covenant that much of the world made to its children has eroded. We must reclaim our children. To do so requires a refocusing of our will, a belief that all children can and will learn, and a bold moral commitment to develop the type of schools needed to prepare students for the futures in which they will live. Educational leaders must prepare themselves and those who follow them to live and prosper in a new global environment of technology, higher-order thinking, information, and fast-paced innovation, moving schools into the future. These are the contemporary superintendent's challenges and opportunities.

Education is a continuing process. School reform is not a partisan issue or tied to election phenomena. It is a long-term effort, and we must support and learn from one another. We must focus on the future of our nation and realize that prosperity for our children is an empty dream unless we provide strong, quality educational improvement for all of our schools. Today, a powerful new worldview is emerging that can fuel teaching and learning for productivity and personal well-being. The vision of change must be powerful enough to focus the public and all levels of the governance system on common challenging purposes, and to sustain that focus over an extended period.

In this book, we have not dealt in lofty idealism, but rather in the realities of today's superintendency, including the unavoidable social, cultural, bureaucratic, and political obstacles. Through trial and error, learning and growing, disappointment and success, many superintendents have improved public education. Their conviction and unflagging enthusiasm leave us encouraged and eternally optimistic.

The superintendent is the most visible advocate of reason and support for the schools, meeting with parent and student councils, business alliances, government officials, and others to advocate and support the cause of education. Superintendents write letters, deliver papers, and testify before committees on behalf of children. Simultaneously, they listen, read situations, and build support networks. The important message is the expression of what their school district stands for and represents.

For these efforts to be credible, superintendents must be aggressive in addressing inadequate performance by students, teachers, and schools. This begins by providing opportunities and support for improvement. But it must also include willingness to eliminate those who show no desire or ability to improve. It requires the conviction to resist the implementation of poorly conceived, no-cost, or cheap solutions that have no chance of success but instead demoralize dedicated educators.

However, despite the overall strength and cogency of superintendents' work, there remains a certain tentativeness, stemming from the wide range of challenges they now face.

An examination of the difficulty of the change process reveals the complex web of values and interpretations that undergirds teaching and learning in our schools. Our analyses of superintendents' stories and experiences do not yield a consensus but rather prompt the refinement of current dialogue and debate. The sheer range of discussion of the sometimes elusive phenomenon of creating twenty-first-century schools is sobering while also perplexing.

The role of superintendents is shifting from one of directing and controlling to that of guiding, facilitating, and coordinating. This is difficult within the current context of intense public pressure and criticism. There is very little consensus on how school improvement should be achieved and little trust that educators are able to make the needed reforms. Yet the future of public education depends on the superintendents' ability to reclaim and take charge of the public discourse needed to improve American schools.

Superintendents' Responsibilities in the Twenty-First Century

The constellation of social, economic, demographic, political, technological, and other factors is changing the world in which we live. These changing contexts create unusual demands as well as opportunities for education leaders—especially school superintendents. Superintendents are asked to build direction, alignment, a culture of visionaries; to encourage risk and experimentation; to set the pace; and to lead by example. Superintendents also demonstrate a deep commitment to protecting and promoting the valuable bridge between yesterday and tomorrow.

It seems everyone today has advice for current and prospective school superintendents. Some of the advice is good, and some of it is misguided, naïve, and narrow. Given the confusion of what our future schools should look like, it's useful to focus ahead, on the coming century.

Despite the crush of competing agendas and distractions, superintendents must bring everyone's attention and efforts to bear on important educational goals for the future. They must lead the way in finding certainty in a school culture that has often been marked by high levels of uncertainty. "The new culture of schools should encourage and expect that the education leaders will orchestrate a program that includes measurable goals as well as regular praise and celebration of progress toward these goals" (Schmoker, 1996, p. 105). Superintendents must position themselves to talk persuasively about results and promotion of a sense of purpose. In doing so, they should focus on outcomes, take risks, and invest in themselves and other people. They will learn by doing and empower people and processes. They must dream of what can be, and not be distracted by nor worry about what has been.

Superintendents are expected to cultivate an ethos that enables teaching and leadership. Exemplary leaders encourage and enlist the support of everyone needed to make the system work. All who have a stake in the vision of a successful school district must be involved in some way. Effective superintendents will be expected to encourage others to act and lead. In short, superintendents must provide conditions that enable the leadership to emerge, producing extraordinary results (Beni, 1996). Being able to make connections with others, to share plans and dreams, and to elicit their help in making dreams reality are basic to the superintendent's leadership.

Superintendents often face overwhelming odds in meeting the challenges of the school district. They must be adroit at identifying and solving specific functional problems as well as analyzing broad issues. In doing so, they must regularly analyze their systems, diagnose problems, and make changes. "Only superintendents can orchestrate the relationships among system functions, such as governance, finance, and management, that will lead to increases in productivity," says Janet Barry, the 1996 Superintendent of the Year. Tending to the system means rooting out the cause(s) of problems (such as the absence of connections among subsystems) and resolving them. Concomitantly, superintendents must create flexible systems. Phillip Schlechty offers these steps (quoted in Marx, 1996) to system leaders to maintain a future orientation while simultaneously dealing with the realities of the present:

- Focus on the future
- Maintain direction
- Act strategically
- Create a results-oriented management system
- Encourage a pattern of participatory leadership
- Foster flexibility in the use of time, people, space, knowledge, and technology
- Encourage innovation
- Provide for continuity
- Provide training, incentives, and social and political support for continuous improvement (pp. 1–2)

Twenty-first century superintendents must become the leaders of the system, not the keepers. This implies bringing constituents together, valuing their input, and, when appropriate, getting out of the way. Education leaders must be careful about the language (the nomenclature) and lead in defining the scope and terms of the debate as education policies are crafted. They cannot be tentative in coalition building.

The success of the school district ultimately resides with leadership that is proactive, not reactive; that is inspired, not simply functional; and that looks to the short- and long-term consequences of actions on future generations for whom the present is held in trust. Superintendents must be made strong by vision, sustained by ethics, and revealed by courage to do what is right in meeting the needs of all children.

Preparing Superintendents

To prepare individuals to take on the complex role of the superintendency, programs for superintendent development have been cropping up across the country. For example, in 1991 the Kentucky State Department of Education asked the National Association of Secondary School Principals and AASA to create a superintendents' leadership assessment center to assist current and prospective superintendents with career planning and development. As a result, a Superintendent's Leadership Development Program was initiated in Kentucky in January 1993. The program emphasizes the skills identified as necessary for success in tomorrow's superintendency. Both associations are now working through state affiliates to get this program adopted in other states. In addition, universities across the country are creating superintendency preparation programs or refurbishing existing programs.

The present condition of the superintendency can best be understood and improved by focusing on the efforts of those who serve in the role of developing twenty-first-century schools. There are many stories where caring, compassion, focus, and just great leadership lifted ordinary educators into the achievement of quite extraordinary outcomes. Such personal values as confidence, honesty, patience, accuracy, enthusiasm, pride, and commitment do allow major obstacles to be overcome. What is needed is a synthesized and coherent view of what is happening in the American superintendency. The battles and opportunities often play a more important role in defining a position than do carefully scribed job descriptions.

This is why it is so important to understand the stories of those who serve in the role and to understand what it feels like to be a superintendent. These personal stories include the challenges and frustrations, and the pains and promises. Through the eyes of those who have been there, we can understand the challenges of improving student learning. We can trace the value of their experiences as they are woven into the fabric of American education today. They become the foundation as we begin to build tomorrow's schools.

Conclusion

American educators will synthesize and translate knowledge and research, experiment, and develop excellent schools to achieve the objectives the future holds. Communities will support, assist, and encourage this effort. American schools must be given the flexibility to be different, to try new methodologies, and to restructure in unique ways. Superintendents provide the leadership to ensure that this happens.

The creative process is a responsibility that requires the leadership of the nation's superintendents. It would be a serious mistake to think that we can rebuild and recreate learning communities without their leadership. This leadership does not develop if we change superintendents every two to six years. Our nation's school districts must have more stable leadership, as do most of our private institutions. We know that meaningful improvement requires at least five to seven years; we need greater continuity at the top of the school district organization to sustain and nurture the continuous improvement process.

Superintendent success will also require the collective engagement of all who have a stake in the enhanced preparation—learning and achievement—of America's youth. The focus is on learner outcomes, curriculum, instruction, assessment, and other factors that make a difference in the teaching and learning process. The American school superintendent is being called upon to take up the challenge of totally rethinking and fundamentally improving American education.

We are at a watershed in history that affects how we function as a society, how we live, how we exchange ideas, and how we learn. In short, we must instill learning as a central value of American society.

We have the opportunity to reinvent ourselves. But what do we want to be? The possibilities are limited only by our imagination. We must strive to do better tomorrow what we do best today.

Appendix A: Superintendent Responsibilities

AASA-NSBA Jointly Determined "Superintendent Responsibilities"

- To serve as the school board's chief executive officer and pre-eminent educational adviser in all efforts of the board to fulfill its school system governance role.
- To serve as the primary educational leader for the school system and chief administrative officer of the entire school district's professional and support staff, including staff members assigned to provide support service to the board.
- To serve as a catalyst for the school system's administrative leadership team in proposing and implementing policy changes.
- To propose and institute a process for long-range strategic planning that will engage the board and the community in positioning the school district for success in ensuing years.
- To keep all board members informed about school operations and programs.
- To interpret the needs of the school system to the board.
- To present policy options along with specific recommendations to the board when circumstances require the board to adopt new policies or review existing policies.
- To develop and inform the board of administrative procedures needed to implement board policy.

Source: Joint AASA-NSBA Committee, 1994.

243

- To develop a sound program of school/community relations in concert with the board.
- To oversee management of the district's day-to-day operations.
- To develop a description for the board of what constitutes leadership and management of public schools, taking into account that effective leadership and management are the results of effective governance and effective administration combined.
- To develop and carry out a plan for keeping the total professional and support staff informed about the mission, goals, and strategies of the school system and about the important roles all staff members play in realizing them.
- To ensure that professional development opportunities are available to all school system employees.
- To collaborate with other administrators through national and state professional associations to inform state legislators, members of Congress, and all other appropriate state and federal officials of local concerns and issues.
- To ensure that all the school system provides equal opportunity for all students.
- To evaluate personnel performance in harmony with district policy and to keep the board informed about such evaluations.
- To provide all board members with complete background information and a recommendation for school board action on each agenda item well in advance of each board meeting.
- To develop and implement a continuing plan for working with the news media.

Appendix B:
Common Ground for Improvement of Public Education

AASA Common Ground for Improvement of Public Education

- A recognition that each side to a controversy has a right to assert its positions vigorously, to be heard and to be taken seriously.
- A recognition that most people on all sides, and particularly parents, are generally motivated by a desire to achieve what is best for children.
- A recognition that vigorous advocacy is characteristic of democracy. However, epithets have no appropriate place in debates over the content and direction of public education.
- Debate over public education is always legitimate. But it comes at a price. And that price should not be extracted unless debate is motivated by a concern for the interest of students and public education, not with personal or partisan political advantage.
- A recognition that parents have a special and immediate interest in what schools do; but equally, there must be an acknowledgment that other constituencies, including the community as a whole, also have a real and direct stake in public education. These interests are sometimes in conflict.

Source: American Association of School Administrators, 1995.

- A recognition that some disputes, particularly those requiring the separation of church and state and respect for religious liberty in public education, have been settled by law. School officials, parents, and others in the community must respect those regulations—recognizing that the law itself is not carved in stone and that some questions are as yet unanswered. The imperative of respect for law is particularly compelling in the case of school officials, who must set an example for the children they are charged with preparing for future citizenship.
- In general, public schools educate and do not engage in narrow ideological indoctrination for the purpose of turning out cadres of identically thinking students.
- Recognition that public schools serve children and parents of a wide variety of perspectives about religion. It is neither the duty nor the right of the public schools to inculcate a particular religious view. By the same token, it is neither the duty or right of public school officials to deliberately undermine particular religious perspectives.
- Schools have at least substantial discretion to accede to parental desires that their own children be excused from lessons that conflict with parental religious beliefs. Prudent exercise of that discretion would greatly reduce conflicts over curriculum.

Appendix C:
Campaign for Reform of
Central Office Functions

- *Goals and standards:* the school board and administrators establish broad goals, high standards, learning objectives, and curricular frameworks for equity and accountability consistent with state guidelines.
- *Equity:* a small, central equity-assurance unit ensures that students who have disabilities or limited English proficiency or who come from low-income families are well served and succeeding.
- *Assistance:* a small intervention unit provides assistance to schools that are failing their students—or, if necessary, closes them.
- *Budget:* a budget or treasury department collects taxes, extends levies, develops systemwide school budget allocations and information, provides reliable computerized budget information, and provides schools with their lump-sum operating funds.
- *Information:* a management information system connects schools to the central office mainframe computer, to each other, and to schools all over the world. A data collection/analysis center—perhaps contracted out to a private consortium of universities and other research groups—collects a variety of student and school data and provides this information to the schools and the public.

Source: Hallett, 1995.

- *Emergency funds:* an emergency funding pool is maintained for unpredictable events, such as major emergency repairs, extraordinary and unexpected energy costs, or substitutes for teachers with extended illnesses.
- *Legal assistance:* a legal/labor unit handles districtwide litigation and centralized union negotiations.
- *Personnel:* a small personnel office carries out background checks and recruits for shortages.
- *Competitive services:* service departments—such as transportation, food services, and payroll—are available if there is sufficient demand among schools for their competitive prices and quality and efficiency of service.

Bibliography

Adler, J. "Kids Growing up Scared." *Newsweek*, Jan. 10, 1994, pp. 42–49.

Adler, M. *The Paideia Proposal*. New York: Macmillan, 1982.

American Association for the Advancement of Science. *Science for All Americans*. Washington, D.C., American Association for the Advancement of Science, 1989.

American Association of School Administrators. *1994 Platform and Resolutions*. Arlington, Va.: American Association of School Administrators, 1993a.

American Association of School Administrators. *Professional Standards for the Superintendency*. Arlington, Va.: American Association of School Administrators, 1993b.

American Association of School Administrators. *Dr. Deming Talks to Educators*. Arlington, Va.: American Association of School Administrators, 1993c.

American Association of School Administrators. *Seeking New Connections: Learning, Technology and Systematic Change*. Executive summary of the invitational seminar. Wye, Md.: AASA and Northern Telecom Integrated Community Networks Group, 1994.

American Association of School Administrators. *Common Ground on Public Education*. Arlington, Va.: American Association of School Administrators, 1995.

Anderson, B. "The Continuum of Systematic Change." *Educational Leadership*, 1993, *51*(1), 14–17. Reprinted by permission of ASCD. All rights reserved.

Asayesh, G. "The Changing Role of Central Office and Its Implications for Staff Development." *Journal of Staff Development*, 1994, *15*(3), 2–5.

Association for Supervision and Curriculum Development. "Refocusing the Curriculum: Making Interdisciplinary Efforts Work." *Education Update*, 1995, *37*(1), 1–8.

Awkerman, G. "Strategic Ends Planning: A Commitment to Focus." In R. N. Carlson and G. Awkerman (eds.), *Educational Planning: Concepts, Strategies, and Practices*. White Plains, N.Y.: Longman, 1991.

Bacharach, S. *Educational Reform: Making Sense of It All*. Needham, Mass.: Allyn and Bacon, 1990.

Barth, D. "The Leader As Learner: Then and Now." *Harvard Graduate School of Education Bulletin,* 1995, *40*(1), 23.

Barth, R. *Improving Schools from Within.* San Francisco: Jossey-Bass, 1990.

Bartlett, D., and Steel, J. *America: What Went Wrong?* Kansas City: Andrews and McMeel, 1992.

Bartlett, D., and Steel, J. *America: Who Really Pays the Taxes.* New York: Simon and Schuster, 1994.

Bateman, F. *Preparing 21st-Century Superintendents: Recommendations on the Urban Superintendency.* Norfolk, Va.: Old Dominion University, 1996.

Bates, J., and Shiver, J. "Eisner Reaps $197.5 Million with Disney Stock Options." *Los Angeles Times,* Dec. 2, 1992, p. A1.

Beales, H. *Satellite Schools: The Private Provision of School Infrastructure.* Los Angeles: Reason Foundation, 1993.

Beni, V. "The Superintendent Enables Teaching and Learning." *NYASCD Impact on Instructional Improvement,* 1996, *25*(2), 40.

Berliner, D., and Biddle, B. *The Manufactured Crisis: Exploding the Myths and Confronting the Real Problems in Education.* New York: Addison-Wesley, 1995.

Berman, P., and McLaughlin, M. *Federal Programs Supporting Educational Change: Factors Affecting Implementation and Continuation,* Vol. III. Santa Monica, Calif.: RAND Corporation, 1978.

Bierlein, L., and Mulholland, L. "The Promise of Charter Schools." *Educational Leadership,* 1994, *52*(1), 34.

Bimber, B. "The Decentralization Mirage: Comparing Decision Making Arrangements in Four High Schools." *Rand Institute on Education and Training Policy Brief.* Santa Monica, Calif.: RAND, 1995.

Bloom, B. *Taxonomy of Educational Objectives: The Classification of Educational Goals. Handbook I: Cognitive Domain.* White Plains, N.Y.: Longman, 1956.

Blumberg, A. *The School Superintendent: Living with Conflict.* New York: Teachers College Press, 1985.

Bok, D. *The President's Report, 1987–88, Harvard University.* Cambridge, Mass.: Harvard University Press, 1988.

Bok, D. "Foundations Seek to Expand Pool of City Schools Chiefs." *Education Week,* 1992, *11*(20), 48.

Booth, J., Bradley, L., Flich, M., Kevugh, K., and Kirk, S. "This Working Life." *Executive Educator,* 1994, *16*(2), 39–42.

Boston, J. "In Search of Common Ground." *Educational Leadership,* 1994, *51*(4), 38–40.

Boyer, E. *High School.* New York: Harper and Row, 1983.

Bracey, G. "The Fourth Bracey Report on the Condition of Public Education." *Phi Delta Kappan,* 1984, *72*(2), 115–127.

Bracey, G. *Transforming America's Schools: An Rx for Getting Past the Blame.* Arlington, Va.: American Association of School Administrators, 1994.

Bracey, G. "The Fifth Bracey Report on the Condition of Public Education." *Phi Delta Kappan,* 1995, *77*(2), 149–160.

Brandt, R. "America's Challenge." *Educational Leadership,* 1991, *49*(1), 11–13.

Brown, F. "Privatization of Public Education: Theories and Concepts." *Education and Urban Society,* 1995a, *27*(2), 116.

Brown, F. "Privatization Issue Takes Nasty Turn." *Washington Post,* July 28, 1995b.

Brown, F., and Hunter, R. "Introduction to Privatization of Public Schools Services." *Education and Urban Society,* 1995, *27*(2), 109.

Brown, T. "The New Science of Leadership." *Industry Week,* 1993, *242*(2) 14–22. Copyright Penton Publishing, Inc. Cleveland, Ohio.

Bryant, M., and Grady, M. "Where Boards Cross the Line." *American School Board Journal,* 1990, *177,* 20–21.

Bursh, P., and Neill, M. "Principles to Guide Student Assessment." *Thrust for Educational Leadership,* 1996, *25*(7), 16–19.

Butler, S. "Privatization for Public Purposes." In W. Gormley, Jr. (ed.), *Privatization and Its Alternatives.* Madison: University of Wisconsin Press, 1990.

Cable in the Classroom. *Education Technology Survey.* Alexandria, Va.: Cable in the Classroom, 1995.

Carlson, R. *Restructuring Schools.* Internal Memorandum. Washington, D.C.: District of Columbia Public Schools, 1989.

Carnegie Forum on Education and the Economy. *A Nation Prepared: Teachers for the 21st Century.* New York: Carnegie, 1986.

Carter, G. "ASCD Looks to New Era of Respect Among Educators, Religious Groups." *ASCD News.* Press release. Alexandria, Va.: Association for Supervision and Curriculum Development, 1995.

Center for Strategic Communications. *New Ideas in Communications.* New York: Center for Strategic Communications, 1994.

Center on Families, Communities, Schools, and Children. *Connecting Policymakers, Practitioners, and the Public: Strategies for Successful Education Reform.* Boston: Institute for Responsive Education, Senate Forum, 1994.

Chance, E. *The Superintendency: Those Who Succeed and Those Who Do Not.* Paper presented at the annual meeting of the University Council of Educational Administration, Minneapolis, 1992, pp. 1–28.

Children's Defense Fund. *The State of America's Children.* Washington, D.C.: Children's Defense Fund, 1991.

Christian, E. "The Tax Restructuring Phenomenon: Analytical Principles and Political Equation." *National Tax Journal,* 1996, *48*(3), 373–385.

Clinchy, E. "Public School Choice: Absolutely Necessary But Not Wholly Sufficient." *Phi Delta Kappan,* 1989, *70*(4), 289–294.

Clinton, W. "Meeting the Needs of At-Risk Youth." Speech to the National Forum for Youth At Risk, Washington, D.C., December 1987.

Commission on Standards for the Superintendency. *Professional Standards for the Superintendency.* Arlington, Va.: American Association of School Administrators, 1993.

Conly, C. *Street Gangs: Current Knowledge and Strategies.* Washington, D.C.: National Institute of Justice, 1993.

Connolly, P., and Vilardi, T. *Writing to Learn Mathematics and Science.* New York: Teachers College Press, 1989.

Covey, S. *The Seven Habits of Highly Effective People.* New York: Simon and Schuster, 1989.

Crosby, P. *The Eternally Successful Organization.* New York: New American Library, 1988.

Crowson, R. "Editor's Introduction." *Peabody Journal of Education,* 1988, *65*(4), 1–8.

Cuban, L. *Urban School Chiefs under Fire.* Chicago: University of Chicago Press, 1976.

Cuban, L. "Conflict and Leadership in the Superintendency." *Phi Delta Kappan,* 1985, *67*(1), 28–30.

Cuban, L. *The Managerial Imperative and the Practice of Leadership in Schools.* Albany: State University of New York Press, 1988.

Cuban, L. *The Urban School Superintendency: A Century and a Half of Change.* Bloomington, Ind.: Phi Delta Kappa Education Foundation, 1989.

Cunningham, W., and Gresso, D. *Cultural Leadership: The Culture of Excellence in Education.* Boston: Allyn and Bacon, 1993.

Daley, S. "School Chiefs Dropping Out, Plagued by Urban Problems." *New York Times,* Dec. 26, 1990.

Daresh, J., and Playko, M. "Aspiring Administrators' Perception of the Superintendency as a Viable Career Choice." Paper presented at the American Education Research Association, San Francisco, 1992. ERIC.

Darling-Hammond, L. "Reframing the School Reforms Agenda." *The School Administrator,* 1992, *4*(9), 22–27.

Deal, T., and Jenkins, W. *Managing the Hidden Organization.* New York: Warner Books, 1994.

Deevy, E. *Creating the Resilient Organization.* Englewood Cliffs, N.J.: Prentice Hall, 1995.

Deming, W. E. *Out of Crisis.* Cambridge, Mass.: Massachusetts Institute of Technology Center for Advanced Engineering Study, 1986.

Detwiler, F. "Surveying the Landscape: Religiously Motivated Opposition to Public Education." *Michigan ASCD Focus,* Spring 1994, pp. 27–29.

Dillon, S. "Publisher Pulls a Textbook in Furor on Sexual Content." *New York Times* (national ed.), Mar. 17, 1994.

Dlugosh, L., Grier, T., Hammon, J., and Houston, P. "The Top Ten Destructive Factors Influencing Public Education." Paper presented at the National Conference on Education, American Association of School Administrators, San Diego, 1996.

Doyle, D. "The Role of Private Sector Management in Public Education." *Phi Delta Kappan,* 1994, *76*(2), 128–132.

Drucker, P. *Managing for the Future.* New York: Truman Talley Books, 1992.

DuFour, R., and Eaker, R. *Creating the New American School.* Bloomington, Ind.: National Education Service, 1992.

Educational Research Service. *Scheduled Salaries for Professional Personnel in Public Schools.* Arlington, Va.: Educational Research Service, 1995.

Elmore, R., and Fuhrman, S. (eds.). *The Governance of Curriculum: 1994 ASCD Yearbook.* Alexandria, Va.: Association for Supervision and Curriculum Development, 1994.

Elmore, R., and McNeil, L. "Contradictions of Control, Part I: Administrators and Teachers." *Phi Delta Kappan,* 1988, *69*(5), 333–339.

English, F. *Curriculum Auditing.* Lancaster, Pa.: Technomic, 1988.

Fidler, M. "Building Learning Communities." *Association Management,* 1994, *47*(5), 40–47.

Finn, C. *We Must Take Charge: Our Schools and Our Future.* New York: Free Press, 1991.

Freedom Forum First Amendment Center. "Clinton Enters Religious Expression Debate." *First Amendment News,* 1995, *1*(4), 2.

Freedom Forum First Amendment Center. *Religious Liberty, Public Education, and the Future of American Democracy: A Statement of Principles.* Nashville: The Freedom Forum First Amendment Center at Vanderbilt University (n.d.).

Fullan, M. *Change Forces: Probing the Depths of Educational Reform.* London: Falmer Press, 1993a.

Fullan, M. "Coordinating School and District Development in Restructuring." In J. Murphy and P. Hallinger (eds.), *Restructuring Schooling: Learning from Ongoing Efforts.* Newbury Park, Calif.: Corwin Press, 1993b.

Fullan, M., and Miles, M. "Getting Reform Right: What Works and What Doesn't." *Phi Delta Kappan,* 1992, *73*(10), 744–752.

Fullan, M., and Stiegelbauer, S. *The New Meaning of Educational Change.* 2nd ed. New York: Teachers College Press, 1991.

Gardner, H. *Frames of Mind: The Theory of Multiple Intelligence.* New York: Basic Books, 1993a.

Gardner, H. *Multiple Intelligences: The Theory in Practice.* New York: Basic Books, 1993b.

Glass, T. *The 1992 Study of the American School Superintendency.* Arlington, Va.: American Association of School Administrators, 1992.

Glass, T. "Exemplary Superintendents: Do They Fit the Model?" In D. Carter, T. Glass, and S. Hord (eds.), *Selecting, Preparing, and Developing the School District Superintendent.* Bristol, Pa.: Falmer Press, 1993a.

Glass, T. "Point and Counterpoint: What Is in the Context of What Might Be?" In D. Carter, T. Glass, and S. Hord (eds.), *Selecting, Preparing, and Developing the School District Superintendent.* Bristol, Pa.: Falmer Press, 1993b.

Glickman, C. "Pushing School Reform to a New Edge: The Seven Ironies of School Empowerment." *Phi Delta Kappan,* 1990, *72,* 68–75.

Glickman, C. *Renewing America's Schools: A Guide for School-Based Action.* San Francisco: Jossey-Bass, 1993.

Glickman, C., Gordon, S., and Ross-Gordon, G. *Supervision of Instruction: A Development Approach.* Boston: Allyn and Bacon, 1995.

Goodlad, J. *A Place Called School.* New York: McGraw-Hill, 1984.

Grady, M., and Bryant, M. "School Board Turmoil and Superintendent Turnover: What Pushes Them to the Brink?" *School Administrator,* 1991, *48*(2), 19–26.

Gursky, D. "Cincinnati Cuts More Than Half of Central Office." *Education Week,* 1992, *11*(35), 1, 13.

Gursky, T. "Staff Development and the Process of Teacher Change." *Educational Researcher,* 1986, copyright by the American Educational Research Association.

Hall, G., and Difforett, G. "State Administrators Association Director's Perceptions of the Superintendent Phenomenon." Paper presented at the American Educational Research Association, San Francisco, 1992.

Hallett, A. (ed.). *Reinventing Central Office: A Primer for Successful Schools.* Chicago: Cross City Campaign for Urban School Reform, 1995.

Hamke, S. "The Theory of Privatization." In S. Butler (ed.), *The Privatization Option.* Washington, D.C.: Heritage Foundation, 1985.

Haynes, C. (ed.). *Finding Common Ground: A First Amendment Guide to Religion and Public Education.* Nashville: Freedom Forum First Amendment Center at Vanderbilt University, 1994.

Hechinger, N. "The Roles of Technology." In S. Rockman (ed.), *The Future: New Visions of Schooling*. Electronic School, 1993.

Heller, R., Woodworth, W., Jacobson, S., Stephen, L., and Conway, J. "Disaster, Controversy—Are You Prepared for the Worst?" *Executive Educator,* 1991, *13*(3), 20–23.

Herd, S., and Estes, N. "Superintendent Selection and Success." In D. Carter, T. Glass, and S. Herd (eds.), *Selecting, Preparing, and Developing the School District Superintendent*. Bristol, Pa.: Falmer Press, 1993.

Hill, P., Wise, A., and Shapiro, L. *Educational Progress as Cities Mobilize to Improve Schools*. Palo Alto, Calif.: Rand Corporation, 1980.

Hirsh, S., and Sparks, D. "A Look at the New Central Office Administrators." *School Administrator,* 1991, *48*(7), 16–19.

Hooper-Briar, K., and Lawson, H. *Serving Children, Youth, and Families through Interprofessional Collaboration and Service Integration: A Framework for Action*. Oxford, Ohio: Danforth Foundation and Institute for Educational Renewal, 1994.

Howlett, P. "Politics Comes to School." *Executive Educator,* 1993, *15*(1), 14–20.

Hult, K., and Walcott, C. *Governing Public Organizations*. Pacific Grove, Calif.: Brooks/Cole, 1990.

James, J. "How to Change. How to Take Risks." Presentation at the National Conference on Education, American Association of School Administrators, San Francisco, 1994.

Johnson, S. *Leading to Change: The Challenge of the New Superintendency*. San Francisco: Jossey-Bass, 1996.

Joint AASA-NSBA Committee (American Association of School Administrators, National School Boards Association). *Roles and Relationships: School Boards and Superintendents*. Arlington, Va.: American Association of School Administrators, 1980.

Joint AASA-NSBA Committee (American Association of School Administrators, National School Boards Association). *Roles and Relationships: School Boards and Superintendents*. Arlington, Va.: American Association of School Administrators, 1994.

Joyce, B. *The Self-Renewing School*. Alexandria, Va.: Association for Supervision and Curriculum Development, 1993.

Joyce, B., Hersh, R., and McKibbon, M. *The Structure of School Improvement*. White Plains, NY: Longman, 1983; Aptos, Calif.: Booksend Laboratories, 1991 (2nd ed.).

Joyce, B., and Showers, B. "The Power of Schooling." *Phi Delta Kappan,* 1987, *68*(5), 352–355.

Juran, J. *Juran on Planning for Quality*. New York: Free Press, 1988.

Kanter, R. "Can Schools be Managed Like a Business?" *School Administrator,* 1991, *48*(2), 64.

Kaplan, G. "Shotgun Wedding Notes on Public Education's Encounter with the Christian Right." *Phi Delta Kappan,* 1994, *75*(9), K1–K12.

Kauffman, S. *At Home in the Universe: The Search for the Laws of Self-Organization and Complexity.* New York: Oxford University Press, 1995.

Kaufhold, J. "What They Don't Teach Superintendents in Graduate School." *The School Administrator,* 1993, *50*(2), 40–42.

Keen, S. *Fire in the Belly.* New York: Bantam Books, 1991.

Kirst, M. "Improving Children's Services." *Phi Delta Kappan,* 1991, *72*(8), 615–618.

Kirst, M. "A Changing Context Means School Board Reform." *Phi Delta Kappan,* 1994, *75*(3), 378–381.

Kirtman, L., and Minkoff, M. "A Systems Approach to Conflict Management." *School Administrator,* 1996, *53*(2), 16–19.

Kline, P., and Saunders, B. "Ten Steps to a Learning Organization." *Executive Excellence,* 1995, *12*(4), 20.

Koppich, J., and Kirst, M. "Editor's Introduction." *Education and Urban Society,* 1993, *25*(7), 123–128. Reprinted by permission of Corwin Press, Inc.

Leithwood, K., Jantzi, D., and Fernandez, A. "Transformational Leadership and Teachers' Commitment to Change." In J. Murphy and K. Louis (eds.), *Reshaping the Principalship: Insights from Transformational Reform Efforts.* Newbury Park, Calif.: Corwin Press, 1994.

LeMahieu, P., Gitomer, D., and Erech, J. *Portfolio Beyond the Classroom: Data Quality and Qualities.* (Center for Performance Assessment Report No. MS-94–01). Princeton, N.J.: Educational Testing Service, 1995.

Levine, D., and Eubanks, E. "The District Administrator." In M. Fullan and S. Stiegelbauer, *The New Meaning of Educational Change.* 2nd ed. New York: Teachers College Press, 1991.

Lezotte, L. "Strategic Assumptions of the Effective Schools Process." In *Monographs of Effective Schools.* New York: New York State Council, Educational Association Research and Development Committee, 1988.

Lieberman, M. *Public Education: An Autopsy.* Cambridge, Mass.: Harvard University Press, 1993.

Lunenburg, F. "The Urban Superintendent's Role in School Reform." *Education and Urban Society,* 1992, *25*(1), 30–44. Reprinted by permission of Corwin Press, Inc.

Macher, K. "Organizations That Learn." *Journal for Quality and Participation,* 1992, *15*(7), 8–11.

Machiavelli, N. *The Prince* and *The Discourses*. New York: Modern Library, 1940. (Originally published in 1532 and 1531, respectively.)

Marx, G. "Superintendency in Crisis Calls for Systems Thinking: State, National Leaders Meet at Annual Conference." *Leadership News,* 1996, *168,* 1, 3.

McArthur, E. *Use of School Choice.* NCES 95–742. Washington, D.C.: U.S. Government Printing Office, 1995.

McCarthy, M. "Challenges to the Public School Curriculum: New Targets and Strategies." *Phi Delta Kappan,* 1993, *75*(1), 55–60.

McCarthy, R., and Bennett, J. "If You're Fired, Here's How to Land on Your Feet." *Executive Educator,* 1991, *13*(4), 14–17.

McCurdy, J. *Building Better Board-Administration Relations.* Arlington, Va.: American Association of School Administrators, 1992.

McEvoy, B. "Against Our Better Judgment: Three Teachers' Enactment of Mandated Curriculum." Paper presented at the annual meeting of the American Education Research Association, San Francisco, 1986.

McGill, M., and Slocum, J., Jr. *The Smarter Organization: How to Build a Business That Learns and Adapts to Marketplace Needs.* New York: Wiley, 1994.

McKenzie, J. *Administrators at Risk: Tools and Technologies for Securing Your Future.* Bloomington, Ind.: National Education Service, 1993.

McLaughlin, M. "The Rand Change-Agent Study Revisited: Macro-Perspectives and Micro-Realities." *Educational Research,* 1990, *19*(9), 11–16.

McNeil, L. "Contradictions of Control: Teachers, Students, and Curriculum. Part 2." *Phi Delta Kappan,* 1988, *69*(6), 432–438.

Meyers, G. C. *When It Hits the Fan.* New York: Mentor Executive Library, 1986.

Midgley, C., and Wood, S. "Beyond Site-Based Management: Empowering Teachers to Reform Schools." *Phi Delta Kappan,* 1993, *25*(3), 245–252.

Miles, M., and Seashore-Lewis, K. "Mustering the Will and Skill for Change." *Educational Leadership,* 1990, *47*(8), 57–61.

Mitchell, D., and Seach, S. "School Restructuring: The Superintendent's View." *EDRS Research Technical Report,* 1991, pp. 1–41.

Mjokowski, C. "Systematic School Restructuring: Implications for Helping Organizations." *Journal of Staff Development,* 1995, 2, 53.

Morris, C. "Pressure Groups and the Politics of Education." *Updating School Board Policies,* 1992, *23*(9), 1–5. National School Boards Association, Alexandria, Va.

Mulligan, D. "Thinking Career Move? Consider Jobs Central." *Conference Daily*, 1996, *15*(1), 1–16.

Murphy, J. *Restructuring Schools: Capturing and Assessing the Phenomena.* New York: Teachers College Press, 1991.

Murphy, J. *Restructuring in Kentucky: Insights from Superintendents.* Nashville: National Center for Educational Leadership, Peabody College at Vanderbilt, 1993.

Murphy, J. "Restructuring in Search of a Movement." In J. Murphy and P. Hallinger (eds.), *Restructuring Schooling: Learning from Ongoing Efforts.* Newbury Park, Calif.: Corwin Press, 1993.

Naisbitt, J., and Aburdene, P. *Reinventing the Corporation.* New York: Warner Books, 1985.

Naisbitt, J., and Aburdene, P. *Megatrends 2000: Ten New Directions for the 1990s.* New York: William Morrow, 1990.

Natale, J. "Growing up the Hard Way." *American School Board Journal*, 1992, *17*(9), 20–27.

National Association of State Boards of Education. *Rethinking Curriculum: A Call for Fundamental Reform.* Alexandria, Va.: National Association of State Boards of Education, 1988.

National Commission on Children. *Beyond Rhetoric: A New American Agenda for Children and Families.* Washington, D.C.: U.S. Government Printing Office, 1992.

National Commission on Excellence in Education. *A Nation at Risk: The Imperative for School Reform.* Washington, D.C.: U.S. Office of Education, 1983.

National Council of Teachers of Mathematics. *Curriculum and Evaluation Standard for School Mathematics.* Reston, Va.: National Council of Teachers of Mathematics, 1989.

National Education Commission on Time and Learning. *Prisoners of Time.* Washington, D.C.: National Education Commission on Time and Learning, 1994.

National Governors' Association. *Time for Results.* Washington, D.C.: National Governors' Association, 1986.

National Information Infrastructure Advisory Council. *Common Ground: Fundamental Principles for the National Information Infrastructure.* Washington, D.C.: Department of Commerce, 1995.

National School Boards Association. *Urban Dynamics: Lessons Learned from Urban Boards and Superintendents.* Alexandria, Va.: National School Boards Association, 1992.

Negroponte, N. *Being Digital.* New York: Knopf, 1995.

Nguyen, L. "Schools Brace for Changes in Population." *Washington Post*, June 8, 1995.

Norton, M., Webb, L., Dlugosh, L., and Sybouts, W. *The School Superintendency: New Responsibilities, New Leadership.* Boston, Mass.: Allyn and Bacon, 1996.

Norwak, S. "New Roles and Challenges for Staff Development." *Journal of Staff Development,* 1994, *15,* 3.

O'Neil, J. "A Generation Adrift." *Educational Leadership,* 1991, *49,* 4–10.

O'Neil, J. "On Lasting School Reform: A Conversation with Ted Sizer." *Educational Leadership,* 1995a, *52*(5), 4–9.

O'Neil, J. "On Schools as Learning Organizations: A Conversation with Pete Senge." *Educational Leadership,* 1995b, *52*(7), 20–23.

Pajak, E. *The Central Office Supervisor of Curriculum and Instruction: Setting the State for Success.* Boston: Allyn and Bacon, 1989.

Patterson, J. *Leadership for Tomorrow's Schools.* Alexandria, Va.: Association for Supervision and Curriculum Development, 1993.

Payzant, T. "Making a Difference in the Lives of Children: Educational Leadership to the Year 2000." Salmon Memorial Lecture at the annual convention of the American Association of School Administrators, New Orleans, 1987.

Ponnuru, R. "Robert Reich Wages War." *National Review,* Dec. 31, 1995, pp. 31–35.

Prince, J. *Invisible Forces: School Reform Versus School Culture.* Bloomington, Ind.: Phi Delta Kappan's Center on Evaluation, Development, and Research, 1989.

Ravitch, D. "National Standards and Curriculum Reform: A View from the Department of Education." *NASSP Bulletin,* 1992, *76*(548), 24–30.

Reagan, R. "Overview of Education Reform Issues." In C. Masshner (ed.), *A Blueprint for Educational Reform.* Washington, D.C.: Free Congress Research and Education Foundation, 1984.

Reichman, H. *Censorship and Selection.* Arlington, Va.: American Library Association and American Association of School Administrators, 1988.

Riley, R. "Education and Goals 2000." Keynote address at the annual conference of the American Association of School Administrators, San Francisco, 1994.

Rist, N. "Race and Politics Rip into the Urban Superintendency." *Executive Educator,* 1990, *12,* 12–15.

Roberts, L. "Constructing a Practical Framework for the Superintendent's Leadership Role in School Reform." Paper presented at the annual meeting of the American Educational Research Association, Chicago, 1991.

Robertson, P. *The New Millennium, the New World Order, the Secret Kingdom.* New York: Inspirational Press, 1994.

Ross, W., and Kowal, J. "Working without a Net." *American School Board Journal,* 1994, *181*(6), 16–19.

Sarason, S. "Foreword." In A. Lieberman (ed.), *The Work of Restructuring Schools: Building from the Ground Up.* New York: Teachers College Press, 1995.

Schlechty, P. *Schools for the 21st Century: Leadership Imperatives for Educational Reform.* San Francisco: Jossey-Bass, 1990.

Schlechty, P. "Shared Decisions that Count." *The School Administrator,* 1993, *50*(10), 20–23.

Schmoker, M. *Results: The Key to Continuous School Improvement.* Alexandria, Va.: Association for Supervision and Curriculum Development, 1996.

Senge, P. *The Fifth Discipline.* New York: Doubleday/Currency, 1990.

Senge, P. "Interdependence: The New Frontier." J. Ellsberry (ed.). *Indiana Principal Leadership Academy,* 1995, *8*(3), 1, 7.

Shannon, T. "The Changing Local Community School Board: America's Best Hope for the Future of Our Public Schools." *Phi Delta Kappan,* 1994, *75*(3), 387–390.

Shepard, L. "Using Assessment to Improve Learning." *Educational Leadership,* 1995, *52*(5), 38–43.

Sizer, T. *Horace's Compromise: The Dilemma of the American High School.* Boston: Houghton-Mifflin, 1984.

Sizer, T. *Horace's School.* Boston: Houghton-Mifflin, 1992.

Spady, W. "Choosing Outcomes of Significance." *Educational Leadership,* 1994, *51,* 18–22.

Sparks, D. "Reflections on the Staff Developer's Future." *The Developer.* Oxford, Ohio: National Staff Development Council, 1994.

Stedman, L. "The New Mythology about the Status of U.S. Schools." *Educational Leadership,* 1995, *52*(5), 80–85.

Steffens, L. "Using Assessment to Improve Learning." *Educational Leadership,* 1990, *52*(5), 38–43.

Steinberger, E. "Margaret Wheatley on Leadership for Change." *School Administrator,* 1995, *52*(1), 16–20.

Stempel, A., and Kelly, C. "Grass Roots Revolution or Palace Coup?" *Basic Education,* 1994, *39*(3), 5.

Toffler, A. *Future Shock.* New York: Bantam, 1984.

Tyack, D. "Health and Social Services in Public Schools: Historical Perspectives." In R. Beheman (ed.), *The Future of Children.* Los Altos, Calif.: Center for the Future of Children, 1992.

U.S. Congress, Office of Technology Assessment. *Teachers and Technology: Making the Connection.* Washington, D.C.: Government Printing Office, 1995.

U.S. Department of Education. *America 2000: An Education Strategy.* Washington, D.C.: U.S. Department of Education, 1991.

U.S. Riot Commission. *Report of the National Advisory Commission on Civil Disorders.* New York: NAL/Dutton, 1968.

Van Horn, C. "The Myth and Realities of Privatization." In W. Gormley, Jr. (ed.), *Privatization and Its Alternatives.* Madison: University of Wisconsin Press, 1990.

Wall Street Journal. "Smarter Jobs, Dumber Workers. Is That America's Future?" *WSJ Educational Supplement,* Feb. 9, 1990. Dow Jones and Company, Inc. All rights reserved worldwide.

Walsh, M. "The Truth Sought in School Was Over Religion." *Education Week,* 1995, *14*(27), 1, 10.

Wang, M., and Reynolds, M. *Making a Difference for Students at Risk: Trends and Alternatives.* Newbury Park, Calif.: Corwin Press, 1995.

Watt, J. "The Devolution of Power: The Ideological Meaning." *Journal of Educational Administration,* 1989, *27*(1), 19–28.

Wehlage, G., Rutter, R., Smith, G., Lesko, N., and Fernandez, R. *Reducing the Risk: Schools as Communities of Support.* Philadelphia: Falmer Press, 1989.

Wheatley, M. *Leadership and the New Science.* San Francisco: Berrett-Koehler, 1992.

Wheatley, M. "Transforming Realities at Work: Stories of Tomorrow's Workplace." *The Developer.* Oxford, Ohio: National Staff Development Council, 1993.

Willier, M. "The Workplace of the Future." *Executive Excellence,* 1995, *12*(4), 5.

Willis, S. "On the Cutting Edge of Assessment: Testing What Students Can Do with Knowledge." *Education Update,* 1996, *38*(4), 1.

Wilson, W. *The Truly Disadvantaged.* Chicago: University of Chicago Press, 1987.

Withrow, F., and Kohls, A. "Learning: A New Dimension in the NII Age." *Technos,* 1995, *4*(1), 22.

Withrow, J. *The Condition of Education.* Washington, D.C.: U.S. Department of Education, Office of Research and Improvement, 1990.

Acknowledgments

The Danforth Foundation created the professional culture in which the ideas for this book were initially discussed. This book benefits from that tradition. The American Association of School Administrators (AASA), the Association for Supervision and Curriculum Development (ASCD), and the National School Boards Association (NSBA) provided forums that facilitated the authors' interaction with superintendents from across the country on the range of issues in this book.

Larry Cuban's work in the early 1970s assisted the authors in crystallizing the direction of this book.

Writing this book involved collecting the experience and knowledge of superintendents about their profession. All of the examples and illustrations, and many of the conceptualizations and understandings, come from these wise and courageous superintendents. Robert Spillane, Gary Wright, and Paul Houston deserve special mention. Given the total number of participants, we are not able to acknowledge individually everyone who helped us, but we are deeply grateful for the generosity and support of all. They provided us with an opportunity to learn from their stories and insights.

One cannot talk about the superintendency without consulting the monumental work that Thomas Glass completed on this topic. Others who strongly influenced the authors' work include Michael Kirst, Joseph Murphy, Terrence Deal, Patrick Forsyth, Peter Senge, Margaret Wheatley, Peter Wilson, Bruce Anderson, Michael Fullan, Thomas Sergiovanni, Charles L. Stater, and A. Harry Passow.

Special thanks are extended to Donn Gresso, Maurice Berube, Denny Wolfe, Robert MacDonald, Robert Sinclair, Cerylle Moffett, and Frank Betts, who provided needed professional perspective.

Fred Bateman, a former superintendent in Chesapeake, Virginia, provided input on the first two chapters.

Lesley Iura, our editor at Jossey-Bass, and Christie Hakim, assistant editor, provided direction, support and encouragement at various key points during the project. Deepest thanks for their advice, for believing in our work, and for shepherding the manuscript through its last phases and supervising its production.

We are indebted to Jerry Hupp, Pierce Granger, Donna Cherry, Susan Litchenstein, and Tom Neighbors, graduate students at Old Dominion University, who conducted important research and assisted in the survey of superintendents. The editing and stylistic advice of Scott Willis is deeply appreciated.

Maritza Bourque and Dawn Hall typed the manuscript and assisted in proofreading documents. Their skills, patience, and dedication are greatly appreciated.

We would especially like to thank our loving families for the encouragement, support, and perspective that they unselfishly provided during this project. Special thanks go to our wives, Lillian Y. Carter and Sandra L. Cunningham, who spend their professional lives in public schools and ensure that we remain reality based. We also thank our parents, siblings, and children (Mike, Kerri, Gene, Jr., and Scott), who continuously remind us of the value of quality education. We cannot imagine this book without their personal, moral, and intellectual help.

Thanks to all who have become a part of this project and for helping us to see it to fruition. We hope that you find this work worthy of the greatness of the people who have had such a profound influence on us. Much of us and a great deal of them is contained herein.

G.R.C.
W.G.C.

Index

CPSIA information can be obtained
at www.ICGtesting.com
Printed in the USA
JSHW061323290822
29726JS00002B/5

9 780787 907990